D1602553

Huntington Library Publications

PROMOTERS AND LANDOWNERS OF THE BOOM YEARS
(*Top, left*) M. L. WICKS; (*Top, right*) DAVID M. BERRY; (*Lower, left*)
WILLIAM N. MONROE; (*Lower, right*) J. DE BARTH SHORB

The
Boom of the
Eighties

IN

SOUTHERN CALIFORNIA

By

GLENN S. DUMKE

Huntington Library

SAN MARINO, CALIFORNIA

Henry E. Huntington Library and Art Gallery
1151 Oxford Road, San Marino, California 91108
Copyright © 1944 by The Henry E. Huntington Library and Art Gallery
All rights reserved
Published 1944. Sixth printing 1991.
Printed in the United States of America

Library of Congress Cataloging-in-Publication Data
Dumke, Glenn S.
   The boom of the eighties in southern California / by Glenn S.
   Dumke.
      p. cm.
   Includes bibliographical references (p.   ) and index.
   1. Real property—California, Southern. 2. California, Southern—
   Economic conditions. I. Title.
HD266.C22S663   1991
333.33'09794'9—dc20   91-8374
                                                         CIP

ISBN: 0-87328-003-2

Contents

v

✒ Contents ⮥

List of Illustrations

Preface

THE boom of the eighties is one of the most frequently mentioned phases of southern California's history. Noticed in all the state and regional histories, the flurry is repeatedly alluded to in the press and in the reminiscences of old-timers. In all these comments, however, the temptation has been to dwell on ludicrous aspects of the movement, and to recount comic or ridiculous anecdotes rather than to subject it to searching analysis. The one book-length description, Theodore S. Van Dyke's *Millionaires of a Day* (1890), is an uproarious lampooning of the antics of the boomers, and, though by an actual witness and participant, is a freehand sketch rather than a sober and strictly factual account. The lone serious study, William Bell Langsdorf's "The Real Estate Boom of 1887 in Southern California" (manuscript, Occidental College, 1932), is an excellent though brief account, but its design compels it to omit consideration of much newspaper and documentary material.

The present work is an attempt to tell the full story, as depicted in public documents, in newspapers and other contemporary accounts, and in the mass of literature on the history of California. The subject presented many difficulties. Because of the period's recency, information exists in vast quantities, and my chief task was one of sorting rather than of searching. The large number of tracts filed prevented, for instance, more than a sampling of those in crowded areas; an attempt to list them all would have been a task of encyclopedic proportions and of no great significance. Despite copious data, however, gaps exist in some of the chief phases of the study. The amount of money involved in realty transactions is certainly a prime index of any land boom; yet accurate totals are absolutely unobtainable, for two reasons: the tendency of lot buyers to record their purchases as made "for the consideration of one dollar," and the fact that land was transferred at such speed that often there were two or three exchanges before the item was finally recorded. These limitations precluded what would have been an interesting aspect of the study—the step-by-step history of important subdivisions. Notwithstanding these restrictions, my endeavor has been to present a clear picture of the boom and to measure its significance in the stream of western history.

In December, 1899, James M. Guinn, foremost local historian of his time, addressed the Historical Society of Southern California as follows:

The history of the cities and towns of Southern California may not be very interesting reading just now to their founders nor to the hosts of dupes who put their faith in the profuse promises of real estate agents, and their money in those paper cities; but years hence when the deceivers and the dupes have passed away, some Macaulay will weave into history a story of our Southern California real estate bubble that will read like a romance.

Although making no pretense to being a Macaulay, I hope the following pages capture a measure of the romance of boom days—the spirit of dusty, noisy auction sales, flag-draped excursion trains, silver-tongued promoters, eager victims, and the ebb and flow of an inflated credit system which even in its farthest aberrations could not permanently injure its basic stock in trade, the land of southern California.

To those who have helped in the building of this account—historians, librarians, civil servants, and California pioneers—I wish to express my sincere appreciation. Dr. John Walton Caughey, Dr. Robert Glass Cleland, and Mrs. La Ree Caughey deserve individual mention, as does the writer's mother, who

acted as his secretary and reduced by half what would have
been a five-year task. A generous grant from the Huntington
Library financed completion of the work.

Abridged portions of the book have appeared in the form
of articles in the Historical Society of Southern California
Quarterly, the *Huntington Library Quarterly*, and the *Pacific
Historical Review*.

GLENN S. DUMKE

San Marino, California
June 23, 1943

The Boom of the Eighties in
Southern California

CHAPTER I

Southern California's Economic Flurries

S OUTHERN California has always grown by spurts. Even in earlier years the region shunned conservative Yankee methods of progress, and its staggering record to date involves a thousandfold increase in population in the historically brief period of a single century. Southern California itself is not completely to blame for this state of affairs. During the fifties the southland reeked with wealth, as a by-product of the gold rush and the consequent demands on the herds of the southern rancheros, and immediately thereafter travelers and tourists took a hand. Many assured themselves of tidy incomes by composing descriptions of their journeys to the Pacific coast; their praise attracted more. tourists, and the newcomers added to the eulogies. Immigrants soon developed the habit of arriving in California in large batches, spaced about a decade apart. Whenever a new group came, there was a boom, and local citizens grew to expect these flurries and to hope for them as fascinating interregnums in

an otherwise placid existence. There have been land booms,
oil booms, and war booms—and, due largely to them, southern
California has become one of the wealthiest and most populous districts in the world. The booms are significant in that
they have been chiefly responsible for the region's fantastic
development, but too often they have been neglected as a
factor in the growth of the modern Pacific West.

The greatest and most interesting land boom was that of the
1880's. Men stood excitedly in line for days at a time in order
to get first choice of lots in a new subdivision. Flag-draped
trains hauled flatcars jammed with enthusiastic prospects to undeveloped tracts far from centers of settlement. Exuberant
auction sales, accompanied by brass bands and free lunches,
helped sell $100,000,000 of southern-California real estate dur-
ing the boom's peak year. Unscrupulous promoters with empty pockets and frayed trousers bought on margin and found
themselves quickly rolling in wealth, while old landowners
who scoffed at the excitement were eventually sucked into
the maelstrom and reduced to poverty. Empty fields and river-
beds and tracts of worthless desert land were platted solemnly
into twenty-five-foot lots—and sold. More than two thousand real-estate agents paced the streets of Los Angeles, seizing
lapels and filling the balmy air with windy verbiage. Business
blocks sprang up like toadstools, and residences sprawled far
beyond earlier city limits. Railroads, formerly sluggish, suddenly traced for themselves with lizard-like speed a complex network of trackage. Schools were so crowded that
double-session work had to be planned, and no less than four
modern colleges owe their existence chiefly to a boom foundation. Settlers who bought in good faith found themselves
stranded on parched and sterile acres, and, undaunted, they
proceeded to organize dozens of irrigation companies which
squeezed every drop of available water from the rugged
ravines of the Sierra Madre and the *ciénagas* of the lowlands

4

and converted the southern valleys into vast luxuriant gardens. It is impossible to tell exactly how many people came to southern California during these exciting months, but more than 130,000 remained as permanent settlers, and the city of Los Angeles increased in size 500 per cent.

In order to understand the progress of this vivid economic flurry, it is necessary to turn back a few brief pages of history. Southern California's modern development actually began in the late sixties, when the drought-accelerated disintegration of the great ranchos brought about an increased devotion to small farms and a more intensive agricultural development. The extension of the Southern Pacific Railroad southward further stimulated the publicity already spread by writers and travelers about the district's charms, and by the end of the decade the first land boom was well under way. This flurry persisted into the early seventies and continued what the droughts had already started—the division of the baronial cattle estates of the southern campos.

Both this boom and that of the eighties had many characteristics in common. In each, there were three foci—Los Angeles, Santa Barbara, and San Diego—with most of the excitement occurring in the "City of the Angels." Rancho subdivision was well under way by 1870; John G. Downey, predecessor of Leland Stanford in the governorship and owner of extensive Los Angeles County real estate, platted 20,000 acres into fifty-acre tracts, and colonists negotiated for other plats, notably Don Abel Stearns's La Laguna and the Azusa and Santa Anita ranchos. Many of the colonists were foreigners—Danes, French, Swiss, British, and Germans. As a result of this interest realty prices rose, and several large parcels sold for twice the amounts they had brought a few years previously, while Los Angeles County realty transactions increased from $40,000 in 1868 to $200,000 in 1869. The most noteworthy project of the decade was the subdivision and sale

5

of the Stearns ranchos, some 70,000 acres in all, including six separate properties, which were marketed by a San Francisco syndicate. James M. Guinn, arriving in southern California in 1869 during the height of the sales campaign, reports that a salesman came aboard the crowded steamer at San Francisco with "an armful of boom literature." Guinn obtained maps and descriptions of the city of Savana, near Santa Ana in the Coyote Hills. Churches, schools, and a city hall were planned, and the promoters insisted that the town had fine prospects. Guinn visited the townsite some weeks later and described it as follows: "A solitary coyote on a round-top knoll, possibly the site of the prospective city hall, gazed despondently down the street upon the debris of a deserted sheep camp. The other inhabitants of the city of Savana had not arrived, nor have they to this day put in an appearance."[1]

Another colony on Stearns ranch property was Westminster, advertised extensively by the California Immigrant Union.[2] Westminster was located between Coyote Creek and the Santa Ana River, six miles southwest of Anaheim. A town of 160 acres was planned, and the surrounding country was laid out in 40-, 80-, and 160-acre farms. Only one of these plats was sold to a person, to avoid large-scale absentee ownership. Purchasers were required to occupy their land and to spend $500 in improvements within two years; they had to be sympathetic with the aims and ideals of the Presbyterian church; and they were expected to provide adequate educational facilities for their children. No liquor was permitted in the colony, except for "sanitary or scientific purposes."[3]

[1]James M. Guinn, "Los Angeles in the Later Sixties and Early Seventies," in Historical Society of Southern California *Annual Publications, 1893*, III, 64.

[2]For a description of this promotional organization see below,Chapter XV.

[3]*All about California and the Inducements to Settle There* (2d ed., 1870) pp. [78-79].

Most Stearns land sold for eight to twenty dollars per acre, depending upon its nearness to towns, its fertility, and its suitability for fruit culture—which was the most popular agricultural occupation. Twenty thousand acres of Stearns ranch property were reported disposed of by 1871.

Other projects during the boom of the sixties included the town of Centinela and the San Pasqual plantation scheme. The Centinela Colony, whose sale was also controlled by the California Immigrant Union, consisted of 25,000 acres seven miles west of Los Angeles, near the present city of Inglewood. Plats of 20, 40, 80, and 160 acres were available as farm sites. A town was laid out which featured a college and a "farm school." The land was said to be suitable for all types of crops, and water was plentifully supplied from Centinela Creek. The promoters expected to purchase, jointly with property owners of the colony, 14,000 sheep, which were to be grazed near by. The San Pasqual plantation was promoted most extensively during April and May of 1870. It consisted of 1,750 acres watered by a costly irrigation ditch. The expectation was that purchasers would buy stock in the enterprise and that, when the citrus groves and vines which the syndicate intended to plant bore crops, the lands would be divided among the colonists. The plan was backed by both San Francisco and Los Angeles capital, and Robert M. Widney, eminent founder of the University of Southern California, was one of the stock salesmen. Despite its sturdy financial support the project failed, primarily because settlers were not yet ready to accept the idea that citrus crops could be grown successfully on upland soil. Other ghost towns, such as Agua Mansa, Queen City, and Santa Maria, as well as more successful settlements like Santa Monica, profited from this early flurry. By 1876 Los Angeles County was reported to have a population of 30,000 persons, and one traveler said, "Subdivisions in various localities have already proven highly successful and flourishing settlements have sprung up on half-barren fields."[4] Land values increased until good farm land was selling for $200 an acre.

San Diego's first boom was due to the energy of Alonzo Erastus Horton, premier promoter of the southern county, who persuaded the lethargic inhabitants of the bay shore to build a city which might rival Los Angeles. Horton used approved promotional methods, and was largely responsible for the creation of the present prosperous municipality. At the same time, Santa Barbara also had its share of excitement, chiefly inspired by the activities of local enthusiasts like the Reverend A. W. Jackson, author of a later tract called *Barbariana*, in which the town instead of heaven became the object of the cleric's proselytizing. Railway-construction prospects increased interest in Santa Barbara property, and lots which had been held at $100 in 1870 brought $5,000 four years later. The Arlington Hotel was built, and the city's population grew, it was estimated, 17 per cent.

This early boom was an important step in the transformation of southern California's economic system. Cleland, outstanding authority on the period, comments:

Despite the successful establishment of settlements at El Monte, San Bernardino, and Anaheim, southern California made little appeal to prospective colonists until drought and bankruptcy, completing the ruin of the cattle industry, brought about the subdivision of many of the large ranchos into farms and homesteads, and led to concerted efforts to stimulate immigration and attract settlers. Such changes led to a wider distribution of wealth, the growth of diversified agriculture, a striking increase in immigration, the construction of new roads, noticeable reduction in lawlessness, and marked expansion in the number of public schools.[5]

[4]Ludwig Louis Salvator, *Los Angeles in the Sunny Seventies* (1929), pp. 29, 47, 77.

[5]Robert Glass Cleland, *The Cattle on a Thousand Hills* (1941), p. 212.

"By 1872," he concludes, "southern California's transition from Mexican cattle frontier to American commonwealth was almost completed."[6]

Interesting as was the flurry of the sixties and early seventies, it bore few of the magnificent attributes of the boom of the eighties. The great boom was an outstanding event of southern California's history. By bringing in a new population, it forced the region one step farther away from the mellow Spanish-Californian culture which had so tinged its earlier development, and, as the third and final step in the break-up of the ranchos, completed the transition from rangeland to agricultural economy.

The boom was built on a seven-year foundation of growing prosperity. The completion of the Southern Pacific to Los Angeles and its subsequent extension through Yuma to Texas increased migration to California, and the winter influx of tourists became a regular occurrence. When the Santa Fe offered competition in the mid-eighties, rates slid downward, and the rate war, coupled with additional inducements to immigrants and colonists, caused an intensified migration which reached a peak in 1886, when railroad fares from Kansas to Los Angeles slumped to the unprecedented low of one dollar. Attracted by the region's prosperity, promoters who had been trained in middle-western booms came to California in droves, and during June, July, and August of 1887 a buying frenzy took place which far outpaced the state's normal rapid rate of land transfer. During these three months alone, over $38,000,000 changed hands in real-estate transactions in Los Angeles County, and the figure for the year was nearly $100,000,000.

High hopes persisted throughout the winter, but in the early months of 1888 the boom collapsed. Because of the con-

[6]*Ibid.*, pp. 241-42.

servatism of the banks, there were few failures, and casualties were limited to those individuals who had plunged foolishly or who had gone too deeply into debt. The receding wave left behind it a multitude of undeveloped townsites and staked-out lots, but also a number of flourishing suburbs. Many of the small towns of southern California were born during the frenzy, and some established settlements were given real encouragement. The boom served to advertise California still more and brought a class of settlers interested primarily in development of the area's resources, rather than in mere realty speculation.

If it is possible thus laconically to characterize the history of such a complex society, the missions and the revolutions may be regarded as events of California's infancy; oil development and the war industry represent the state's maturer years; and the intervening realty booms of the late nineteenth century may be looked upon as the growing pains of California's adolescence.

CHAPTER II

Agriculture in
the Southern Counties

A N IMPORTANT reason for the boom's intensity and one
of the chief shock absorbers for the ensuing collapse
was the basic strength of the agricultural economy
which underlay the flurry. The boom was, essentially, a land
boom, and land resources were emphasized in many ways.
The beauty of the countryside, mineral exploitation, and
products of the soil all found places in promotion literature,
and, of the three, agricultural production ranked highest in
contemporary consideration.

Southern California in the seventies was just beginning to
realize its agricultural potentialities. Politics, mining, and stock
raising had occupied most of the region's attention during its
first century. Now, however, the rapid growth of population,
the clearing up of older issues such as land titles, sectional
differences, and filibustering, and the gradual emergence of
the district from the depression into which it had been plunged

by the dying throes of the livestock industry, fitted southern California for fresh activity.

The possibilities of agriculture, especially in the form of vineyards and citrus groves, were gradually becoming evident. Bankrupt rancheros replaced cattle with crops. Benjamin D. Wilson, a former stock raiser less financially pressed than many of his neighbors, in 1873 considered a herd of one hundred cattle too large. Sentiment favored a no-fence law, whereby the responsibility for controlling stock was placed directly on the shoulders of the ranchero, and not on those of his farmer neighbors. Subdivision of the ranchos, the consequent decline in land values, and some important discoveries relevant to fruitgrowing gave a tremendous impetus to horticulture. Citrus fruit, it was found, could be shipped long distances by rail without spoiling, and many wary landowners thereupon increased their orange acreage. New artesian sources were located, and their utilization stimulated irrigation development and led to the reclamation of numerous otherwise worthless areas. The uplands, carefully avoided by earlier settlers, were found to be frost-protected and ideal for citrus fruits. And, finally, the pleasing discovery that most of the land in the southern valleys was rich and fertile made agricultural potentialities appear unlimited. Land prices rose, and California grew more and more famous.

The wine industry was by all odds the foremost agricultural enterprise of southern California before the boom. Wine was the only commodity available in carload lots in 1876. Much of it was poor, but this characteristic apparently did not destroy its market. Production rose from 1,300,000 gallons in 1875 to 14,000,000 gallons in 1889, and in the latter year there were 150,000 acres devoted to vineyards and 120,000,000 vines bearing. Two of the foremost vineyardists in the Los Angeles area were Matthew Keller, who had 137 acres in the heart of the present city, and Benjamin D. Wilson.

Wilson's large holdings in the San Pasqual area eventually passed to his son-in-law, J. De Barth Shorb, who became one of the chief grape growers of Los Angeles County and a member of the state Viticultural Commission. As late as 1889 Shorb produced 500,000 gallons of wine annually, and his sales extended to England and Germany.

Citrus growing gradually transcended wine making in importance. The deteriorated mission stock had been partially regenerated by seedlings from Hawaii and Central America, but in 1856 the Los Angeles assessor listed only 151 bearing orange trees. One pioneer in citrus growing was a Dr. Halsey, who started in 1854 a nursery of oranges and limes on the former Rowland estate. He soon sold out to William Wolfskill, who in 1857 planted several thousand trees—the largest citrus grove in the United States. Leonard Rose, a German, bought from Wolfskill a quarter section near San Gabriel, and made a showplace of his orange groves and vineyard. Dr. Thomas Balch Elliott, founder of the modern city of Pasadena, started a grove on the east edge of the Arroyo Seco in 1874. Other early growers were Dr. Joseph Shaw and Matthew Keller.

Despite the awakening of interest, progress was slow. Oranges were considered too perishable for long shipment, and Hawaiian oranges and Sicilian limes offered severe competition in the San Francisco market. Also, the fruit was not of very good quality, even as late as 1875. Van Dyke, contemporary historian of the boom, says: "Nothing worthy of the name of orange could be seen in California. Thick-skinned, sour, pithy, and dry, it was an insult to the noblest of fruit to call the California product by that name. . . . The lemons, great overgrown things, with skin half an inch thick over a dry and spongy interior, were more worthy of pity than contempt."[1]

[1] Theodore S. Van Dyke, *Millionaires of a Day* (1890), pp. 31 ff.

ᴥ The Boom of the Eighties ᴥ

Not until the Department of Agriculture sent two seedlings of the Washington navel orange to Mrs. L. C. Tibbetts of Riverside, in 1873, did the citrus boom really start. This, together with the other encouraging agricultural discoveries previously mentioned, caused a rapid increase in planting. In the seventies David M. Berry, colonizer of Pasadena, told his patron, Dr. Elliott, that "the fruit growers here are a much more prosperous class than the commercial men. The same time and labor devoted to fruit here that we give at home to business would make us happy and rich in a short time."[2] Berry also claimed that there was great profit in the citrus nursery business, evidencing a rapid expansion of the orange industry. He reported one sale of a quarter acre of orange seedlings for $4,000, and he felt confident that he could "double all investments in trees within a year."[3] By 1880 over 1,250,000 citrus trees were growing in southern California; six years later 500 carloads of fruit were shipped out of the state. In 1887 was formed the first citrus co-operative association, the Orange Growers' Protective Association of Southern California, headed by J. De Barth Shorb. That group failed after a short life but has been succeeded by other and more powerful co-operatives. By 1889, 12,667 acres were devoted to orange culture in the six southern counties, and the industry was worth more than $2,000,000.

Other crops increased as well, and the enthusiasm for agriculture was reflected by the construction in 1878 of a pavilion on Temple Street for the display of farm products. Enough had been done to prove conclusively that California was not dependent on fruitgrowing alone for its prosperity. There were 6,000,000 bushels of wheat produced in 1860; twenty

[2]David M. Berry to Thomas Balch Elliott, Sept. 18, 1873.

[3]*Idem*, May 13, 1874.

years later the production had increased fivefold throughout the state. Barley production increased twentyfold during the thirty-six years following 1852, and oats, flax, ramie, jute, and sugar beets gained in popularity. An agricultural census of 1882 showed the existence of 450,000 orange trees, 48,350 lemon, 64,380 walnut, and 33,000 apple. There were also peach, olive, quince, pear, plum, almond, and fig trees in thousands; and potatoes, dairy products, and honey were advancing in importance. The olive industry obtained a secure foothold in the south, and by 1887 there were about 1,000 acres planted to this crop. Fruit drying began on a small scale in 1874, and by 1887 millions of pounds of peaches, prunes, and apricots were being thus prepared.

Unprofitable fads, however, interrupted steady development. William Workman tried cotton culture during the Civil War, and Matthew Keller planted six acres to cotton, just north of the present University of Southern California campus. His crop was good, but he found no market. Later, ambitious plans were made by an organization, calling itself the California Cotton Growers and Manufacturers Association, which planted 10,000 acres at Bakersfield and imported a Negro colony to work the plantation. The imported labor failed to do the job expected of it, and the experiment was not a success. California cotton proved profitable only after several decades had passed.

Sericulture was also given a brief but hopeful trial. In 1864 the state legislature, inspired by enthusiasts, offered a bounty of $250 for every planting of 5,000 two-year-old mulberry trees, and a bounty of $300 for every 100,000 salable cocoons. By 1869, 10,000,000 trees had been set out. The chief instigator of silk growing in California was Louis Prévost, who organized the California Silk Center Association, bought 8,500 acres of land near Riverside, and so boosted the popularity of the venture that for a time silkworm eggs sold at ten dollars per ounce. The undertaking failed when Prévost died and the bounty was stopped by the legislature.

In fact, practically every means of utilizing the land's resources was tried at least once in southern California. There was a miniature oil boom after the Civil War, and Salvator, the Austrian traveler, was shrewd enough to predict that petroleum would constitute "the greatest mineral wealth of Los Angeles."[4] Mining existed on a small scale and produced precious metals, marble, and cinnabar. Race horses were bred on various southern ranchos, notably on "Lucky" Baldwin's Santa Anita and on Leonard Rose's Sunnyslope. A good index to the rising economic importance of the southern counties was the rapid development of transportation facilities, including both railroads and steamship lines, which raised land prices and helped to settle the back country.

Agricultural development brought prosperity, prosperity brought fame, and fame attracted new settlers. Of all the causes of the boom, agricultural expansion was the most substantial and constituted a foundation solid enough to withstand the blow of the collapse. Without the real agricultural prosperity upon which the boom was based, speculation would have shattered the region's economic structure and might permanently have stunted its growth.

[4]Salvator, *Los Angeles*, p. 92.

LOS ANGELES AND SAN GABRIEL VALLEY RAILROAD—HIGHLAND PARK BRIDGE (ABOUT 1885)

CHAPTER III

Railroad Competition

T HE immediate cause of the great boom is generally con-
ceded to be the rate war between the Southern Pacific
and the Santa Fe railroads, which occurred in March of
1886. Although the former had arrived in southern California
eleven years previously, resistance to its monopolistic abuses
built up a tension which made the ensuing competition even
more frantic than it would have been had the two lines run
a neck-and-neck race for entry. The reduction of fares to
unheard-of levels stimulated the migration of hordes of people
who would otherwise have confined their interest in California to reading about it.

The Central Pacific Railroad, the first overland route from
California, was essentially a San Francisco enterprise, and during its formative years it made no provision for the southern
half of the state. There came a time, however, when its founders
realized that, in order to maintain their monopoly of California's
railroad business, they must tap the potentially prosperous

17

areas south of the Tehachapi, and their interest in this project increased when competing lines threatened to enter the state by its desert gateway. As a result, the Southern Pacific Railroad was incorporated in December, 1865, by the owners of the Central Pacific. The new line was authorized to proceed down the coast and to receive aid from any counties below Santa Clara, and later it was given permission to meet the Atlantic and Pacific Railroad, approaching the coast from Albuquerque along the thirty-fifth parallel. The coastal survey was soon abandoned, however, in favor of an inland route by which the railroad entered the San Joaquin Valley through Pacheco Pass. Despite three hearings before the Secretary of the Interior and vigorous protests by citizens of the neglected southern coast counties, the new survey was approved by the state legislature in 1870. The federal government thereupon withdrew 7,500,000 acres of valley land, in alternate sections within twenty miles of each side of the proposed line, for a subsidy.

The owners of the Southern Pacific, otherwise known as the "Big Four,"[1] were exceptionally skilful and fortunate in intercepting opposition. There were two immediate threats of competition. The first was the already-mentioned Atlantic and Pacific, building west from Texas; but the Southern Pacific's authorization to meet that road near Fort Mojave, coupled with the Atlantic and Pacific's financial embarrassment due to the panic of 1873, ended the menace. The second was the Texas and Pacific, hastening westward under Colonel Tom Scott's proddings to reach the ocean somewhere in southern California. In this case, the Southern Pacific obtained permission to build a line over Tehachapi Pass, to extend via Los Angeles to Fort Yuma, there to preclude entrance of Scott's railroad into the state. The race was to be a fair one;

[1]The Big Four consisted of Mark Hopkins, Leland Stanford, Charles Crocker, and Collis P. Huntington.

that is, the provisions of the authorization obtained only if the Texas and Pacific did not enter California first. But Collis P. Huntington, who had been responsible for passage of the bill permitting the Tehachapi branch, was confident that the Southern Pacific could beat its eastern rival. The panic again helped the Big Four. Scott was forced to request a subsidy from Congress, in addition to his land grant, and when this was refused, the Southern Pacific faced no more opposition. On December 1, 1881, the California line joined the Texas and Pacific, not at the California border, but at Sierra Blanca near El Paso; and two years later it had completed an extension to New Orleans.

Whether the Southern Pacific would pass through Los Angeles was, for some time, a serious problem. The railroad was in the habit of requiring financial inducements from each town it favored with its presence, and the city fathers of Los Angeles were at some pains to determine whether the line would be worth the subsidy proposed. That the city had been seriously hampered by the crudity of its transportation facilities was freely recognized. The fact that San Francisco boasted the only near-by customhouse necessitated transshipment of all imports; mail was often seven or eight months in reaching Los Angeles from the East, and letters were occasionally sent back to Panama from San Francisco to await a boat for San Pedro or San Diego. Stage and freight rates from the harbor were excessive.

Some attempts had been made to remedy the situation. As early as 1850 Congress was memorialized by Senator Thomas Benton to make San Pedro a port of entry, in the hope of reducing the San Francisco-Los Angeles freight charges, which were sometimes double the rates between San Francisco and New York. Benton's request was granted in 1854. A trimonthly boat from San Francisco was inaugurated, and Phineas Banning, founder of Wilmington and an early owner of Santa Catalina Island, made various improvements in harbor transportation, which culminated in 1863 in the organization of the Los Angeles and San Pedro Railroad. This line was completed in 1869, and six years later a Santa Monica-Los Angeles route was chartered by John P. Jones, the Nevada mining Midas, as a portion of his projected Los Angeles and Independence Railway.

The advantages to be gained by a transcontinental railway connection seemed worth the sacrifice involved, and in November, 1872, Los Angeles voted the subsidy for the Southern Pacific. Included were a 5 per cent levy amounting to $600,000 on the assessed valuation of land and improvements in the county, sixty acres for a station site, and stock held by the city in the Los Angeles and San Pedro Railroad. The 5 per cent rate was deemed excessive by many, and there were prophecies of imminent bankruptcy. The railroad, in turn, agreed to build south over Tehachapi Pass into Los Angeles, then east to San Bernardino to connect with the Texas and Pacific at Yuma. To satisfy the southeastern part of the county, a branch to Anaheim was promised. On September 6, 1876, the golden spike was driven at Soledad in the presence of 350 Los Angeles citizens and fifty San Francisco residents. The San Fernando tunnel, an excavation almost 7,000 feet long, was hailed as "The Greatest Project Now Under Construction in the United States,"[2] and week-end excursions visited its site. The arrival of the railroad in Los Angeles helped to mitigate the depression which had resulted the year before in the collapse of the local board of trade.

But the Southern Pacific was not an unadulterated blessing to the region. There was much dissatisfaction with its "octopus" methods. In building south through the San Joaquin Valley, the railroad had not hesitated to change its route to avoid towns which refused it subsidies. Many of these deserted

[2]*Los Angeles Herald*, Jan. 1, 1876 (supplement).

settlements were thus doomed to stagnation. The same practice was continued east of Los Angeles, and when San Bernardino refused a subsidy, the tracks were laid to the south,
through the Slover Mountain Colony (later known as Colton), which agreed to give a square mile of land for a station.
Through a whole decade San Bernardino struggled along
without a rail connection, and not until the arrival of the
Santa Fe did prosperity return. This unhappy system, coupled
with the control of large areas of land granted it by the government, made the Southern Pacific sole arbiter of which
sections of the state should be developed, and its power was
strongly resented by local citizens.

In addition, the railroad exacted excessive rates as a pre-
rogative of its monopoly. The Tariff Association of California
tried for years to encourage water competition or the entrance
of a competing railroad, and a Railroad Commission was
formed in the seventies. But the Southern Pacific continued
to charge "all the traffic would bear." The Santa Monica line,
with its loading wharf, pleased local merchants because it
saved a half day in the boat trip north. But in 1877 the Southern Pacific bought the Santa Monica road, stopped the trains,
and tore down the wharf. When freight shipped on the
Southern Pacific was marked for transfer to San Diego by
way of the California Southern Railway, a line connecting
with the Southern Pacific at Colton, instructions were usually
ignored and the freight taken to San Pedro for shipment to
San Diego on the lines of the Pacific Mail Steamship Company. Rates between Los Angeles and Colton were as high
as between Los Angeles and Chicago. The only solution for
the angry shippers of California seemed to be the organization
of a competing railroad.

This hope for competition became a reality in 1885, with
the completion of the Santa Fe to Los Angeles. The Santa Fe
made an unpropitious start in 1859, but unexpected profits

from the cattle trade of western Kansas enabled further expansion and, under the skilful leadership of William B. Strong, it built westward rapidly, joining the Atlantic and Pacific at Albuquerque in 1873. The road reached El Paso in 1881, Guaymas in 1882, and Needles in 1883. Here, on the border of California, it was halted by the Southern Pacific's coastal monopoly, and it faced three alternatives. The first was to construct a line parallel to the Southern Pacific as far as San Francisco, but that scheme was rejected as too costly. The second was to relinquish forever plans to reach the Pacific Ocean in California, but the Santa Fe was reluctant to give up, because the result would be eventual absorption of its western extensions by the Big Four. The third alternative was to purchase the Mojave-Needles division of the Southern Pacific and obtain terms on the use of Southern Pacific tracks as far as San Francisco.[3] That was the plan agreed upon, and the line to Guaymas was used as a lever to extort concessions from the Huntington interests. The latter realized that a steamship line from the Mexican port might not be ultimately successful, but the end of the monopoly loomed, in any case, and all things considered, the Big Four deemed it best to give in. The Mojave-Needles division was turned over to the Santa Fe, and in return the plans for the Guaymas steamship line were abandoned.

Two other lines facilitated the Santa Fe's entrance into California. The California Southern, backed by San Diego and National City businessmen in close co-operation with the Santa Fe, was completed from National City to Colton in November, 1882, and reached San Bernardino the following year. The railroad had misfortunes: floods in 1884 washed out thirty miles of track in Temécula Canyon, and company equipment was later sighted floating far out to sea. In addition,

[3]Lewis B. Lesley, "The Entrance of the Santa Fe Railroad into California," *Pacific Historical Review*, VIII, 93-94.

the refusal of the Southern Pacific to co-operate occasioned some loss of revenue. But connection was made with the Santa Fe's desert extension, and in June, 1885, the California Southern was purchased by Topeka interests. The other line which aided the Santa Fe was the Los Angeles and San Gabriel Valley Railroad, built to the San Gabriel River in February, 1887, by James F. Crank of Los Angeles. Crank had built his line with the object of transcontinental connection, and it provided the Santa Fe with a paying right of way into Los Angeles. Santa Fe trains, however, had entered that city as early as September, 1885, on track leased from the Southern Pacific, but not until it obtained its own roadbed did the Santa Fe start the rate war which in turn began the boom.

The Santa Fe quickly consolidated its new trackage in southern California, including several local lines which it bought, into the California Central Railroad. This company, chartered in January, 1887, was composed of eight short lines and the San Gabriel Valley road and comprised 183½ miles of right of way. Before 1890, however, the California Central joined the California Southern and a Redondo Beach line, to form the Southern California Railroad. "It has been well said that the history of the Santa Fe Railway is the history of its combinations with other roads."[4]

The manner in which the railroads contributed to the boom was by means of a rate war which occurred shortly after the Santa Fe reached Los Angeles on its own roadbed. The Santa Fe quit the Transcontinental Traffic Association in 1886, and thereupon a steady decline of rates began. Early in 1887 the Santa Fe suggested a pooling arrangement with the Southern Pacific, whereby the former would take fifty per cent of the southern-California business and twenty-seven per cent of

[4]Rockwell D. Hunt and William S. Ament, *Oxcart to Airplane* (1929), pp. 165-66.

the northern. When its offer was refused, the Santa Fe decided to exert pressure which would destroy once and for all the Big Four's monopoly in the state.

Normal rates from the Mississippi Valley to southern California fluctuated in the neighborhood of $125. By 1885 they were down to $100, and when the Santa Fe drove its golden spike at Cajón Pass on November 9, 1885, they immediately dropped to $95. There was thus a precedent of cutthroat competition, but the battle rose to sudden fury in March of 1886. On the fifth of that month, the *Los Angeles Times* reported:

Still Cutting

The Railroads Get the Knife in a Little Further

San Francisco, Mar. 4. All overland roads this morning made open rates on limited tickets to eastern points as follows: Boston, $47; New York, $45; Chicago, $32.

A Second Cut in Fares

Prices of limited tickets were cut for the second time to-day to the following figures: Chicago, $25; New York, $40; Boston, $42.

The climax came on March 6, when both the Southern Pacific and the Santa Fe settled down to a finish fight over the fares between Kansas City and Los Angeles. In the morning the Southern Pacific met the Santa Fe at twelve dollars. The latter then dropped to ten dollars, and the Southern Pacific followed suit. The Santa Fe cut again to eight, and was met. Then the Southern Pacific, through some apparent misunderstanding, underbid itself, cutting to six dollars, then to four. Finally, shortly after noon, the Southern Pacific announced a rate of one dollar. Santa Fe officials claimed they sold no tickets for less than eight dollars, but intentionally set a trap into which the Southern Pacific neatly fell.[5] These ridiculous levels did not persist long, and on March 10 it cost ten dollars to travel to Chicago or St. Louis, and twenty-three dollars to go to New York. For approximately a year, however, fares remained below twenty-five dollars to Missouri River points and did not soon regain their former heights.

Rate cuts were by means of rebates at destination; that is, the passenger would receive the benefit of any cuts which were made during his journey. The railroads lost heavily on local traffic; passengers going to near-by points would buy transcontinental tickets at bargain prices and drop off at their respective stations. Freight rates suffered a corresponding decline. Coal went down to one dollar per ton, and Harris Newmark, a Los Angeles businessman, shipped a trainload of Liverpool salt for sixty cents per ton. Later in the year these reductions were applied to short hauls. The result was to decrease the cost of living in California and to make profits greater on exported goods.

There has been some suggestion of the possibility of deliberate connivance between the two railroads to bring about the rate war, with a view to increasing travel and immigration and to selling railroad lands. Such a conclusion seems, however, improbable. Astute railway managers would not have sacrificed huge immediate profits by a planned fight with one another, merely to better their chances for a highly speculative future.

"The result of this war," says Netz, one of the historians of the boom, "was to precipitate such a flow of tentative migration, such an avalanche rushing madly to Southern Cali-

[5]*Los Angeles Times*, Mar. 7, 1886; see also William B. Langsdorf, "The Real Estate Boom of 1887 in Southern California" (MS, Occidental College, 1932), pp. 13 ff.

fornia as I believe has had no parallel."[6] Southern Pacific officials predicted that 120,000 people "of high quality" would come to California by rail by the end of 1887, but "persons who are informed by studying the statistics say that this estimate is too low."[7] Sacramento soon required six instead of four trains daily, and Los Angeles two instead of one. Service was doubled, not only on the Southern Pacific and Union Pacific, but also on the Denver and Rio Grande, Burlington, and Iowa routes. In 1888 the *San Francisco Call* estimated travel to the coast over all lines but the Santa Fe at 78,437 fares. Of these, 32,392 did not return. The Santa Fe brought in some 65,000 persons. Willard, historian of Los Angeles, sums up by asserting that the Southern Pacific's arrival increased the city's population one hundred per cent, and the ensuing arrival of the Santa Fe increased it 500 per cent.[8]

The railways offered many inducements to travelers. The "emigrant car" aided poorer settlers by providing folding seats which could be flattened into beds, and cooking accommodations. "Emigrant houses" furnished a week's free lodging while travelers earned enough to continue their journey. Railway agents maintained informal employment services. The "land-seeker's ticket" was a method by which the fare paid would be applied on the purchase of railway-owned western land. Railway land was sold by installments, and special reduced rates were given colonists who traveled and settled together.[9]

The pièce de résistance of the railway advertising menu

[6]Joseph Netz, "The Great Los Angeles Real Estate Boom of 1887," in Hist. Soc. of Sou. Calif. *Annual Publications, 1915-16*, X, 56.

[7]*Pasadena Daily Union*, Sept. 5, 1887.

[8]Charles Dwight Willard, *The Herald's History of Los Angeles City* (1901), p. 310.

[9]Edna Monch Parker, "The Southern Pacific Railroad and Settlement in Southern California," *Pac. Hist. Rev.*, VI, 111-14.

was the excursion, started on a large scale by the Santa Fe in 1886. During early 1887 directed trips entered California at the rate of three to five per day, and each regular train had many sections. As a result freight traffic was delayed, and schedule revision became necessary. California newspapers exulted over the number of excursionists. The following announcement is typical:

The Fall Excursion

The first of the regular fall excursions from the East to California left Kansas City yesterday (the 7th), and will come via the lines of the Union, Central, and Southern Pacific to Los Angeles, where it is due on the 12th inst. After that date an excursion will arrive every other day throughout the season.[10]

By these various methods the railroads capitalized on the attractions of southern California, which had first been brought to the attention of the public by the rate war. The railroads were therefore the immediate, if not the most important, cause of the boom, and their influence was cataclysmic in its results. When the railroads fought, the boom started. It remained for the people in California and their local advertising methods to keep it going.

[10]*Pasadena Daily Union*, Sept. 8, 1887.

CHAPTER IV

Advertising

ANOTHER basic cause of the boom was the extensive advertising and publicity campaign which carried information about southern California to all parts of the world. During the decades of the seventies and eighties the southern region first developed the publicity consciousness which has characterized it ever since and which has been largely responsible for its phenomenal growth. Neither agricultural development nor railroad competition would have attracted immigrant hordes unless the way had been paved by widespread propaganda.

The new population had heard about California from many sources: accounts of returning gold seekers, descriptions written by eager travelers and residents, railroad propaganda, material from western newspapers and other agencies, and, finally, letters from friends and relatives who had found the southland to their liking and had become permanent citizens. All of these sources except the first will be considered; return-

ing miners were for the most part either disappointed and thus
not good advertisers, or else primarily interested in the northern half of the state.

Probably the earliest tenuous hint of southern-California
advertising which filtered into the eastern mind was that
provided by travelers' and others' descriptive accounts. An
immense number of these were written after the gold rush
and before the boom, and they range from the encyclopedic
Resources of John Hittell to the jocund and slightly mocking
"Golden Hesperides" of Charles Dudley Warner.[1] Although
the spirit varies, the content is much the same in all—high
praise of miscellaneous benefits and of the following attributes
of the region: climate, rapid disappearance of the frontier,
agricultural potentialities, cheap living costs, healthfulness,
picturesqueness, and money-making opportunities.

The climate was, and is, a perennial favorite. Warner was
enthusiastic: "This is Paradise. And the climate? Perpetual
summer (but daily rising in price). . . . The night temperature
throughout California is invariably in great contrast to that
in the daytime; nearly everywhere fire is necessary at night
the year round, and agreeable nearly all the year, even in
Southern California."[2] Another visitor adds: "The architecture
of this region will remind you that you are in a land where
it is never very cold. The dwelling is a secondary matter here,
and it results that many people are satisfied to live in very
small and slight houses."[3] William Henry Bishop, who traveled
during the boom, was even more outspoken: "The temperature, this late November day—on which there are telegrams
in the papers of snow-storms at the North and East—is per-

[1] *Atlantic Monthly*, LXI, 48-56.

[2] *Ibid.*, p. 50.

[3] Charles Nordhoff, *California: for Health, Pleasure, and Residence* (1873),
p. 139.

fection. It is neither hot nor cold. A sybarite would not alter it."[4]

There was need to abolish the idea prevalent in eastern minds that California was still frontier territory. Much space was devoted to assuring timid newcomers of the safety of life in the West: "The whole number of persons in the whole southern half of the State (where thousands sleep all summer on the open ground) injured by snakes and poisonous reptiles, animals, etc., in the last ten years is not equal to the number killed by lightning alone in one year in one county in many Eastern States."[5] Charles Nordhoff—a traveler-publicist and grandfather of the modern novelist—whose volume, *California for Health, Pleasure, and Residence*, was given "more credit for sending people to California than anything else ever written about the section,"[6] went so far as to say that "There are no dangers to travelers on the beaten track in California; there are no inconveniences which a child or a tenderly reared woman would not laugh at . . . when you have spent half a dozen weeks in the State, you will perhaps return with a notion that New York is the true frontier land, and that you have nowhere in the United States seen so complete a civilization."[7]

As southern California had few precious metals to exploit, and as the cattle business suffered a sharp decline in the sixties, more and more of the advertisers turned to agriculture as the real basis of the southland's prosperity. "Possibly Southern California should be described as a garden rather than an agricultural region," says Warner. "There is . . . no doubt that nearly every kind of wine known to the market is made

[4]*Old Mexico and Her Lost Provinces* (1889), p. 436.
[5]Theodore S. Van Dyke, *Southern California* (1886), p. 151.
[6]Morrow Mayo, *Los Angeles* (1933), pp. 70 f.
[7]Nordhoff, p. 18.

from the same field."[8] Nordhoff makes an even broader statement: "After a thorough examination, I believe Southern California to be the finest part of the State, and the best region in the whole United States for farmers."[9] Van Dyke notes the variety of products which could be grown: "Southern California seems to produce with proper care nearly every kind of tree, shrub, grass, herb, or tuber that is at all common or useful in the temperate zone, together with a large number of those of the tropics."[10]

There were, of course, extravagant claims. Bishop, for instance, asserts that ten or even five acres were "a comfortable property. . . . Half an acre in lemons is sufficient for the support of a family. It is in evidence here that returns of from $500 to $1,000 an acre are had from orange, lemon, and lime, after the trees have arrived at full bearing."[11] And Warner recounts the tale of a vigorous booster who claimed that vine growth was so rapid that melons were bumped along and bruised on the ground. "If you want to pick a melon in this country, you have to get on horseback."[12] These tall stories were somewhat neutralized by criticism of more levelheaded promoters, like Van Dyke, who states: "It is just as true that beets here reach the size of one hundred pounds and over, that sixty bushels of wheat are raised to the acre . . . as that in the Mississippi catfish have been caught weighing fifty pounds. . . . So, too, those who call it the land of 'perpetual' or 'eternal' sunshine do not mean that literally, but suppose the reader capable of making the proper exceptions."[13]

[8] *Atlantic Monthly*, LXI, 53.
[9] Nordhoff, p. 130.
[10] Van Dyke, p. 189.
[11] Bishop, p. 435.
[12] *Atlantic Monthly*, LXI, 49.
[13] Van Dyke, p. 188.

31

Another advantage of the region was the cheapness of living costs. Nordhoff claims that living expenses (before the boom) were less by a third than in any eastern state. California was at this time, he says, "the cheapest country in the United States to live in."[14]

A most important talking point for southern California was its healthfulness. Bishop remarks:

> Invalidism is heard of with considerable frequency as an excuse for the migration hither. Certainly many advantages offer to the invalid. The climate permits him to be almost constantly out-of-doors. The sky is blue, the sun unclouded, nearly every day in the year, and he can go into his orchard and concern himself about his Navel or Brazilian oranges, his paper-rind St. Michaels, and his Tahiti seedlings, with little let or hindrance.[15]

Much attention was given to the aid of the climate in the treatment of tuberculosis, or, as it was then called, "consumption." One writer says: "The purity of the air of Los Angeles is remarkable. Vegetation dries up before it dies, and hardly ever seems to decay. Meat suspended in the sun dries up, but never rots. The air, when inhaled, gives to the individual a stimulus and vital force which only an atmosphere so pure can ever communicate."[16] There was, it must be admitted, some mild criticism, but never enough to detract in any measure from the praise bestowed.

The Spanish and Mexican periods had given California a picturesque aura which was capitalized by the advertisers. Los Angeles was described as "cosmopolitan," and said to be "the product of one era of barbarism, two or three kinds of

[14]Nordhoff, p. 18.

[15]Bishop, pp. 450-51.

[16]Benjamin C. Truman, *Semi-tropical California* (1874), pp. 33-34.

A NEW DEPARTURE

EXCURSION!

A THROUGH CAR

FROM

LOS ANGELES to BOSTON, Mass.

SEPT. 25th, 1886

LOWEST PRICE.

QUICKEST TIME.

BEST ACCOMMODATIONS.

I shall leave Los Angeles September 25, for Boston, Mass., with a special party, making the trip without change of cars. Returning, leave Boston November 3, 1886. Tickets sold to any point for one way or the round trip. For particulars address me at

California Southern Railroad Office,

239 N. Main St., Los Angeles.

N. C. CARTER.

EXCURSION BROADSIDE (REDUCED)

civilizations, and an interregnum."[17] Warner praises Camulos Rancho and Santa Barbara for their preservation of the older Latin atmosphere.

The possibilities of profit in California investment were not by any means neglected. Warner facetiously remarks: "It has been a subject of regret ever since that I did not buy Southern California when I was there last March, and sell it out the same month. I should have made enough to pay my railway fare back . . . and had money left to negotiate for one of the little States on the Atlantic coast."[18] Another writer boasts that Los Angeles "takes the first place by all odds for booms in lands and building."[19]

Finally, there were plenty of general statements which attempted to sum up the glories of California for the prospective settler. A typical example is the following: "In this newer and nobler life which is growing up here upon the shores of the Pacific . . . it seems to . . . [the writer] he can discern the fair promise of a civilization which had its only analogue in that Graeco-Latin race-flowering which came to the eastern shores of the Mediterranean centuries ago."[20]

But travelers' accounts, whether in books or magazines, were not the only means of advertising California. Much of the publicity was financed by railroads, primarily the Southern Pacific, for two main purposes: to sell their own granted land, and to induce a large population, whose future business and travel would be profitable, to settle along their lines. One of the most effective methods used by the railroads was the employment of agents, who wrote, lectured, and planned

[17]Benjamin F. Taylor, *Between the Gates* (1878), p. 261.

[18]*Atlantic Monthly*, LXI, 48.

[19]William H. Thomes, *California—As It Is and Was* (1887), p. 30

[20]Walter Lindley and J. P. Widney, *California of the South* (1888), p. 72.

exhibits in various parts of the world, expounding the glories of the West. A noted example was Jerome Madden, Southern Pacific land agent at San Francisco. His books, *California: Its Attractions for the Invalid, Tourist, Capitalist, and Homeseeker* and *Lands of the Southern Pacific*, attained a wide circulation. The same railroad maintained other agents in many parts of the United States and Europe. The companies also co-operated with immigration agencies like the California Immigrant Union, and subsidized editors and writers. An interesting illustration of the latter was the Southern Pacific's financing of Marcus D. Boruck's *Spirit of the Times*, a San Francisco weekly. Land advertisements were often written up in the form of pseudo news articles and inserted in ordinary news columns. Among writers paid by the railroads were Charles Nordhoff and Benjamin Truman, whose pointed allusions in their various volumes to the lines retaining them leave little doubt as to their chief interest. In addition, railroad companies published pamphlets and folders which were distributed by station agents throughout the country. One of the more ambitious efforts of the Big Four was the *Southern Pacific Sketch Book*, which attained a circulation of 10,000 copies.

Western newspapers did their share in advertising the southland. Their circulation was, of course, more limited than that attained by descriptive accounts and railway propaganda, but it was much more direct and served to guide the enthusiasm of the newcomer into proper paths of investment. Newspaper advertising reached its zenith in 1886 and 1887, and many were the tricks which promoters employed to urge their wares. There were several types of newspaper advertisements, and some exhibited a strangely modern approach to the advertising problem. First, there was an abundance of realtors' announcements, which were little more than expanded business cards—for example:

◈§ *Advertising* §◈

Office of

E. H. Lockwood

Cor. Colorado St. and Fairoaks Ave.

Dealer In

GILT EDGE REAL ESTATE[21]

Newspaper copy writers also delighted in lengthy descriptions of various tract offerings. A long-winded discussion in the *Pasadena Daily Union* waxed rather confidential:

This is an era of town building in Southern California, and it is proper that it should be so, for the people are coming to us from the East and from the North and from beyond the sea, and for the great multitude whose faces are turned with longing eyes toward this summer land and who will want homes among us, we must provide places. And while there is much room in Pasadena and in Monrovia and in other pleasant towns, yet Pasadena prices, and even Monrovia prices are rather high for the purses of many who will come, and these places are rapidly filling, and the prices are getting higher.[22]

There followed an even longer description of the location of the proposed town, its benefits for the sick, a pledge as to the prohibition of saloons, and a presentation of the stock issues offered. The town thus treated was La Verne, which is not yet a metropolis. Some of the descriptions included glib statements which today seem rather humorous, such as, "Elsinore is the center of a coal mining and manufacturing district, which makes it a natural business center.[23] Still others resorted to poetry, of which the following effusion is perhaps the most brilliant:

[21]*Pasadena Daily Union*, Oct. 10, 1887.

[22]*Ibid.*, Sept. 5, 1887.

[23]*Ibid.*, Oct. 29, 1887.

Go wing thy flight from star to star,
From world to luminous world as far
As the universe spreads its flaming wall.
Take all the pleasures of all the spheres,
And multiply each through endless years,
One winter at Vernon is worth them all.[24]

A favorite trick of the newspaper advertisers was to make a flamboyant announcement to arouse the curiosity of the reader, and to follow it up with a more detailed explanation. As early as October, 1887, the following advertisement was printed:

Linda Rosa!   Linda Rosa!
            —WHERE IS—
Linda Rosa!   Linda Rosa![25]

Nobody knew—but during November the explanation appeared as a half page of copy that began:

Linda Rosa! Linda Rosa!
WHERE IS LINDA ROSA?
WE GIVE YOU THE PARTICULARS NOW

It is nestled in the far-famed Temecula Valley, the home of Allesandro and Ramona. It is situated in San Diego County on the line of the California Southern Railroad, which being connected with the Atlantic and Pacific, and Atchison, Topeka, and Santa Fe lines, gives us not only a direct Eastern outlet, but also one with the port of San Diego.[26]

Another example of this type of announcement reads:

[24]*Los Angeles Times*, July 3, 1887.

[25]*Pasadena Daily Union*, Oct. 29, 1887.

[26]*Ibid.*, Nov. 25, 1887.

HO! FOR THE CORSON TRACT

For the accommodation of all desiring to examine these
Lots, whose attractions and good quality it is
not desired to hide under a bushel

A FREE CARRIAGE DAILY

(except Sunday) will leave the Santa Fe Station
at 1:36 p.m.[27]

The use of pseudo news articles to advertise realty offices,
railway land, or tract offerings was widespread. The *Los
Angeles Times* included on its front page such items as the
following:

Bargains in Real Estate

Do not fail to read the advertisement of J. C. Byram and Co.,
in the "wants" column of today's Times. This firm is having great
success in handling city, suburban, and ranch property. You will
make no mistake in placing any kind of real estate in their hands
for sale or exchange.[28]

Special supplements, like that of twelve pages issued by the
Times on New Year's Day, 1886, contributed to the publicity
about southern California. In this particular issue, the types of
people who would benefit by life in the region were listed in
detail, with an eye to eastern readers. The *Herald* had a supplement of eight pages on the same day. An examination of
local newspapers shows a great increase in real-estate advertising during 1886 and 1887, reaching a peak during the latter
year. There was a sharp decline in 1888, however, when the
boom broke, and by July of that year the only land advertisements printed resembled the following, in which the realtor
begged for business:

[27]*Ibid.*, Sept. 7, 1887.

[28]*Los Angeles Times*, Mar. 7, 1886.

37

~§ The Boom of the Eighties §~

WANTED! WANTED!
Resident Lots and Acre
Property Listed With
Us For Sale
Good Property Will Sell
Arnold & Mills Co.[29]

Among local agencies which aided the newspapers in their dissemination of propaganda were chambers of commerce, boards of trade, realty syndicates, and the California Immigrant Union. The annual reports and statistical pamphlets issued by these groups constituted a worthy addition to boom advertising, and the parent organizations became veritable experiment stations in discovering new uses for California land. The outstanding publication was the Union's booklet, *All about California and the Inducements to Settle There*, which went through at least three editions and carried to all reached by the Union's far-flung tentacles detailed information on California's development.

A fourth type of publicity was evident in the activities of enthusiastic newcomers, who exerted their influence chiefly by personal correspondence. Often, of course, there is no possibility of learning just what arguments they used to persuade friends and relatives to come to California, but a survey of postal activity, particularly during boom years, shows that many letters traveled eastward. And as the population of California continued to increase magnificently, the assumption is perhaps safe that some migration, at least, was due to the urgings of these personal missives. Letters mailed in Los Angeles alone increased from 2,083 per month before the boom to 21,333 at its height. Pioneer settlers like Benjamin D. Wilson praised California in their letters. "No Country can be more

[29]*Pasadena Daily Union*, July 27, 1888.

38

healthy than this," he wrote his brother as early as 1854. "Here besides the finest climate in the world we produce every species of grain and fruits in the greatest abundance."[30] Prospective immigrants often wrote Wilson asking for information about agriculture and living conditions, and his replies were consistently enthusiastic. His son-in-law, J. De Barth Shorb, answered many of these requests for information. "Los Angeles County," said Shorb in a characteristic reply, "is the third county in the State in point of productiveness and it is only in its infancy of development."[31] He also thought "Los Angeles City the best place to start a bank in this vicinity, or at any point in California." But he added, "A more economical disposition of a larger banking capital could be easier made by simply renting an office and loaning on real estate securities which in this county affords such first class security."[32] Harrison Gray Otis was another California resident whose eastern contacts made his influence as an advertiser important. A typical Civil War veteran in his forties, he arrived in California in 1882 from Ohio, looking for a place to make a new start. His editorship of the *Grand Army Journal,* while in the East, gave him an influence among army men which he utilized effectively to persuade them to move to California.

These four types of publicity—descriptive accounts, railroad propaganda, newspaper and local agency material, and, finally, the work of enthusiastic residents—combined to make southern California perhaps the best-advertised portion of the country during the third quarter of the last century. Quaint as this advertising was, it illustrates better than anything else

[30]B. D. Wilson to [Wiley R. Wilson], April 12, 1854. See also John Walton Caughey, "Don Benito Wilson: An Average Southern Californian," *Huntington Library Quarterly,* II, 285-300.

[31]J. De Barth Shorb to J. F. Slevin, March 22, 1880.

[32]J. De Barth Shorb to A. Wellington Hunt, June 6, 1877.

the economic tendencies of the period, and it forecasts the astounding success of modern publicity methods in the same region. That it seems primitive is no sign that it was in-effective. Besides statistics, the best evidence of its value was the critical attitude of the northern half of the state. "Our brethren of the city and would-be state of the Angels under-stand how to advertise," wryly announced the *San Jose Times-Mercury* in 1885. "The average Eastern mind conceives of California as a small tract of country situated in and about Los Angeles. . . . The result shows the pecuniary value of cheek."[33]

[33]Glenn Chesney Quiett, *They Built the West* (1934), p. 275.

CHAPTER V

The Boom in Los Angeles

THE larger causes of the boom having been described,
it now remains to examine the progress of the flurry
in the areas chiefly affected. Outstanding as a center
of boom enthusiasm was the city of Los Angeles itself, the
nucleus of the entire frenzy. Strange to say, the city has never
been given full credit for the part it played during these exciting years. This neglect is easier to understand when one
realizes that, during the past eighty years, the normal growth
of Los Angeles has been so fantastically rapid that any acceleration, however striking, fails to stand out against the equally
striking background. Pioneers who lived through the flurry
often insist that there was no boom in the city itself, that the
upswing was a purely suburban phenomenon, but county
records prove them incorrect. Los Angeles was the true focus
of the boom: urban capital financed the boom towns of the
countryside; city realtors originated the most picturesque
promotion schemes; the biggest auction sales were held within

the city limits; most of the buyers, even of country property, boarded excursion trains at a Los Angeles station.

During 1886-88, there were filed in Los Angeles County alone some 1,770 tract maps, subdivisions, and replats—397 maps in 1886, 1,079 in 1887, and 294 in 1888. For the most part these maps were for territory either within, or closely adjacent to, the city limits of Los Angeles and Pasadena, and in each of the three years Los Angeles had a clear majority. Of the 397 plans filed during 1886 Los Angeles listed 174; in the year of the boom's height, 1887, fully a third of the maps—about 375—were of city property; and in the year of the decline, 1888, almost half (119) were for urban territory. Such figures are indisputable evidence that Los Angeles partook copiously of the feast. In 1886 the *Tribune* bragged, "Los Angeles is booming, and is likely to boom for years to come."[1]

The boom of the eighties was not by any means the only one which Los Angeles experienced. "The growth of the city," says Guinn, "has been irregular, by fits and starts,"[2] and he lists four periods preceding 1880 when the economic upswing was sharp enough to be defined as a boom; none of them, however, was so important or so extreme as that of 1887. One took place in the early fifties as a reflected flurry of the gold rush. Another occurred during the last years of that decade, when a spurt of building activity, sponsored by Californios who were now rich enough to indulge in realty manipulation, resulted in the erection of such structures as Stearns's Arcadia Block and the Temple Block. Ten years later immigration increased sharply, and the assessed valuation of city property rose above $2,000,000, largely as a result of the railway propaganda which was to achieve the con-

[1] Oct. 25, 1886.

[2] James M. Guinn, *Historical and Biographical Record of Southern California* (1902), p. 155.

struction of the Southern Pacific to Los Angeles. And the peak of another building boom was reached in 1874, when construction figures attained a new high mark of $600,000.

In the mid-seventies people became definitely interested in Los Angeles real estate and groped toward the development of modern publicity methods. A centennial celebration on July 4, 1876, advertised the city very effectively, and property sales increased in a lively fashion. Mayor William Workman had purchased Boyle Heights land in 1867 for five and ten dollars per acre; now he sold it for $200 per acre. Business started the slow movement toward the south and west which in recent years has been intensified.

During the early eighties signs of imminent prosperity became evident in the rapid arrival of new business enterprises and in the astounding growth of old ones. A table published in the *Tribune*[3] in October, 1886, presented the increase in the number of businesses and individual fortunes in the course of these years:

Value	1882	1884	1886
Over $100,000	7	9	14
$50,000—100,000	9	24	27
25,000— 50,000	43	51	49
10,000— 25,000	109	186	229
5,000— 10,000	248	331	373

Examples of phenomenal price rises are numerous, and, unless environmental circumstances are considered, are none too significant. They do show, however, the increasing ease with which money was spent for real estate during the boom. The father of Joseph Netz, one of its historians, purchased thirty-two acres at the corner of Vernon and Central Avenues in 1883 for $12,000 and sold them two years later at a loss. The

[3]Oct. 25, 1886.

same property brought $40,000 in 1887. Twenty-five acres on Seventh Street near Figueroa were unsuccessfully offered in 1886 at $11,000; the next year they brought $80,000. Land at Sixth and Main streets, quoted at twenty dollars per front foot in 1883, sold for $800 per foot in 1887.

Prices continued to ascend, and by 1886 the city boom was on in full force. Railway statistics promised an influx of 4,000 persons during the year, and optimism, particularly among realtors, was rife. Land advertisements in the newspapers gradually grew larger during the summer, and by fall were occupying far more than their share of column inches. New realty firms were organized by the dozens, and their proprietors gladly granted cheerful interviews. Two of the more important development companies founded during this year were the Southern California Land Company, which took offices in the Baker Block, and the Los Angeles Land Bureau. The former presented the Howes Tract on Jefferson Street, and the Childs, Urmston, City Center, Williamson, and Columbia Colony subdivisions. The Land Bureau's sales methods illustrated that cunning naïveté so characteristic of Victorian business methods; in December the concern called a free meeting at Armory Hall to discuss "Southern California, Her Present and Future, with special reference to LOS ANGELES AND HER SUBURBS,"[4] which, like so many public meetings of those years, doubtless degenerated into an auction sale or at best a description of tract offerings before the evening was done.

The direction in which the city tended to grow was in 1886 still a question of commanding interest, although signs and portents of the modern southwestern expansion became more and more evident. Barren lands in the vicinity of the University of Southern California rose to $1,000 per acre, and Moses L. Wicks, as active in real estate as he was in trans-

[4]*Ibid.*, Dec. 31, 1886.

portation and banking, stated that Los Angeles was growing toward the sea, and that was "the direction to invest in."[5] The prediction was made that west Los Angeles would be the "aristocratic quarter"—a prognostication borne out by the recent establishment of Beverly Hills, Westwood, Bel-Air, and the Palisade developments. There was still much interest, however, in east Los Angeles and Boyle Heights, and construction of the Buena Vista Street bridge was believed not unlikely to boom that section greatly. The new city hall on Fort Street (now Broadway) gave a mild incentive to eastward expansion, and the year ended with the complete sale of an entire east Los Angeles tract, the Alexander, which brought $14,000 to its developers. Business property, although increasing steadily in value, was relatively quiet during the boom. For example, the corner of Ninth and Flower Streets was on sale for $6,500, the corner of Eleventh and Hope for the same amount, and a lot near Ninth and Hope for $7,000— these were, however, far from the center of activity.

With the arrival of hordes of newcomers, housing facilities became strained during the first year of the boom, and landowners were repeatedly urged to build rental property. Despite agitation, they generally refused, preferring to take advantage of rising sales prices rather than risk large sums in soaring construction costs. Fortunate owners of rentable houses were, however, enjoying handsome revenues, and realtors' profits in 1886 were composed largely of rental commissions. Reluctant as they were to build to rent, many investors proved quite willing to build to sell, and during the year about one hundred new houses per month were erected, representing an estimated investment of $5,000,000. Boom frenzy had not yet entirely eliminated that class of purchasers who planned to occupy the property they bought, and as a

[5]*Ibid.*, Oct. 10, 1886.

result hill lots and the spacious flats of west Washington Street were highly popular.

The increase in volume of realty transfers was steady during most of 1886, starting at $1,018,578 for January, rising in February, declining somewhat for two months, and then rising again. During the latter part of the year, monthly transfer totals were usually over $3,000,000. Clearly the boom, though still decorous and restrained, had started, and 1886 demonstrated what could be accomplished by proper promotion and enthusiastic response. Optimism throbbed hard that winter, and Los Angeles exuberantly awaited the spring. Somehow it seemed to know that the climax had not yet been reached, and that the rainbow's end was sturdily anchored in the plaza of the City of the Angels.

The year 1887 was the kaleidoscopic peak of boom excitement for all of southern California. When 1886 saw an influx of thousands of tourists and immigrants, promoters felt justified in predicting prosperity ahead. But the spring of the next year brought with it, not a recurrence of mere thousands, but the arrival of tens of thousands, who crowded the trains to overflowing and loudly demanded a place to stay and spend their money. The population of Los Angeles was estimated to have increased from 11,000 to 80,000 during boom years, and most of the increment undoubtedly came in 1887. Inhibitions and conservatism vanished. The gold was there for the taking, and aggressive noisiness carried the day.

The year dawned with a cold snap, but local citizens impatiently refused to be discouraged by such an un-Californian occurrence. The turnover of real estate attained a breathtaking pace. By April the city realized that it was in the throes of the most tremendous flurry it had ever experienced, and editorial writers were already predicting the permanence of the frenzy. One stated that the boom would continue as a normal result of the increase in population. "Never again,"

he said, "will real estate at points eligible for business purposes or for pleasurable occupation, be as low as sometimes
it has been on the market."[6] "To call it a craze or a bubble,"
proclaimed the *Tribune,* "is the veriest nonsense."[7] Optimism
was unquenchable. Business found itself stimulated by the
reduction in freight rates due to the Santa Fe's arrival, and
buying enthusiasm was kept at high pitch by the publication
of simmering statistics in the newspapers. Ambitious plans
were made for civic betterments, including a new courthouse,
a city hall, improved sewers, pavements, and schools; the
Pavilion was the scene of a colorful April flower show which
proclaimed the glories of California horticulture. Newspapers
were filled with items announcing the formation of new land
companies, irrigation enterprises, and real estate firms of which
there were an estimated 2,300 within the city limits; established concerns, such as the Los Angeles Land Bureau, did a
thriving business with offerings like the Governor Stoneman
Tract, emphasized during early May.

For the first time business property became the subject of
widespread speculation. In April an undeveloped tract of
fifty-four acres on Main Street was offered for $100,000, and
the advertisement stressed that it was "fine for subdivision."
Spring Street property was popular, a two-story building on
a sixty-one-foot lot being offered for $87,000, and business
frontage bringing $700 to $2,000 per front foot. City lots
ranged from $200 to $25,000 each. Urban residence property
meanwhile encouraged wild gambles. So attractive had countryside developments become that city realtors were obliged
to explain the advantages of metropolitan investment. One
advertisement read: "What do you prefer? In the new city
of Multicraze, thirty miles from Los Angeles, three miles

[6]*Ibid.,* Apr. 4, 1887.

[7]*Ibid.,* May 29, 1887.

from the nearest residence, amidst beautiful desert sand, sage brush, and large stones, a lot 45 x 130 for $350. [or] We will sell you, one mile from Los Angeles city limits, surrounded by magnificent improvements, rich, level, loamy land at $350 per acre."[8] Another realtor argued: "Why go forty miles away . . . when you can purchase half-acre lots in South Los Angeles at $160 in installments."[9] A favorite trick was to offer residence lots in blocks of three or five, perhaps with the object of inserting a "dud" with salable property. In this spirit three lots near Hope and Temple streets were priced at $7,500. Residences on Hill between Ninth and Tenth brought $8,500 to $12,000 each; houses on Grand Avenue between Seventh and Tenth earned from $5,000 to $10,000 for their owners; Temple Street land was marketed at $950 to $3,500; and "country property" near Lincoln Park, in the form of lots on Pasadena Avenue, sold at ten to fifteen dollars per front foot. At the same time, acreage surrounding the city had risen from seven to fifty dollars per unit. No longer were the hills favored by purchasers; they were suitable only for occupation, and the buyer who bought to sell wanted land easy of access and simple to survey.

Insatiable promoters began to analyze their sales and concluded that newcomers were contributing the bulk of boom profits. They chided native sons for their timidity, and reminded them that easterners were buying "at prices which enabled them to reap the bulk of the great advance."[10] The boom, it seemed, was based largely on fresh capital. The new arrivals accepted as gospel truth the propaganda flung at them from all sides and eagerly wrote to friends and relatives urging them to move West. The Los Angeles post office handled

[8]*Ibid.*, Apr. 19, 1887.
[9]*Ibid.*
[10]*Ibid.*, May 15, 1887.

CITY OF THE BOOM—LOS ANGELES IN 1889

the mail of 200,000 transients between August and December of that hectic year, and postal receipts rose from $19,000 in 1880 to well over $50,000 at the boom's peak. A city directory published in 1887 listed 55,488 citizens, but it is certain that, though the wildest estimates must be discounted, the true population far exceeded this figure. Los Angeles was a crowded, seething city of promoters, amateur and professional; hotels bulged with occupants, prices soared to astronomic levels, and everywhere—on the streets, in print, in homes and clubs—the incessant topic was land, the land of southern California.

Transfers in 1887 were soon being recorded at the rate of thirty to seventy daily, involving totals in excess of $100,000. Some days brought record sales. Amounts noted from April 15 to April 30 will serve as an index of the rapid turnover:

April 15, $398,871	April 23, $143,707
16, 175,828	24, 827,925
17, 433,988	26, 266,676
19, 249,424	27, 240,814
20, 305,793	28, 141,250
21, 258,117	29, 498,418
22, 317,035	30, 278,164[11]

Monthly sales fluctuated in the neighborhood of $5,000,000 from January to March, but in April rose to $7,174,908. From then on there was a steady rise. In May the *Tribune* remarked that the day was a poor one when a quarter of a million dollars in property failed to change hands. In June transfers totaled $10,899,120, and the parallel July figure was $11,930,354. The peak months of the boom—June, July, and August—brought $38,000,000 in real-estate transfers to Los Angeles County. Truly the late summer and early fall of 1887 in Los Angeles

[11]The *Los Angeles Tribune* and *Los Angeles Express* published daily and weekly transfer summaries during these years.

49

need yield to few rivals as a period of feverish business, ready cash, and lush prosperity.

But the summit was reached in 1887. After that, the boom proceeded to slip downgrade, and promoters were fully occupied explaining drooping sales figures and dwelling happily on the past—emphasizing, of course, their opinion that there was no logical reason why the flurry should not surpass itself during the following summer. Their manful strivings were in vain. Easterners, satiated with hysterical advertising, responded in ever-diminishing numbers, and the winter tourist crop was painfully small. Unfortunate incidents occurred to discourage optimists. For instance, January was a month of flooding rains which temporarily disrupted railway communication, and some property owners decided that the time had come to sell out. Advertisements became plaintive, then desperately noisy, then subsided into mere feeble glimmerings of their old enthusiasm. The boom was over, and the machine was running down.

However, 1888 was not a year of complete disaster. Many there were who ardently believed that nothing could destroy southern California's prosperity, and these excitedly patronized the shaky market. Others, more conservative, congratulated themselves on having recognized the boom for what it was at the start, and continued their agricultural and business developments with calm faith in the basic sturdiness of southern California's economy. Cautious newcomers began to realize that climate would not support them permanently and, instead of speculating in risky residential tracts far from the city limits or in inflated business blocks, began to request "mediocre-priced business property,"[12] with a view to developing a permanent source of income rather than mere speculative profits. A rumor that removal of the post office

[12]*Los Angeles Express*, Feb. 4, 1888.

to Broadway near Seventh was contemplated caused "quite a little ripple in realty . . . down there,"[13] and one sale of business frontage consummated in that district brought $875 per foot. The buyer, however, soon became aware of his mistake in purchasing so far from the center of town, for the rumor proved false. He immediately sold for $112 per foot and considered himself fortunate to have saved as much as he did. Residence land was not entirely neglected, meanwhile. The west side prospered, often boasting weekly sales totaling $100,000 to $200,000, but the consensus was that no single section of the city was especially favored by purchasers. Eastside sales were stimulated by the proposal of the Los Angeles and San Gabriel Valley Railroad to erect a station at the corner of Aliso and Los Angeles Streets. In March a lot on Washington near San Pedro was listed at $2,000; a lot on the east side of South Vermont at $750; and similar offerings, near Seventh and Santa Fe, at $450 each. Prospects of the southern outskirts were improved by local railway expansion there, and districts such as Vernon maintained fair sales records throughout the year. Col. Griffith G. Griffith, donor of the park which now bears his name, put the undeveloped Los Feliz Rancho on the market and embarked on an efficient sales campaign which resulted in an upswing in that region.

Other encouragement was not lacking. Excursion parties continued to arrive, even if they did not buy as freely as they had the previous summer, and predictions of a rejuvenation of the boom were limited only by newspaper space available to print them. Realtors were cheered by the growing relative importance of suburban sales, and one recklessly prophesied that residence lots at $1,000 would soon be a thing of the past. The city's six streetcar lines flourished, demonstrating that although people were no longer eager to buy they were

[13]*Ibid.*, Feb. 11, 1888.

51

still willing to go and look, and optimists pointed to passenger traffic between Pasadena and Los Angeles as heavier than "on any other line of road in use."[14] There was also a building spurt of no small proportions during the opening months of the year. Investigators agreed that this was the biggest house-building craze Los Angeles had ever experienced, with some 260 new residences under construction in January. In addition, several new business blocks were projected, among them a 90,000-dollar structure at the northwest corner of Spring and Second Streets; a 95,000-dollar building on the east side of North Main, near Temple; and three other less imposing edifices, scaled at $40,000 to $60,000 each. A survey of nine of the city's leading architects showed that they had $247,000 of residence building on order, and the total of business and residence property then in course of construction amounted to $729,000. One abortive project which received much publicity was that for a hotel at the corner of Tenth and Main; the planned cost was $750,000, and the structure was to cover a two-acre area. The architect was said to have "adopted the very free treatment of the Franco-English Renaissance,[15] and the building was to have four stories and 400,000 square feet of floor space. Each detail of the proposed hostelry was discussed with palpitating enthusiasm on front pages of newspapers; it had been talked of during many months of 1887, and now that it was to become a reality Los Angeles promoters felt they would have to bow no longer to San Francisco in magnificence of hospitality. Construction did begin, and the 80,000-dollar foundation was built, but the boom sickened and died before more of the inn could be brought

[14]*Commercial Bulletin of Southern California*, Jan. 28, 1888.

[15]*Los Angeles Express*, Jan. 14, 1888. Newmark says the structure was to be the Hotel Splendid; but Harry Ellington Brooks describes a newspaper competition which resulted in the name "Balboa."

to completion. Later the masonry and lot were offered free to anyone willing to go on with the structure.

Notwithstanding the slump, Los Angeles sales for the week ending February 24 exceeded by $500,000 the combined sales of Sacramento, Oakland, and San Jose and topped by more than $850,000 those of San Francisco. Other sections of the state quite openly attempted to profit by this activity in Los Angeles; they delegated agents to establish offices in the city and tried to divert some of the freely flowing capital. Among them was one J. E. Yoakum, who advertised his headquarters at 16 South Main Street as a "Bureau of Information for Tulare and Fresno Counties." That his sponsors were not too sanguine of success may be concluded from the fact that they permitted him to deal also in local real estate.

But the boom was clearly on the decline. Despite favorable auspices, the first months of 1888 brought with them misgivings. No longer was optimism unqualified. Flaws were discovered by even that most civic-minded group, the real-estate men. There was, for instance, an attempt by a syndicate to sell to the city the land on which St. Vincent's College had stood. St. Vincent's, having decided that boom prices made its five-acre campus near Sixth and Broadway too valuable for educational purposes, in 1886 had sold it for $100,000, moving to a new site at Washington and Grand. About the middle of January, 1888, the syndicate that had bought the old campus proposed to sell the land to the city for the inflated sum of $450,000, taking in part payment the city-hall property, valued at $300,000. "The sublime and wholesale character of this scheme," sneered the *Express*, "lifts it so far above ordinary, everyday jobbery as to entitle it to a considerable measure of respect."[16] Even its own land, Los Angeles decided, could be overvalued. By assertions like the

[16]*Ibid.*

following, promoters tried vainly to persuade themselves that there was no ground for misgiving:

All leading agents report a very healthful but not an exceedingly brisk market. "It seems to be the idea," said one of them, "that values are too high. All newcomers, you will find, get here with that delusion to muddle and bother them, and it takes a residence in town or near it of a fortnight or so before they come to the conclusion that Los Angeles real estate, city or county, is one of the best buys in the world. Only the advanced lines of the visiting army have yet entered the market."[17]

Grumblings and forebodings grew louder. "The market," a realty reporter frankly admitted, "is not what it used to be," and, although he attempted to modify his gloom with the statement that "It is a staple, solid market, and nine-tenths of the sales made may be chronicled as bona fide transactions," his depression was clearly evident.[18]

Sales statistics verified the apprehension. January realty transfers began bravely at $1,000,000 per week, and the month's sales amounted to nearly $7,000,000. February and March showed small increases, but the year's peak was reached in March, at the level of $7,699,917. Then the decline set in: from $5,500,000 in April there was a slight rise to $6,600,000 in May, followed by a quick plunge in July to $4,700,000— only about a third as much as that month yielded in the previous year. The totals of daily transactions exhibited exaggerated fluctuations, which were perhaps as good an index as any that the end was in sight. The glorious twentieth of January, 1887, whose sales reached the astounding total of $1,679,945, was seldom approached, even in the spring, and by the end of the year was only a pleasant memory.

The real effect of the boom on the city can perhaps best

[17]*Ibid.*, Feb. 4, 1888.
[18]*Ibid.*, Feb. 11, 1888.

be explained through assessment statistics. In 1886 Los Angeles was assessed at $18,000,000; 1887 saw an increase of $10,-000,000 in the valuation; another $11,000,000 was added in 1888; and by 1889 the total was $46,000,000. That sum rose by $3,000,000 during the following year, thereby showing the lag between the business cycle and government recognition of it, and not until 1891 was there a decline to the 1889 figure. Clearly, the city was far richer after the boom than before, and citizens merely accepted the lift the flurry had given them as an easy step to higher levels of sound prosperity. This happy ending was not so evident in rural districts; there, the end of the boom often brought disaster. Only the essential strength of the urban business structure in Los Angeles enabled it to neutralize the decline.

The obvious next step, following the boom's chronology, would be a review of the subdivisions and tracts in Los Angeles. Such a summary, however, is precluded by the very number of plats filed. *Howell's Tract Directory*, published in 1888, contains 278 pages, not of individual lots but of tract offerings, and these approximate 1,700 in number. To devote even a paragraph to each would fill a good-sized volume, and in lieu thereof it seems best to stress two or three of the most interesting subdivisions. One of these was the Wolfskill Orchard Tract, loudly acclaimed throughout the boom. The Wolfskill family, who began their California residence in 1831, owned 120 acres in south Los Angeles, near the river. A section of this holding, lying between Third and Seventh, and Alameda and San Pedro Streets, was platted into lots, and a strip 300 by 1,900 feet was donated to the Southern Pacific for a railroad station. The tract was advertised as being covered with orange and walnut trees in full bearing, and the depot, for some obscure reason, made the offering immensely popular, "though how a passenger station could be expected to give great value to property in the neighborhood is scarcely comprehensible."[19] Lots near it brought $200 per front foot, and even some of those an appreciable distance away in the river bottom were sold at $500 each. Sale of the Wolfskill property was controlled by the Los Angeles Land Bureau, which engineered many other successful boom campaigns.

The most interesting subdivision was the Electric Railway Homestead Association Tract, whose promotion was much more efficient than its management. It consisted of 280 acres, or 1,210 lots, between Ninth and Pico, west of Vermont Avenue. Lots were priced at $290, ten dollars down and ten dollars per month. In a hollow on the property about 110 houses were built, costing $600 to $4,000 each, and were offered as prizes to lot purchasers; one house was given away with every seven lots sold. The hollow was soon deeply furrowed by water erosion, and in the rainy season "some of the houses looked like miniature castles on the Rhine."[20] The promoters also provided an electric railway, the first to be constructed in Los Angeles and the second in the state; it was built by Col. F. H. Howland, and was called the Maple Avenue and Pico Street line. A former president of the Los Angeles Chamber of Commerce described a trip on the road as a "succession of starts and stops," and admitted that he had been obliged, at least once, to walk back from Pico Heights to town.[21] Later, prospective buyers were taken to the tract in carriages, served port wine, and shown J. R. Millard's nearby Pico Street home as an example of how Electric Homestead property could be improved. The project soon failed, however, despite the energy of its promoters. As early as February, 1888, an article in the *Express*, entitled "An Electric

[19]Harry Ellington Brook, "Reminiscences of 'The Boom'," *Land of Sunshine* (Feb., 1895), p. 46.

[20]Netz, in Hist. Soc. of Sou. Calif. *Annual Publications, 1915-16*, X, 61.

[21]Hunt and Ament, *Oxcart to Airplane*, p. 190.

Homesteader Growls," assailed the poor management of the subdivision. The anonymous writer, who signed himself "A Thirsty Lot Owner," stated that he wrote to deny the truth of an article previously published by the *Express*, which had described the Electric Homestead organization as "a company that actually lives up to an agreement and meets an emergency." This, the letter writer grumbled, was false. The railroad gave extremely inadequate service, and both the management and the method of sale of lots were, in his opinion, "questionable." His strongest protest, however, was that the company had not supplied water as promised. There were a hundred families on the tract without sufficient water, and, he insisted, they "had been put off long enough with fair promises." The tract went from bad to worse, and Howland, builder of the railway, died in poverty.[22]

Other tracts widely advertised during the boom were the Kohler and Frohling subdivision, near Seventh and Central; the Alexander Weil Tract, west of Alameda, between Central and Tennessee; and the Vignes Tract, now the site of gasworks, salvage companies, and manufacturing plants, which was at the time advertised as ideal for "parties desiring a home."[23] There were also many attempts to create new towns under the protecting wings of Los Angeles. Melrose and Dayton Heights were in the western part of the city; Wilderson, Edna Park, Bettner, and Rowena adorned the southern flatlands. Advertising for the last-named suburb reached poetic heights: "You need not till the soil," exulted the promoters; "you can look on while the earth sends forth her plenty."[24] Vernon, Vernondale, and Downey also attracted much attention. North of the city lay Hollywood, recorded

[22]*Los Angeles Express*, Feb. 4, 1888; *Los Angeles Tribune*, Oct. 31, 1886.

[23]*Ibid.*, Oct. 25, 31, 1886.

[24]*Ibid.*, May 26, 1887.

February 1, 1887, and largely sponsored by Ivar Weid and
H. H. Wilcox, chief landowners in the foothills. In May
Wilcox started a large villa estate, and Lincoln Avenue was
planned to be "the finest drive in Los Angeles County, being
100 feet wide and five miles long."[25] Two hundred acres of
residential lots were put on the market. Highland Park, in the
rolling hills west of the Arroyo Seco, claimed to be "to Los
Angeles what the Campagna . . . is to Rome—the admiration
of the artistic world."[26] Kenilworth, on the lands of the
Rancho Los Feliz, was given a magnificent start, but failed
to survive even in name. Most of these localities are now incorporated in the city itself.

The boom, therefore, was not a wholly suburban phenomenon. The city of Los Angeles was its true nucleus, and
urban encouragement was chiefly responsible for its intensity.
Tracing the boom's course in thriving Los Angeles is relatively difficult, but the city was definitely the actual center
of the flurry, and its suburban manifestations, however, striking and picturesque, were merely rivulets flowing from the
copious source of supply, the ever active City of the Angels.

[25]*Ibid.*, May 15, 1887; Edwin O. Palmer, *History of Hollywood* (1937),
I, chaps. 8 and 9.

[26]*Los Angeles Tribune,* Jan. 5, 1887.

CHAPTER VI

Speculation on the Shore

ALTHOUGH the boom's effect on urban property was very great, its spectacular aspects were most evident in the suburbs. In outlying communities unscrupulous promoters made their greatest profits; in the ghost towns of the southern counties reckless investors suffered their largest losses. True, risks there were greater, as everyone realized, but, on the other hand, the profits were so huge when an embryo metropolis really succeeded that speculation became rampant in this type of development. In some cases promotional claims were justified; Glendale, Burbank, Azusa, and Monrovia may be cited as examples of the successful boom town. But the files of the County Recorder's office are crowded with maps and deeds of the towns that failed. The boom assumed its most extravagant aspects in the suburbs.

The sanguineness of promoters attained astonishing heights. Even before the full force of the excitement reached urban Los Angeles, there were subdivisions recorded in outlying districts, and during 1887 and 1888 the town-platting mania reached its climax. According to a later investigation, about sixty new towns were laid out during these two years, most of them were surveyed, many of them given a "flying start" with promoter-subsidized improvements, such as hotels, parks, banks, and stores. These sixty towns embraced a total of 79,350 acres of land, or 500,000 lots, sufficient, according to Guinn, to support 2,000,000 persons, but their combined population in July of 1889 was a mere 2,351. The discouraging aspect of these figures is of course due to the number of ghost towns included in the list, and the statistics are misleading in a way, for many of the communities started by the boom, although they had a very small population in 1889 at the time the survey was made, have since vindicated the confidence of their backers in no uncertain manner. The height of the epidemic of town platting was reached in the fall of 1887, when single days saw five or more "additions" or new towns recorded. These suburban municipalities, although each was supposed ultimately to rival Los Angeles in importance, were usually located discreetly on a main boulevard or avenue, or on one of the railroad lines which by this time crisscrossed the southern counties.

To separate the sales figures of Los Angeles city and its environs is difficult. In the county as a whole transfers were valued at $98,084,162 in 1887, but, as most of the property was sold on credit, many additional transfers went unrecorded; that is, the same piece of property would be transferred several times in a week or month, and only the ultimate owner would bother to record his purchase. Because of that tendency, Guinn thinks a safer figure for the total county transactions would be $200,000,000, and double that for all of southern California. Unimproved land adjacent to the city sold for $2,500 per acre, and land that brought no more than $100 per acre in 1886 rose to $1,500 in 1887. Perhaps some

idea of the interest in real property can be obtained by mortgage figures for the decade from 1880 to 1890. Mortgages in
these years amounted to $542,704,054 for the state as a whole;
Los Angeles County alone accounted for $61,146,896. During
this period there were 331,803 encumbered lots in the state,
and 45,926 of them were in Los Angeles County. The only
counties in California whose lot mortgages surpassed in value
their mortgages on acreage were Alameda, San Francisco,
Los Angeles, and San Diego. It is safe to say that many of
these southern lot mortgages, if not most of them, were made
on small-town property.

With such an intense interest in suburban real estate and
new-town platting during these years, the fact seems clear
that the boom in urban property, although the nucleus of the
southern-California boom, was only part of it. And one must
turn to the smaller communities to fill out the picture of the
speculative excitement. One group of them was situated on
the southern slope of the Los Angeles plain, between the city
and the sea. This district, forming as it did the route to what-
ever harbor Los Angeles would eventually adopt, naturally
attracted the attention of promoters; and, indeed, many small
towns were planned in the region, but only a few of them
attained later significance.

One of the latter was Inglewood, which received its start
during boom years and has since experienced a gradual but
intermittent growth. It was platted by the Centinela-Inglewood Land Company, organized in 1887 with the stated
purpose of building a town near Centinela Springs.[1] Surveys

[1]The ambitious aims of the company were described in the following
terms: " 'To lay out, survey and map villages, towns and cities; and to buy
and sell the lots and blocks or subdivisions; . . . to erect and maintain
hotel or other buildings and water and gas works, pipes, mains, reservoirs,
and appliances within or for the benefit of such villages, towns or
cities. . . .' " This excerpt from the articles of incorporation is quoted from
William W. Robinson, *Ranchos Become Cities* (1939), p. 141. For the town
plat see Los Angeles County "Miscellaneous Records," XXXIV, 19-36.

were made in August and September of 1887. The company listed lots from $200 to $750, with residence property in the lower brackets; orchard land could be obtained for $600 to $1,500 per acre, and ordinary farm acreage varied from $200 to $400. Eleven miles of water pipe were laid, and free lumber was offered to those first improving their property. The Redondo Beach railway, completed in the spring of 1888, increased interest in the project, and by the time the boom had reached its climax, there were several small businesses, a planing mill, a brickyard, a projected "College of Applied Sciences," and, last but not least, five real-estate offices. The name was derived from either Inglewood, Canada, or Englewood, Illinois.

The patriarch of the town was a wealthy Canadian named Daniel Freeman, who had arrived in 1873, and the Land Company listed among its directors several of the most active names in southern-California real estate, including those of Dan McFarland, Edward C. Webster of Pasadena fame, L. T. Garnsey, and Leonard Rose. The organization was capitalized at $1,000,000, divided into 10,000 shares at $100 each, and advertising expenses alone exceeded $20,000 in 1888. One of the company's most interesting schemes was the donation of an eight-room "Eastlake style" house to General John Frémont. The gift was readily accepted but never occupied by the recipient. The closest relationship the Frémonts ever had with Inglewood was through the organization by Mrs. Jessie Benton Frémont of a seed and floral company there, which prospered for a time. The Land Company built a large hotel which never flourished. During early days barley and truck farming supported the village, which had a boom-time population of 300. The boom's collapse had little effect on Inglewood, because speculation had never been as rife as in some other towns, but the decline's blighting hand was felt in the failure of the hotel and the end of the College of Applied

Sciences. In 1890 Freeman obtained the unsold land of the company on quitclaim.

One of the highly-publicized boom towns in this area was The Palms, on the Rancho La Ballona. It was one of the half-way points between the city and the beach settlements, and its growth was greatly stimulated by the harbor flurry started by the Santa Fe Railroad at La Ballona Slough. The Palms was subdivided in 1886 and recorded in December of that year. It was bounded by Washington, Overland, and Manning Streets, and incorporated about 500 acres of land, worth approximately $40,000.[2] The town was originally designed as the municipal center for a grain-growing area, and the earliest newspaper notices stress the fact that a grain warehouse was being built. The town was platted so that the Los Angeles and Santa Monica Railroad ran directly through it, and there were provisions in the title deeds for the exclusion of saloons. The increase in realty turnover in 1887 caused a resubdivision, and land northwest of Washington Street was added to the original plat. In April the promoters boasted that eight miles of streets had been graded, parks laid out and planted with 6,000 shade trees, and that owners completing improvements on their property were being presented with adjoining lots. The promoters added that soft water was available in abundance twenty-seven feet below the surface of the ground. The town at this time comprised some 350 lots in two sizes (50 by 150 feet and 150 by 300); the remainder of the tract was divided into plots ranging from three to fifteen acres. Portions of The Palms were later acquired by Los Angeles and Culver City, and its modern fame rests on its adjacency to the Metro-Goldwyn-Mayer motion-picture studios.

Practically every town that sprang up along the seacoast

[2]For advertisements of The Palms, see the *Los Angeles Tribune*, Dec. 6, 9, 1886. The subdividers of the plat were C. J. Harrison of San Jose, E. H. Sweetser of Santa Monica, and Joseph Curtis.

of Los Angeles County, and many of those farther south, utilized the lack of important harbor development in southern California to stress its own prospects. Some had logical claims: the best of these were advanced by San Diego and Newport Harbor. Other towns based their arguments on intensive hope and wishful thinking. Shallow half-moons in the bluff coastline, like that at Santa Monica, were transformed by boom literature into landlocked bays; and mud flats, such as those at La Ballona and Anaheim Landing, were pictured as future centers of Pacific trade. Certain enthusiasts went so far as to forecast vast dredging projects which would transform interior villages, like Sunset and Chicago Park, into busy shipping centers.

Perhaps the most characteristically speculative of these seaside harbor projects was that at La Ballona, the present Playa del Rey. La Ballona was not a fly-by-night project; the mouth of Ballona Creek had been touted since 1885 by prominent citizens, among whom was Moses L. Wicks, and the Santa Fe Railroad was known to be deeply interested in its development as a shipping point to compete with the Southern Pacific's Santa Monica wharf. In 1886, when property values started to rise, the Ballona Harbor and Improvement Company was organized. Capitalized at $300,000, it immediately employed an engineer, Hugh Crabbe, to plan a harbor that would " 'float the fleets of the world.' "[3] Ballona Harbor was designed in rectangular shape, with a pile-lined channel 200 feet wide to deep water. The inner harbor was to be two miles long, 300 to 600 feet wide and six to twenty feet deep. A right of way was immediately granted to the Santa Fe's subsidiary, the California Central, and two piers were constructed. The town was to occupy the cliffs surrounding the harbor. "This," said Wicks, "is the biggest scheme ever pro-

[3]Robinson, p. 118.

REDONDO BEACH IN 1880—PROSPECTIVE HARBOR FOR LOS ANGELES

posed to benefit Los Angeles, and if carried out it will be worth millions to the company."[4]

Local citizens generally supposed the Santa Fe Railroad was backing the project directly, but subsequent announcements (in April, 1887) denied this. Periodic reports of the company's progress were given to the newspapers, however, and many people thought that southern California's dream of a good harbor was to be fulfilled here. By April a steam dredge had been ordered, and work had begun on the south side of the projected channel. A few days later an article entitled "Ballona Booming" stated that the railroad had been built seven miles toward Los Angeles, and that material for the harbor construction was expected daily. The *Tribune* was supremely confident: "Great competing railroads, each controlling a commodious and safe harbor all by itself—what may not then be expected in the way of commercial progress?" But Ballona Harbor was not destined to be the ocean mart of the southland; the boom's decline ended the solvency of the improvement company and with it all hopes for a great port. Not until 1902 was the district revived as a recreational area, under the name of Playa del Rey.

Santa Monica is an excellent example of an established municipality stimulated by the boom. Development had begun in the early seventies, with the purchase of most of the land surrounding the bay by Col. Robert S. Baker, a former cattle rancher from Tejón. He attempted an abortive settlement known as Truxton, located on the palisades, but investors failed to arrive until John P. Jones, the Comstock millionaire, joined Baker in 1874. Thenceforth the town prospered. By October, 1875, Jones's vigorous promotion had brought a population of 1,000 to Santa Monica, and the settlement boasted 119 buildings. The Los Angeles and Independence

[4]*Los Angeles Tribune*, Oct. 11, 1886.

65

Railroad was started, and a wharf built to fulfill hopes that
Los Angeles would find its harbor here. "It is evident to all
that Santa Monica Bay is well protected," the local *Outlook*
pathetically insisted.[5] Other railroad schemes were not lacking: some fervid citizens predicted that Tom Scott's San
Diego line would be switched to a northern terminus at Santa
Monica; others felt that better prospects were promised by the
extension of the Los Angeles and Independence Railroad to
Colorado, there to connect with the Utah Southern. But,
despite this enthusiasm over business prospects, the backers
of Santa Monica kept constantly and sensibly in mind the
town's advantages as a resort. A tract pamphlet's quotation
from the *Outlook* stated: "Last Sunday we saw nine gentlemen in bathing at Santa Monica. The date was December 5th.
They informed us that the temperature was about the same
that prevails during the summer."[6] On such a hardy spirit of
self-hypnosis has modern chamber-of-commerce psychology
been built! Although Jones's ambitious plans failed, and his
sale of the Los Angeles and Independence Railroad to Central
Pacific interests in 1877 definitely ended Santa Monica's infant development, still a solid foundation was laid, and with
the help of confident old-timers, such as Williamson Dunn
Vawter,[7] and enthusiastic newcomers, like Abbot Kinney,
Santa Monica was in a much better position to take advantage
of the coming activity than less-developed localities.

The actual boom struck Santa Monica in 1886. During that
year five subdivisions were recorded, and a building en-

[5]Quoted in Coronel pamphlets.

[6]*Ibid.*

[7]Vawter was a Hoosier who bought sixty acres in Santa Monica and
established a general store there. He identified himself with civic development, operated the earliest lumberyard in the town, and chartered the first
street railway and national bank. He was a member of the board of trustees,
after incorporation of the town, and with his son was responsible for subdividing the eastern portion of Santa Monica.

thusiasm gripped the citizens as prices began to mount. The Hotel Arcadia, named after Col. Baker's wife, Arcadia Bandini Stearns Baker, daughter of an old Spanish family, was built in that year. It was erected by a certain J. W. Scott, who purchased some land in 1885 for $3,000, subdivided it into forty lots, sold thirty of them for $30,000, and with that sum constructed the hotel on the remainder of his property. The edifice was completed in 1887 and became one of the foremost resort hotels on the Pacific coast, equaled, in Santa Monica's opinion, only by the Del Monte. Houses and business blocks were built in proportion, and on November 30 Santa Monica was incorporated as a city.

During 1887 twelve plats were filed at the County Recorder's office, and the building flurry continued. Steere's Opera House, St. Augustine's Episcopal Church, several business blocks, and a number of residences were erected. The Southern Pacific proposed to reconstruct Jones's wharf, in order to compete with the prospective Santa Fe-controlled harbor at La Ballona, but, when the latter failed to materialize, the Southern Pacific was no longer interested. On March 3 an auction of property between Ocean Avenue and Twentieth Street netted $42,000, and the following week a second auction bettered that record. A similar sale on April 13 brought $18,000, and in May the outlook for Santa Monica was described as "bright"—with reservations, for there was a lack of enthusiasm among the moneyed interests over Santa Monica's future as a harbor. Local optimists, however, were soothed by the signing of a contract for a 50,000-dollar bank structure and the opening of additional tracts. On June 2, Ben Ward, the noted Los Angeles auctioneer, presided at another successful auction, whose visitors were advised to bring both their appetites and pocketbooks; during the same month the Santa Fe Tract, consisting of fifty-three acres in South Santa Monica formerly belonging to the Vawter family, was subdivided and sold for $53,000. The Wave Crest and Ocean Spray tracts were also opened, the latter on the present site of Ocean Park, and some lots in these developments attained the then respectable figure of $1,350.

Railroads played an important part in Santa Monica's boom, as they did elsewhere at this time. As early as January, 1886, a flurry was incited by a rumor that the Santa Fe was about to construct an extension, a wharf, and a three-story hotel in South Santa Monica. Property values rose accordingly, but in October the district was disappointed by the announcement that the Santa Fe had finally decided on Ballona Slough. In 1887 Moses L. Wicks became interested in a short-lived project designed to connect Ballona and Santa Monica by rail, thus giving the Santa Fe a connection with the Southern Pacific. An outgrowth of the boom was the construction of the Los Angeles Pacific Railroad, one of the early interurban lines running from the beach to the San Fernando Valley.

By August the " 'free lunch-free music' stage of auction sales had been reached,"[8] and the end of boom activity was in sight. Probably because Santa Monica was not a boom town in the usual sense, it suffered less from the subsequent decline than did many of its neighbors. The First National Bank, backed by Vawter, was successfully established in 1888; Senator Jones, his finances refurbished, built a 30,000-dollar home and stated his intention of remaining a resident; and a board of trade was organized which advertised the region very effectively. Despite the slump, over $125,000 in building improvements was recorded in 1888, and the beach still held its attraction for the inland masses. Santa Monica actually gained more than it lost by the boom: its population and property values increased measurably, and added buildings and civic improvements were there to stay. A special result of boom

[8]Luther A. Ingersoll, *Ingersoll's Century History: Santa Monica Bay Cities* (1908), p. 170.

enthusiasm in the Santa Monica area was the establishment of the National Home for Disabled Volunteer Soldiers on 300 acres of the former Wolfskill property. Jones and Arcadia Baker donated the land, and the government accepted it. Barracks, a hospital, and housing facilities for 1,000 men were provided. The Soldiers' Home virtually started the town of Sawtelle and greatly pleased Santa Monica businessmen.

Farther down the coast, Redondo Beach was promoted vigorously as another potential harbor for Los Angeles. A 100,000-dollar iron pier was built and a hotel (large engravings of which adorned most Redondo advertisements) was planned. The Santa Fe Railroad completed a branch from Los Angeles to Redondo, via Inglewood, in 1888. Inglewood promoters were interested in Redondo, and in 1888 the two developments were merged under the name of the Redondo Beach and Centinela-Inglewood Land Company. In process of expansion, this organization published an announcement in January, 1888, which read in part as follows:

To the Public
In our management of Inglewood and Redondo Beach we find that the high price of building material, and especially of lumber, is a most serious obstacle to building and development.
For the purpose of furnishing material for cheap homes at Redondo Beach and Inglewood we found it necessary to enter the field of lumber merchandising. . . .

Six million feet, they added, were "to be furnished as needed,"[9]—an evidence of the versatility of southern-California promoters. Redondo Pier was for a time used commercially, but recently the area has been devoted almost entirely to resort purposes.

Only brief mention need be made of boom activities in and around San Pedro. "The harbor district," says a recent in-

[9]*Los Angeles Express*, Jan. 3, 26, 1888.

vestigator, "was somewhat less affected than other localities and towns in the southern part of the state by the land craze of 1887." The chief stimulation occurred because "shipping agents, chandlers, and others profited by the immense imports of raw material, especially lumber, which accompanied the building boom."[10] San Pedro was incorporated as a city in 1888, There was an attempt to extend the Gould railroad system to the vicinity in 1887,when Jay Gould in May bought an option on Rattlesnake Island; six days later the Union Pacific bought the island for $175,000.

Farther south the second largest city in present Los Angeles County was getting its faltering start. The promoter of the Long Beach area, William Erwin Willmore, was ahead of his time; his misfortune was to begin the boom six years too early, and his ambitious ventures, characterized by all the fanfare of later publicity, failed miserably. "If poor Willmore could only have held on a little longer," laments one writer, "the grand land boom . . . would have included Willmore City in its sweep."[11]

Willmore was an Englishman impressed by realty possibilities in the southland. In 1880 he obtained an option on 4,000 acres of the Bixby rancho along the coast and planned a typical colony—a town beautified by trees, parks, and broad boulevards, and surrounded by ten-, twenty-, and forty-acre farm plots. Willmore employed every possible advertising method: he listed his land with the California Immigrant Union, advertised in more than a hundred newspapers and thirty-five magazines throughout the nation, and employed a recruiting agent whose job it was to organize excursions to the "American Colony," as Willmore dubbed his project. The excursions were not very successful; the agent worked

[10]Hallock F. Raup, *Rancho Los Palos Verdes* (1937).

[11]*Ranchos of the Sunset* (1925), pp. 32-3.

nearly a year before enough colonists could be gathered to make a worth-while party, but after several had broken their agreements a group of sixty finally arrived in Los Angeles on February 24, 1882. They employed some of the earliest tourist cars (hitched to a freight train), brought their own bedding, cooked on a community gasoline stove, and held religious services en route. After a sight-seeing tour around Pasadena, they were taken to Long Beach and seemed delighted with their situation.

The colony had evidently been well planned. Willmore offered his farm land at prices varying from twelve dollars and a half to twenty-five dollars per acre, and there was plenty of water available. Willmore stressed in his advertisements his desire to attract experienced farmers and dairymen: "The favorable location, fertility of the soil and ready market for all products raised will make it possible to carry on these important industries very extensively and profitably."[12] But despite its advantages Willmore City and the American Colony did not prosper. A year's work exhibited only one small store and a dozen houses on the lands; floodwaters washed out the horsecar line that connected the area to the Southern Pacific tracks at Wilmington; and the Methodist Resort Association failed in 1883 to fulfill Willmore's hopes that its annual camp meeting would be held in his city. He failed to make his payments to the Bixbys, and abandoned the project in 1884.

Development of the region was not to languish, however. The first tenuous hints of the coming flurry were making themselves evident in property values, and a new organization, the Long Beach Land and Water Company, headed by Robert M. Widney, took up where Willmore had left off. The company renamed Willmore City, calling it Long Beach, took advantage of boom sales to create a seaside resort instead of

[12]*Ibid.*, p. 4.

an agricultural colony, and had the town well established by 1888. The quality of Long Beach's population was favorably compared with that of Santa Monica, cultural advantages were stressed, and every effort was made to bestow upon Long Beach the reputation of being "an educational watering-place."[13] "All agree," said the *Los Angeles Tribune* in 1886, "that only first class railroad facilities are needed to make Long Beach one of the best resorts for all seasons of the year, in the world."[14] The town planned by Widney and his associates included many of the improvements suggested by Willmore: a thirty-foot setback to buildings, planting of numerous trees and hedges, strict control of livestock, regulation of beach camping, and no "objectionable or inappropriate bathing suits."[15]

In April of 1887 another colony scheme was promulgated. The California Co-operative Colony obtained 7,000 acres of the Cerritos Rancho from the Bixbys, about six miles inland from Long Beach. The colony was operated on the subscription basis: 200 shareholders, to be known as "founders," would each buy a 140-dollar share of stock at a fifty per cent discount. Each share would entitle the holder to a business or residence lot in the projected town, and the privilege of purchasing not more than four ten-acre plots of surrounding farmland at a discount. For subsequent investors the farm tracts were offered at fifty dollars per acre, one-third down. "Purchasers," stated one advertisement, "need not 'camp out' while looking at this tract. It lies at the threshold of Southern California's metropolis. . . . The Early Bird Catches the Worm."[16] This somewhat dubious description

[13]Lindley and Widney, *California of the South* (1888), p. 139.

[14]Dec. 17.

[15]*Ranchos of the Sunset*, p. 31.

[16]*Los Angeles Tribune*, Apr. 14, 1887.

of the land was apparently effective, for before the month was out another co-operative venture, called the California Land and Investment Association and featuring a settlement named Brockton, had started negotiations for 7,500 adjoining acres. Neither of these projects was ultimately successful. Oil development, the expansion of Long Beach, and the southward extension of the Los Angeles industrial area were necessary to populate the section, and some parts of it have matured only in very recent years. One of the incentives to expansion of the second colony had been a projected railway from the San Gabriel Valley to Long Beach, and the failure of that plan chilled enthusiasm for Brockton to a low temperature.

If any region in southern California had legitimate reasons for publicizing harbor prospects, that region was Newport Beach. Its harbor is some three miles long, averages more than half a mile in width, and with suitable dredging could have been made into an excellent commercial port. The distance from Los Angeles (about fifty-five miles) injured its prospects, however, although with improved transportation that difficulty could probably have been overcome. The bay region, with its inlet channel extending more than four miles toward Santa Ana, was known in its early years by the unflattering title of Gospel Swamp. Development was largely due to James and Robert McFadden, who bought beach land in 1886 and began a lumber and shipping business at Newport. The low opinion held of the district was amply shown by the terms of purchase: the property was described as "swamp and overflow" land, and was sold by the state for one dollar an acre.[17] Although the beach was used by Santa Ana Valley residents as a summer camping place, there were few permanent residents, and the Santa Ana boom failed to reach this far. The

[17]H. L. Sherman, *History of Newport Beach* (1931), pp. 18 ff. For the route of the Santa Ana and Newport Railroad, see Los Angeles County "Miscellaneous Records," XXXIV, 47.

McFaddens built a pier in 1887 and connected their lumber-yard with valley towns by the Santa Ana and Newport Railroad, and in 1888 the federal government made a halfhearted survey of the bay. Upon completion of the railroad there was some real-estate activity in the early nineties, but prospects were so poor that the McFaddens, angered by Southern Pacific competition, sold their interests. It may be concluded that the boom, as such, never reached Newport Harbor—which is strange, considering that regions less well-endowed benefited greatly from it.

The speculation mania proved powerful enough to span the twenty miles of ocean between the mainland and Santa Catalina Island. George Shatto purchased the island from the Lick estate, in August of 1887, for $200,000. He established a town, Shatto City, which went unrecorded and was shortly renamed, at his sister's suggestion, Avalon. He instituted regular excursions from the mainland on the steamer "Ferndale"; profited greatly from the publicity of resident writers like Charles Frederick Holder; held auction sales and disposed of some 200 lots; and built a two-storied, verandaed hotel, the Metropole. Shatto labored under a mortgage of $133,000, however, and when the boom broke he sold the island to a British mining syndicate, which paid $40,000 of the agreed $400,000, became disappointed in mining prospects, and defaulted. The island was finally transferred to Phineas Banning in 1892.

The boom on the southern-California seashore extended from Santa Barbara to San Diego,[18] and even affected less important places, such as Pismo Beach, at greater distances. The flurry was responsible for the development of already-established towns, the indirect beginnings of several modern beach cities, and an increased interest in the construction of a port

[18]See below, Chapters XII and XIII.

74

for Los Angeles. The Pacific Ocean was a good talking point, whether for resort or commercial purposes, and realty promoters utilized it in their accustomed efficient style.

CHAPTER VII

Suburban Centers of the Boom: The San Gabriel Valley and Pasadena

O F ALL the suburban regions, the one struck hardest by the boom was the forty-odd miles of fertile valley land lying between Pasadena and San Bernardino. There were two main reasons. First, and probably most important, was the fact that the San Gabriel Valley was the natural route for any railroad line extending east from Los Angeles. Both feasible passes which cut the Sierra Madre, Cajón and San Gorgonio, were reached from the valley, and both the Santa Fe and the Southern Pacific used this logical route. The result was that these rail lines formed the nuclear threads of valley settlement and greatly stimulated local promotion activities. The second reason for the area's responsiveness to realty publicity was its favorable soil, climate, and water supply. From the citrus groves around Pasadena, now crowded out by residence plats, to the sandy grape lands near Fontana, the valley is composed of a series of alluvial fans watered by underground streams and in some cases by surface creeks flowing from mountain canyons. As soon as the prevailing distrust of foothill lands for citrus growing was dispelled by the settlement of several successful colonies in these regions, agricultural development went forward rapidly. And thus was provided one more basis for exuberant publicity.

Perhaps no other area in southern California was more prolific in its production of boom towns than the San Gabriel Valley. By April, 1887, crowded trains of the Santa Fe lines were stopping at the following places: Sycamore Grove, Highland Park, Garvanza, Lincoln Park, South Pasadena*, Raymond, Pasadena*, Olivewood, Lamanda Park, Huntington, Sierra Madre*, Arcadia,* Monrovia*, Duarte*, Azusa*, Gladstone, Alosta, San Dimas*, Lordsburg*, Palomares, Claremont*, Ontario*, Magnolia*, Cucamonga*, Etiwanda*, and San Bernardino*. Anyone familiar with the territory at present will note, however, that only those starred are now worthy of being called "towns," and even some of these are mere rural hamlets.[1]

Settlements were not, of course, limited to those lands adjacent to the California Central. The Southern Pacific also encouraged its share of municipalities. Among the more prosperous was Alhambra, a settlement which grew up near the San Gabriel Mission lands and which was stimulated by the boom. In early 1887 Alhambra was occupying much space in advertising columns. "ALHAMBRA TO THE FRONT!"—"The Booming Suburb and the Equal of Pasadena!"—declared one of these outbursts. Among the most highly publicized subdivisions here was the Stoneman Tract, promoted by the Los Angeles Land Bureau. Other plats were equally successful, however, for sales to May, 1887, totaled $62,000. Values continued high in this region, for as late as June, 1889, J. De Barth Shorb was selling part of his holdings for more than $1,000

[1] *Los Angeles Tribune,* Apr. 20, 30, 1887. Lordsburg is now La Verne, and Magnolia later became Upland.

per acre. If the boom seemed slow in starting, it reached a rapid peak: only one tract map was recorded in 1886 for Alhambra, but during the following year twenty-two were listed; in 1880 there were not enough people in Alhambra to give it a place in the population statistics in the census of that year, but a decade later there were nearly 1,000 permanent residents.

The great Rancho Santa Anita, purchased in 1875 by Elias J. Baldwin from Harris Newmark, a Los Angeles business-man, experienced a steady rise in land values. Newmark had paid $85,000 for the property, which included not only the oak-dotted slopes of the present Santa Anita area but also the land on which Arcadia and a part of Monrovia now stand. Baldwin interviewed Newmark, as the story goes, with a tin box under his arm, prepared to pay $150,000 cash; but New-mark's business agility raised this figure by $50,000. Newmark had previously offered the land to the Indiana Colony[2] for twenty dollars per acre, or $100,000 in gold. That was in 1873, and David M. Berry, colony agent, apparently liked the re-gion. "It is a grand property," he said, "and if I owned it I think I could easily make it worth $1,000,000. Everything seems favorable about it." Not the least favorable factor was the possibility that it might be "bought for greenbacks"—an important item when dealing with easterners in the year of the panic.[3]

Baldwin's use of the ranch as a breeding ground for cham-pion race horses, his disputes with his neighbors over irrigation facilities, and his later financial embarrassments are well known. Not so well known was his determination to make the boom pay for his investment losses. He began the subdivision of Arcadia with the enthusiasm of any promoter; he planted

[2]The Indiana Colony was the group which originally settled Pasadena.

[3]David M. Berry to Thomas Balch Elliott, Sept. 5, 1873.

with long lines of stately eucalypti what is now known as the "Double Drive," hauling water for this purpose in barrels from Santa Anita Canyon. He organized a company and constructed a 50,000-dollar hotel, the Oakwood, which, efficiently operated by Comstock and Lawrence, summer proprietors of his Lake Tahoe hostelry, became the fashionable objective of coaching parties from Los Angeles. So successful were Baldwin's methods that the *Louisville Courier-Journal* used him as an example of California aggressiveness. After stating that he had sold 600 lots in four days without the aid of advertising, one article concluded: "You can judge of the enterprise of the people of California."[4]

Perhaps the most successful small boom town of the San Gabriel Valley was Monrovia. The guiding spirit behind the town was William N. Monroe, a railroad-construction engineer who first came to southern California in 1875 and associated himself with civic enterprises to the extent that he became a member of the Los Angeles city council in 1880. Monrovia, however, was not a one-man project. Edward F. Spence, a former mayor of Los Angeles, John D. Bicknell, a prominent local attorney, and James F. Crank, the interurban-railway builder, joined Monroe in the spring of 1886 and laid out a sixty-acre town on land from the Rancho Santa Anita, purchased from Baldwin, and from the Rancho Azusa de Duarte on the east. In addition to the sixty-acre municipal area, about eight square miles of farm and orchard lots were laid out.

The first auction-excursion was held on May 17, 1886 and was a pronounced success. Inside lots, about 50 by 160 feet, were sold for one hundred dollars each, corner lots were fifty dollars higher, and outlying five-acre tracts were disposed of at $250 per acre. According to Wiley, historian of the Monrovia area, "at the time Monrovia was founded . . . speculators

---

[4] *Los Angeles Tribune,* May 23, 1887.

were becoming interested in realty surrounding Los Angeles to a distance of from twenty to thirty miles."[5] Monrovia grew rapidly. Whereas in 1886 only nine tracts or additions were recorded, during the following year this figure was more than quadrupled. The town was incorporated in November, 1887, with a population of 500; two hotels were erected; small businesses were established in profusion; and street railways were built. Monrovia was popular with investors not only because Monroe himself lived in the town, kept open house, and had as his guests prominent wealthy men who in many cases were thus induced to buy land, but also because water was distributed free to property owners. The construction boom caused a shortage of labor, and the faith of Los Angeles financiers in Monrovia was early demonstrated by the organization in 1887 of the First National Bank, with Joseph F. Sartori, subsequent leader in Los Angeles banking circles, as one of its founders.

The fact that "the rise in price of Monrovia lots was the most phenomenal of any boom town" was due largely to judicious advertising.[6] In December, 1886, the *Tribune* devoted one and a half columns to enthusiastic description of Monrovia, and later in the month the Grand View Hotel was opened by a glittering banquet and ball—an 1886 version of a modern *première*.[7] Monroe sold his lots cheaper than did many adjacent subdividers, with the express provision that property be improved; thus unprofitable speculation was avoided, and values rose rapidly. Lots that went for $150 in mid-1886 were bringing offers of $5,000 to $8,000 by the end of that year. Lots later purchased for $5,400 were sold in five months at a profit of $7,000. In May, 1887, an anniversary

[5] John L. Wiley, *History of Monrovia* (1927), pp. 47 ff.

[6] Netz, in Hist. Soc. of Sou. Calif. *Annual Publications, 1915-16*, X, 65.

[7] *Los Angeles Tribune*, Dec. 6, 22, 1886. Some adverse publicity occurred in January, when Col. Sam Keefer, the hotel's proprietor, committed suicide.

celebration was held, and the progress of the town recounted. The California Central, it was boasted, ran four through passenger trains a day to Monrovia; and rails for the first streetcar line were laid on May 18. That day also saw the successful auction of the E. F. Spence Addition, which attracted two trainloads of prospective buyers—more than 1,000 persons. Indeed, the railway company ran out of free tickets. Yet most of the buyers were residents of Monrovia. One hundred and sixty lots were sold, netting $10,810. The boom continued to progress during the early months of 1888. An interesting criterion of municipal success is to be found in the statement that "some idea of the city's growth is conveyed in the fact that at this time a man named Brown was employed a half-day each week to collect garbage for five dollars per week."[8] Though by May the flurry was declining, the census of 1890 showed that the population had almost doubled, and Monrovia is still one of the most enterprising towns of the foothill area.

Near by, Sierra Madre and Duarte experienced their share of excitement. According to one local reporter, a "lively boom" in Sierra Madre was in full swing by May, 1887. Statistics bear out his assertion: lots worth $36,000 were sold there in less than twenty-four hours. Another factor in the foothill boom was the Sierra Madre Villa, described as the "first Southern California hotel whose fame extended to all parts of the world." It was built in the later seventies and housed such celebrities as William Tecumseh Sherman, Phillips Brooks, John L. Sullivan, and Minnie Maddern Fiske.[9] Duarte, an earlier settlement which was not quite so active during the boom as some of its neighbors, boasted itself "staid, prosperous, and lovely," and urged prospective investors to "get

[8]Wiley, pp. 66 ff.

[9]*Los Angeles Tribune*, May 6, 1887, Dec. 8, 1886.

in on the ground floor." The most eagerly-advertised tract here was the Blankenhorn and Chippendale. Appeals were made to "Butchers, Bakers, Grocers, Blacksmiths, and Tradesmen Generally" to settle in Duarte, and in April the custom was started of publishing periodic letters (emulated by other suburban towns during the boom) in the *Los Angeles Tribune.*[10] These letters were not outstanding for originality or statistical accuracy, being usually verbose and provincially egotistic, but they were symptomatic of the boom and somewhat representative of local advertising methods. The Duarte correspondent used much space, in his first missive, in accusing Monrovia, West Duarte, and Azusa of trying to appropriate Duarte's fame and established prosperity. He also petitioned the Los Angeles and San Gabriel Valley Railroad to run a two-mile spur past West Duarte, to connect the older town with the railroad's main line, but this plea was not answered. Most of the sales in and around Duarte were of acreage property, which was immediately platted; and probably the absence of large numbers of town lots accounted for the fact that there were only two realtors in Duarte at the time. A comparison of tract maps and additions recorded shows the relative intensity of the boom in these two towns: Sierra Madre filed six maps in 1886 and nineteen in 1887; Duarte, one in 1886 and six in 1887. Glendora, a few miles east, was also affected by the boom, to the extent that acreage preempted from the government in 1877 sold for $1,000 per unit in 1887; other land, which had sold for two and a half to fifteen dollars per acre in 1879, was cut into 1,500-dollar lots in 1887.

Azusa, located on the rocky uplands of the Dalton Ranch near the San Gabriel River, is an excellent example of a town which had nothing to recommend it save publicity. Despite

[10]*Ibid.*, Jan. 16, Apr. 5, 13, 17, 1887.

its mediocre location the region was the subject of some of
the earliest colonizing ventures. Henry Dalton in 1855 tried
the lottery method of disposing of his ranch lands. He offered
prizes, in real and personal property, amounting to $84,000,
including 240 "elegant lots in the town of Benton" (another
ghost town existing only in its promoter's imagination) and
twenty-four "superb forty-acre farms on the Rancho of
Azusa."[11] Dalton failed in his promotion scheme, and the
founding of a successful town on the ranch had to await the
efforts of Jonathan S. Slauson, in the great boom of the
eighties. In December, 1886, a group of Los Angeles businessmen, led by Slauson and including in their number John D.
Bicknell, the attorney who helped found Monrovia, organized
the Azusa Land and Water Company, with a capitalization
of $500,000. The company bought 4,000 acres of the Rancho
Azusa, platted a town, and began to sell lots in April, 1887.
The acreage purchased included, in the main, good agricultural land and adequate water facilities, but Slauson located
the town "where it was practically all sand, gravel and boulder wash. When somebody asked him why he placed it at
that particular spot, he remarked," 'If it's not good for a town,
it isn't good for anything.' "[12]

Many stories surround the Azusa boom. The town was
publicized to such an extent that buyers stood in line all night
before the sale opened; the person who held second place in
line supposedly refused an offer of $1,000 to give it up, and
the eager investor who held fifth place reluctantly sold his
location for $500. Lots totaling $280,000 found buyers the
first day, and the sale was continued for two additional days.

[11]Cleland, *Cattle*, p. 212 n.

[12]William Spalding, *History of Los Angeles City and County* (1931),
I, 267.

[13]James M. Guinn, "The Great Real Estate Boom of 1887," in Hist. Soc.
of Sou. Calif. *Annual Publications, 1890*, I, 15 f.

"Not one in a hundred had seen the townsite," says Guinn. Fewer still expected to live there.[13] The sale continued throughout the summer, although nearly half of the town lots platted were disposed of during the first three days. At the end of two months, the promoters reckoned their profits at $1,175,000. Slauson stood loyally by his new town—as well he might, considering its financial success—erected a brick building and hotel and announced with satisfaction: "This may be cited as the climax of the Big Boom."[14] The promoters had their difficulties, however. They were violently attacked by the *Times* for their business methods and defended with equal violence by the *Tribune*, which summed up its rebuttal with the statement: "The Times is worse than a mad dog, and does more to create bad blood in the community."[15]

In general, the most spectacular aspects of the boom were evident in the San Gabriel Valley. The area was unique in having two important competing railway lines as magnets for settlement. Older towns, such as San Gabriel, experienced a rise in property values with the consequent listing of many new tracts and additions; but it was in the new boom towns, like Monrovia and Azusa, that the era's most characteristic aspects could be found.

At the western end of the San Gabriel Valley lay Los Angeles' closest competitor as a center of boom enthusiasm— the city of Pasadena. Throughout the period Pasadena rivaled Los Angeles in the relative vigor of its upheaval, in promotion activity, and in general excitement. Considering Pasadena's late origin, it might well be argued that the boom was relatively more intense within her borders than in the older and more firmly established city, but, whether or not such a point of view is justified, the boom in Pasadena remains one

[14]*Los Angeles Tribune*, Apr. 4, 1887.

[15]*Ibid.*, May 3, 1887.

of the most interesting and significant events of the time.

A survey of tract maps filed in the Los Angeles County recorder's office is enlightening with regard to this comparison. During 1886 and 1887, 549 plats, replats, and additions were filed for Los Angeles; the same period saw the recording of 433 similar maps for Pasadena. These figures are ample proof of the selling frenzy which gripped the "Crown City" during the boom's height; but they tell little of the formative factors which influenced Pasadena's growth and saw it rise from a barren ranch to a prosperous citrus colony, and then suddenly blossom forth into one of the principal cities of the Los Angeles area. Perhaps part of the answer to the problem of why Pasadena was so strongly affected by the boom lies in its earlier successes. From first to last, Pasadena has been a real-estate broker's ideal.

Pasadena lies on the old Rancho San Pasqual, which was owned jointly in the early seventies by Benjamin D. Wilson and Dr. John Griffin. In May of 1873 a group of Indianans under the leadership of Dr. Thomas Balch Elliott formed an organization known as the California Colony of Indiana, for the purpose of locating a suitable area in California and settling thereon. To that end a committee of investigation, consisting of David M. Berry, John H. Baker, Nathan Kimball, and Albert Ruxton (a surveyor), was sent to California in August. To pay the expenses of these emissaries and to defray other costs, each member of the colony was assessed monthly up to twelve and a half dollars. The panic and depression of 1873 wrecked the colony organization, but Berry stayed in California to represent Dr. Elliott and a few interested persons and, with the aid of California capital, formed the San Gabriel Orange Grove Association, which in 1874 was responsible for the founding of Pasadena. The choice of location was not a speedy process; Berry, chief agent, investigated most of the available land in southern

California before deciding on San Pasqual, but his trials and tribulations are reserved for discussion in a later chapter. The San Gabriel Orange Grove Association was capitalized at $50,000 and divided into 200 shares of $250 each. Every shareholder was entitled to seven and a half acres of the subdivided lands and a 1/200 interest in the unplatted remainder (about 2,462 acres), with water rights. The subdivided portion consisted of 1,500 acres, laid out in fifteen- and thirty-acre farm tracts. As soon as the association made up its collective mind to buy, Wilson and Griffin came to an agreement regarding their joint ownership. Wilson desired to develop his own lands, and took 1,600 acres east of the present Fair Oaks Avenue, while Griffin took 3,962 acres west of that line and turned them over to the association. The total purchase price was $25,000, and payment was completed within one year. The property was distributed by lot, and an assessment of ten per cent was levied for water development.[16]

In 1876 Wilson opened the tract east of Fair Oaks Avenue, under the name of the Lake Vineyard Land and Water Company. A good ranchero, he now proved himself an equally good real-estate man and sold hundreds of acres, aided by an excellent publicity campaign. One of his efforts to enhance the value of his property is described in his correspondence with a New Jersey hotel proprietress. He offered her a ten-acre site on Oak Knoll ridge if she would agree to construct a "Sanitarium-hotel." The proprietress was not only willing, but eager, and offered enthusiastically to spend between $10,000 and $20,000 on improvements. The venture failed, however, when the prospective builder was unable to raise money on her eastern property.[17] Land values in Pasadena and vicinity rose steadily. The correspondence of J. De Barth

[16]Thomas Balch Elliott, "History of the San Gabriel Orange Grove Association" (holograph MS, Elliott papers).

[17]Caughey, *Huntington Library Quarterly*, II, 299.

Shorb, Wilson's son-in-law who succeeded to his interests, shows a consistent faith in the future of southern-California land. Shorb habitually refused offers, on the ground that prices were rising—despite his constant struggle, particularly in the early eighties, to cope with the encumbrances on Wilson's property. As early as March, 1880, Shorb demanded $30,000 above commission for his Oak Knoll property (180 acres with 1,500 orange trees and more than 20,000 grapevines), and he warned prospective buyers that the gross price would rise to $40,000 by April. Newcomers who wished to purchase land for twenty dollars an acre were no longer welcomed. "The county is full of buyers," he concluded, and among them were the Pasadena colonists, who desired to purchase some of his lands adjacent to their property.[18] Shorb, however, would not take less than fifty dollars per acre for this land, and he was evidently not anxious to sell at all, stating that in his opinion $125 could be obtained by 1881. "Those who have held on during all the past dark days should not now be too anxious to realize," was his advice, and unlike many others he himself followed it religiously.[19] By September of 1880 he was asking for his acreage sixty dollars, cash, or seventy dollars, with terms. "Everything is booming now," he said in October, ". . . in anticipation of the nearly completed Southern road";[20] and by March of the following year his acreage was bringing from $75 to $100. Oak Knoll was sold in November, 1881.

The colony settlement on the bank of the arroyo had, meanwhile, not been idle.[21] In 1880, when Pasadena had only

[18] J. De Barth Shorb to C. J. Hopkins, Mar. 25, 1880.

[19] J. De Barth Shorb to William Mathews, July 7, 1880.

[20] J. De Barth Shorb to James W. Hart, Oct. 22, 1880.

[21] The naming of Pasadena was a complicated procedure. "Indiana Colony" was unsatisfactory: Berry objected, "Nine tenths of the members are *not* from Indiana, and the name . . . sounds too much like colds, coughs,

a general store, a post office, and a twice-weekly stage to Los Angeles, the enterprising settlers divided 3,000 acres of their holdings into five-acre lots and sold them at fifty and sixty dollars each. Prices were still low. One buyer purchased twenty acres on California Street, east of Marengo Avenue, for $2,000, and the best lots east of Fair Oaks and south of Colorado Street sold for forty-five dollars, with corners yielding sixty dollars. Good land was still selling at one hundred dollars per acre in 1883, and just the year before a misguided citizen had traded three acres on the northeast corner of Fair Oaks and Colorado for a mule team. About 1885 the boom started, due largely to the arrival of the Santa Fe. Sales increased, the Raymond Hotel was completed in 1886, and in May of that year Pasadena was incorporated as a city. The Raymond was one of Pasadena's chief assets; it welcomed 35,000 guests during 1886 and 1887 and held balls which attracted society from miles around. The foundations of the hotel had been laid in 1883 by Walter Raymond, son of a travel-agency manager, who had been impressed with the possibilities of the resort-hotel business in California. The boom also gave two other hotels to Pasadena: La Pintoresca, destroyed by fire twenty years later, and the Green. The latter was built by Edward Webster, who erected a station and presented it to the Santa Fe free of charge as an inducement to the railroad's laying its tracks near the hotel. George G. Green financed construction and after the boom broke took over the management of the building. Despite depression, the hotel lived on, and Green shortly added a wing to the structure. It remains today one of the stateliest relics of Pasadena's boom.

In March, 1886, the spark was struck which set off the explosion—the auction of five acres of mid-town property

chills, etc. to suit us." A Chippewa Indian word was finally proposed by a friend of Dr. Elliott and was accepted. (David M. Berry to Thomas Balch Elliott, Nov. 27, 1873.)

donated by Benjamin D. Wilson for a school. Appreciation in value made this area too valuable for school grounds, and permission was obtained from Wilson's heirs to subdivide and sell it. The five acres were cut into thirty-five business lots, of which three were reserved for a town hall and library. Thirty-two of the lots were sold at the auction, bringing in some cases more than one hundred dollars per front foot. In all, $44,772 was realized. Among the important tracts in Pasadena were the Painter and Ball, which occupied 2,000 acres in the northwest section of the city; Los Robles, bought by Gen. George Stoneman from Wilson and John Downey in 1872; Oak Knoll, which was the name given to Shorb's property and adjacent lands, amounting to 7,100 acres, bought by New York speculators in 1886 and 1887; San Marino, presented to Shorb by Wilson as a wedding present; and, on the brink of the arroyo in the western part of town, Linda Vista, purchased by J. D. Yocum in 1883. The progress of Pasadena even during 1886 was remarkable. By the end of that year there were fifty-three active real-estate agencies, land was selling at $1,000 per acre, and in eleven months 1,500 acres had been subdivided. Population had increased to more than 6,000, restaurants were feeding 1,000 customers per day, and crime, the hallmark of rapid growth, was rampant. Five trains were run daily to Los Angeles, with special theater trains three nights a week; the agricultural and business interests of Pasadena demanded between fifteen and thirty freight cars per day, many private teams, and the constant activity of three express companies. Both the Southern Pacific and Santa Fe railroads were surveying near Pasadena for new lines, and there were already four and one-half miles of street railway in existence. Land sales for the year were estimated at $5,000,000, and between 400 and 500 new buildings, requiring the labor of 1,200 carpenters, were erected.

The climax was reached in 1887. "How fast Pasadena is

catching up with Los Angeles," remarked the *Tribune* in May, "will be seen from the fact that two years ago she was about one-twelfth as large; now she is more than one-sixth."[22] Writers like E. P. Roe added to the encomiums. In May a "tremendous boom" was started on Raymond Avenue by announcement of plans for a 100,000-dollar opera house to be built there, and during the same month was inaugurated a new railway timetable, providing for twenty-two regular trains running daily between Pasadena and Los Angeles, plus extra ones. Thirty thousand dollars was allocated for improvements in the Oak Knoll area. In September three random examples of sums involved in daily real-estate transactions amounted, respectively, to $25,450, $34,930, and $46,669. Single sales often reached large figures; seventy-four lots, in one instance, brought $22,140. The boom had its drawbacks as well as advantages. "The rapid selling of real estate," complained the *Tribune's* correspondent, "has had the effect of leaving many fine places uncultivated, they changing owners so fast that no one kept them long enough to work them. The result is that Pasadena orchards do not present so fine an appearance as two years ago."[23]

A more-or-less indirect result of the boom was the work of Thaddeus S. C. Lowe, a versatile eastern scientist, who came to Pasadena in 1888 to construct a gas plant. Lowe was attracted by the scenic possibilities of the mountain range which towered over the city, aided the early construction of an observatory on a near-by summit, and four years later built the Mount Lowe Railway, a transportation curiosity which was a tourist magnet for many years.

Neighboring areas profited by Pasadena's magnificent prosperity. South Pasadena was one of these, although there was apparently never a definite plan for the development of an

[22]*Los Angeles Tribune*, May 6, 1887.
[23]*Ibid.*, Apr. 16, 1887.

independent city to the south. The first hint of a separation occurred in 1885, when O. R. Dougherty purchased ten acres near Mission Street, subdivided it, and advertised his place of business as the South Pasadena Land Office. Resentment of certain settlers over the location of Pasadena's business district probably was responsible, as much as anything else, for the second town's development. "Although there was no studied effort," says Carew, "on the part of anybody for separation, almost before the inhabitants in that section knew what was happening, the settlement was being called South Pasadena."[24] Its incorporation as a city, in February, 1888, was brought about by its strong desire for legal weapons to combat liquor dealers.

Altadena, that portion of Pasadena nestling in the foothills, had a more complex history. In the seventies fourteen hundred acres of seemingly worthless land was deeded as a good-will gift by Benjamin D. Wilson to the San Gabriel Orange Grove Association. In 1880, some of this land was pre-empted by two settlers, Peter Gano and Stanley P. Jewett, and the rest was purchased by Capt. Frederick J. Woodbury and his brother John, of Marshalltown, Iowa. The brothers in 1881 had bought the land and water rights of Rubio Canyon and in the following year acquired 937 acres of the original grant. They started immediately to develop the eastern portion, and John Woodbury planted the far-famed deodars on the present "Christmas Tree Drive." The boom gave the brothers Woodbury an opportunity to subdivide, and on February 9, 1887, the Pasadena Improvement Company was organized for the purpose of developing Altadena. Its holdings included the land formerly belonging to Gano and Jewett, the Woodbury property, a section owned by the California Olive Company, Rubio Canyon and its water rights, and a portion of the

[24]Harold D. Carew, *History of Pasadena and the San Gabriel Valley* (1930), I, 345 ff.

water rights of Millard and Las Flores canyons. John Woodbury became president, and Edward C. Webster, secretary.
The town was named after a nursery belonging to a friend
of the Woodburys. From that time onward the growth of
Altadena was steady, its rolling ground and picturesque
canyons providing attractive sites for expensive homes. In
1888 Pasadena made a faltering attempt by an extension provision to engulf within its municipal boundaries Altadena and
the foothills, but the scheme was foiled by Altadena citizens.

Garvanza on the south and Lamanda Park on the east also
enjoyed a flourishing growth, reflected largely from Pasadena. A one-day sale which took place in May of 1887 will
serve as an example of Garvanza's enthusiasm: it resulted in
the disposal of 110 lots for the fair sum of $25,275. Lamanda
Park was the northwest corner of Leonard J. Rose's Sunnyslope Ranch; its name was contrived by combining his first
initial with Amanda, his wife's name. Rose subdivided the
property in 1885 and later other capitalists became interested
in it, notably James F. Crank, the railroad man. Lamanda
Park was given excellent publicity in newspapers, but it has
never outgrown its status as a suburb.

The Pasadena boom was thus a fair second to Los Angeles'
own flurry, being important enough to foster suburbs in its
turn. Outside of Los Angeles itself, the frenzy struck hardest
in Pasadena and the eastern valley, and their modern prosperity is very largely due to boom-time development. Here
the vaunted attractions of southern California were displayed
to their best advantage—fragrant citrus groves, fertile, watered
soil, and shaded avenues backed by the snow-tipped peaks of
the Sierra Madre. Not unnaturally, therefore, most of the
passengers who boarded excursion trains at a Los Angeles station headed northeast toward the blooming orchards of the
"Crown City" or the rich, cheap acres of its pleasant hinter-
land.

CHAPTER VIII

Glendale, Burbank, and the

San Fernando Valley

For some inexplicable reason most of the communities to which the boom gave birth and which still exist are reluctant to be known as "boom towns." Perhaps there is a stigma in owing one's origin to a period of abnormal growth, or possibly the citizens of these towns merely consider it rather commonplace to be allocated to a year in which so many other cities had their birthdays. However that may be, historians are often intensely interested in denying the boom origin of their communities. The historian of Glendale, John C. Sherer, early tries to convince his readers that "Glendale was not a boom town." He admits, nevertheless, that "it had its experience in fluctuating values."[1]

If Glendale was not a boom town, there were no such in southern California. True, settlers had already planted farms and orchards on the lands of the Rancho San Rafael, but most of the other towns created by the flurry were built around

[1]John Calvin Sherer, *History of Glendale and Vicinity* (1922), p. 53.

93

just such loose nuclei. The San Rafael property had been taken from its original grantees, the Verdugos, by a sheriff's sale in 1869, the foreclosure resulting from the operation of the exorbitant interest rates of that period. The land was bought by Alfred B. Chapman, who, it might be remarked to his credit, reserved 200 acres for the unfortunate Verdugo heir; and the ranch was later partitioned among twenty persons. The present city of Glendale arose on lands belonging to Chapman, Andrew Glassell, Ozro W. Childs,[2] and Cameron E. Thom. Newcomers were attracted to the fertile valley; they included Harry J. Crow, who bought land west of Glendale Avenue and south of what is now Broadway, and B. F. Patterson and E. T. Byram, who bought out Childs's interest. The chief industry of the region at that time was the raising of fruit, especially of peaches, apricots, and prunes, with some oranges and lemons along the foothills. According to Sherer, this early agricultural activity was never very profitable, and the only way to make it pay was to "peddle as well as produce."[3]

About 1883, investors began to buy Glendale land with an eye to speculation rather than orchard planting. Among the most active of these new arrivals was Moses L. Wicks, the Los Angeles attorney who identified himself with so many boom enterprises. In that year he bought 10,500 acres for over $50,000, from Benjamin Dreyfus and others. During the same year he purchased from Valentine Mand 800 acres near the foothills, including a share in the water rights of the mountain canyons. Wicks immediately began to plat and sell his

[2]Childs, a Vermonter, born in 1824, migrated to California in 1850 and became a tinware merchant at the mines. Later he moved southward and was a storekeeper and nurseryman in Los Angeles. Real estate next occupied his attention, and he profited greatly from the boom. He built the Los Angeles Opera House in 1884 and the Childs Block on Temple Street some months afterward. He died in 1890.

[3]Sherer, p. 57.

land. Meanwhile, the new settlers of the Glendale region commenced to feel the need of a name for their settlement, and at a schoolhouse meeting held in 1883 a debate finally resulted in the selection of its modern title. Despite the satisfaction of local residents, it took eight years to persuade the Post Office Department that the name should be used, objections being raised on the grounds that other "Glendales" already existed. But the choice of a name was not the only co-operative activity of the citizens. On August 30, 1886, the Glendale Improvement Society was organized for the purpose of promoting the town's welfare. The society was one of many which sprang up during boom years and, like other groups stimulated unduly by realty activity, died afterward of malnutrition. During its brief life, however, it was responsible for much civic progress. A transportation committee organized shortly after its inception was instrumental in securing access to Los Angeles by means of the Los Angeles-Glendale Railway, an interurban line built by two Arkansas engineers in 1887, which ran down Crow (Glendale) Avenue to San Fernando Road and the Los Angeles boundary; there was a connection by bus with the Verdugo Hills. The line was subsidized by Cameron Thom, Erskine Ross (Thom's nephew), and Andrew Glassell, each of whom contributed about $5,000. The railway later became part of the Terminal Railroad, which in turn sold out to the Los Angeles, San Pedro, and Salt Lake Railway. Publicity in the Los Angeles papers was a paramount objective of the Improvement Society, and in 1887 members pledged eighty dollars to aid in the establishment of the town's first newspaper, the *Glendale Encinal.*

In the early months of 1887, Ross, Thom, Byram, Patterson, and Ben Ward (the auctioneer) pooled their interests and on March 11, filed the first plat of the "Town of Glendale." The town contained over sixty blocks and occupied

95

the center of the present city, from Lexington Street to below Colorado Street, and from Central Avenue to five blocks (on an average) east of Glendale Boulevard. The east-and-west streets were numbered. Advertisements in Los Angeles papers stressed that the town was only six and a half miles from the courthouse and that a motor railway was under construction. Blocks averaged two and one-half acres each, lots were large, streets varied from sixty to eighty feet wide, with twenty-foot alleys between them, and water was available for every lot. A Southern Pacific station and a 50,000-dollar hotel were promised. One advertisement concluded:

Glendale is right in the wake of the solid improvement. Four miles beyond is the new candidate for favor, the Town of Burbank, and still beyond and at the head of the valley which bears its name, can be found the growing town of San Fernando, and you have to go through Glendale to reach the vast acreage of San Fernando. . . . No cobblestones, river bottom, or wash lands.[4]

Ben Ward was the agent. By May 274 lots had been sold, and a price rise was promised shortly.

The hotel which the advertisements pledged was erected under the same stimulus that had led to building the Pasadena inns. Unlike them, however, it failed miserably when the boom burst. Thom, Ross, and Crow invested approximately $60,000 in the structure. In 1889 the building became a seminary, known as St. Hilda's Hall, under the sponsorship of the Episcopal diocese of southern California. After four years the institution closed and in 1905 was sold to the Battle Creek Institute for a sanitarium. Thom, Ross, and Crow salvaged only $12,000 from the wreck of their venture. Another point of similarity to Pasadena lay in the fact that a

[4]*Los Angeles Tribune*, May 1, 1887.

96

sister community grew up on the south—in this case a straw-
berry-raising center known as Tropico. The largest landowner in these bottom lands was W. C. B. Richardson, and
the head office of the Strawberry-Growers' Association was
located here. The settlement was tacitly separated from Glendale by the Southern Pacific Railroad's erection of a station
in the strawberry fields. Japanese farmers later acquired the
district's chief industry, and the town itself was engulfed by
Glendale in 1918.

Burbank was laid out early in April, 1887, on lands of the
Providencia Rancho. The town was first advertised under
the ranch name, and its size (17,000 acres) and its location
on the main Southern Pacific line from the north were emphasized. The fact that six passenger trains passed through
daily was also stressed, but the advertisements carefully omit-
ted any mention of whether or not the trains stopped. In May
nine business and residence buildings were projected, but the
Providencia Land and Water Company, which stood behind
the venture, appeared equally interested in the sale of farm
plats as in the disposal of city lots. Notices accented the soil's
adaptability to oranges, lemons, limes, and olives, notwithstanding Glendale's limited success with such crops. During
the summer of 1887 promoters promised rapid expansion,
including the erection of at least fifteen new buildings. The
boom continued through the early months of 1888, and excursions were still arriving in March. Promoters boasted that
these were "pleasure excursions" and that Burbank sales
methods differed from those of surrounding communities.
One article proclaimed:

We have never had a [real] excursion, never employed a brass
band or had a street parade; have offered no lottery schemes to
tempt purchasers to invest, but without any show or parade we
have in a few months sold over 900 Town Lots and 2000 acres of

97

land adjoining, aggregating nearly $600,000. In less than ten months a grain field has been converted into a growing prosperous town of over 250 BONA FIDE INHABITANTS.[5]

By that time there were a sixty-room hotel, a streetcar line, and a dummy interurban line nearly completed.

The La Cañada region was the subject of seven plats during the years 1886-87. The 6,000-acre La Cañada Rancho was owned by Dr. J. L. Lanterman and Col. A. W. Williams, who subdivided it in 1880. Their method was unique in that the entire tract centered on Michigan Avenue (the present Foothill Boulevard), and the property was divided into forty-six plats, each one-fourth of a mile wide, facing this thoroughfare. Adaptation of the patroon system was aided by the establishment of the grape industry in 1884 and by the platting of La Crescenta by Dr. Benjamin Briggs, of Indiana, who had come to California with the idea of founding a health resort near the mountains. The name "La Crescenta" was derived from the formation of the alluvial fans at the base of the hills. Development was rather slow, although a school was constructed in 1887; a typical boom hotel was not built until 1890. Montrose was located on part of the Briggs land, which had been sold by his daughter to a real-estate company. That purchase, plus the Lanterman subdivision and another tract called the Beach Addition, constituted the present town of Montrose, which was, however, a post-boom development. In general, the La Cañada Valley was not affected to any extent by the boom, although a small hotel was built at Crescenta Cañada, in the center of the valley, as a hopeful nucleus. A windstorm demolished the structure in July, 1887, before the speculation mania had reached its height.

A large part of the San Fernando Valley had been owned

[5]*Los Angeles Express*, Jan. 3, Mar. 10, 1888.

by Pío Pico, who was bought out in 1869 by the San Fernando Farm Homestead Association. This group obtained for $115,000 the southern half of the valley, some 60,000 acres, after bringing a friendly action for partition against the Celís heirs. The organization was backed by San Francisco capitalists, among them, Isaac Lankershim (who bequeathed his name to a valley highway and settlement) and Isaac Newton Van Nuys. The area was originally devoted to sheep raising and later was planted to grain, but the drought years of the sixties injured it materially. In 1880 the Los Angeles Farm and Milling Company succeeded to the holdings of the Farm Homestead Association, and, as a result of emphasis on grain growing and processing, the boom was late in arriving. However, in 1888 Isaac Lankershim organized the Lankershim Ranch Land and Water Company and bought from the Farm and Milling Company 12,000 acres in the eastern end of the valley. The tract was subdivided into small farm sites and put on the market at prices ranging from five dollars to fifty-five dollars per acre. The population center was the town of Toluca, born during the boom and later renamed, first, Lankershim, and then, more recently, North Hollywood. The Lankershim Orchard Tract, as it was called, was promoted actively but failed at the time to grow into a large settlement. In 1888, however, sales in excess of $200,000 were reported, and the town of Toluca boasted a hotel, a school, some stores, and several houses. The region was advertised as possessing "natural subirrigation" from the Los Angeles, Pacoima, and Tujunga rivers. Large-scale development was postponed for future decades, however, and the boom's chief function was to call attention to the potentialities of this part of the valley.

The northern half of the valley was never under the control of the San Fernando Farm Homestead Association but, instead, was acquired by Senator Charles Maclay of Santa Clara and his partner, George K. Porter, a San Francisco shoe manufacturer. They received 56,000 acres of valley land lying between the present communities of Chatsworth and Roscoe. Benjamin F. Porter, George's cousin, shortly purchased one-half of the latter's three-fourths interest, and a small part of Maclay's one-fourth interest. Most of the land except that northeast of the mission was devoted to wheat culture. Berry, the Pasadena colony agent, was mildly interested in San Fernando Valley land and examined the district carefully. In 1873 he reported to his sponsor: "San Fernando ranch of 55,000 acres is well adapted to semi tropical fruits, but it will cost a good deal to build reservoirs to hold the winter rains, for irrigating trees. The owner owes $40,000 and must sell enough to meet that in one sale."[6] The area adjoining the mission was platted by Maclay into the town of San Fernando, on September 15, 1874. The town area embraced 1,000 acres and featured straight streets and twenty-five-foot lots, generally priced between ten and fifty dollars. Land was reserved for a Southern Pacific station. The ranch land, comprising about 36,000 acres, was sold at five to forty dollars per acre, and the purchaser of a forty-acre plat acquired water rights. A circular issued by the California Immigrant Union stressed the fact that "The soil of the Maclay San Fernando Ranch is without exception the richest on the Southern Coast."[7] The Southern Pacific made inducements to settlers. "We have concluded to carry," the railway announced in 1874, "heads of families who are to be residents of the new town at half the regular rates between Los Angeles and San Fernando, also to carry lumber from Los Angeles to San Fernando at half the regular rates." That the town of San Fernando was to be the official railway terminus for the Southern Pacific's construction north from Los Angeles, until the southward-building branch reached it from

[6]David M. Berry to Thomas Balch Elliott, Sept. 9, 1873.
[7]Coronel pamphlets.

the San Joaquin, was hailed as a stimulus to rapid growth; as
the excavation of the route through Soledad Canyon was
expected to be a long task, San Fernando would profit for
some months from this delay. Prospective investors were
urged to come by sea, if they lived in San Francisco, and to
land at Truxton, Baker's town on the Santa Monica palisades;
steamer rates were advertised as ten dollars and six dollars—
"and sometimes less when there is opposition."[8]

The auction which Maclay tried to hold on completion of
the new railway station was evidently not a great success.
"A plat of the town was in evidence," says one critic, "and
some attempt was made at an auction sale of lots, but the
crowd was not very enthusiastic. . . . A few lots were knocked
down, but they were probably sold to by-bidders."[9] Despite
that unpropitious start, the town progressed rapidly. Two
hotels, the Kittridge House and the Fernando, were constructed; a general store was put up by Maclay himself, and
the town became the freighting terminus for the northern
trade. Sales of farm land proceeded enthusiastically—so much
so, in fact, that Elliott and Berry experienced difficulty in
marketing their Pasadena property. Berry grumbled in May,
1874: "The San Fernando Colony is selling land at low figures
and we cannot make everybody come to our terms." Subsequently he wrote: "I want to take forty acres in San Fernando
at $10 an acre." In August he stated: "There will be plenty of
buyers next winter but lately San Fernando has offered such
inducements that we can do nothing. Besides we began so late
that we cannot make a show of good things yet to attract
people."[10] The completion of the Southern Pacific from San
Francisco to Los Angeles greatly aided San Fernando. While

[8]*Ibid.*

[9]Spalding, *History of Los Angeles*, I, 208.

[10]David M. Berry to Thomas Balch Elliott, May 16, 18, Aug. 5, 1874.

other areas complained of high freight rates and the consequent throttling of hoped-for new business, San Fernando profited from what freight there was. The beginning of the boom in 1886 saw the town fairly well established as the nucleus of valley settlement. Substantial brick buildings were under construction, 4,000 acres were being farmed, and prices were rising steadily. "The time is not far distant," predicted the *Tribune*, "when San Fernando will be a healthy and dangerous rival of Pasadena."[11] Charles Maclay built a two-story hotel in October, 1886, and a 2,000,000-gallon reservoir promised an adequate water suppy. During the boom more than ten new tract maps were filed for San Fernando and its vicinity.

Maclay was not satisfied with his first platting project and soon organized a company which took over 20,000 acres northeast of San Fernando Road. Forty-acre farm plats were laid out, and the townsite of Pacoima was surveyed, but this development was never so successful as San Fernando. The area to the west of the mission came under the control of two development companies: one, the Porter Land and Water Company, acquired most of the land southwest of the town, and the other, the San Fernando Valley Improvement Company, bought from Benjamin Porter the site of Chatsworth Park and platted it in 1888.

New settlers continued to come and the valley throve, but it was never so quickly settled as the regions east of Los Angeles. While the San Gabriel boom was largely concerned with the formation of towns, the San Fernando boom chiefly involved the sale of farm properties. An attempt was made to use the Southern Pacific track as the thread along which a row of settlements could be built, and there was even a halfhearted attempt, in 1886, to promote Tehachapi. But the

[11]*Los Angeles Tribune*, Oct. 26, Dec. 20, 1886.

land was not as well suited for colonization and settlement as the valley flats, and promoters satisfied themselves with stressing the town's resort possibilities. San Fernando remained the capital of its valley domain for many years, and only under the stimulus of war industry are the smaller communities reaching north to meet it.

CHAPTER IX

Pomona and the

Irrigation Settlements

P OMONA was another colony town. It originated in the boom of the seventies, under the auspices of the Los Angeles Immigration and Land Co-operative Association, a company formed in December, 1874, and capitalized at a quarter of a million dollars. The typical colony share-purchasing scheme was utilized—in this case 2,500 shares at one hundred dollars each were distributed. Pomona's founders included men who were interested in other realty projects—notably L. M. Holt, publicist and editor of Riverside, and Harry Crow, who owned acreage in south Glendale. The company surveyed and subdivided 2,500 acres of the San José Rancho, reserving 640 acres for the town and laying out the rest in forty-acre farm plots. When the Southern Pacific Railroad arrived in 1874, Pomona became the temporary shipping point for Riverside, and business improved measurably, with the result that a hotel, new business blocks, and numerous residences were built. The first auction was a three-day affair, from February 22 to 24, 1876; land was sold at an average price of sixty-four dollars per acre, and the first day of the sale grossed $19,000. Pomona, however, did not have a completely untroubled existence: the drought of 1876-77 almost ruined the town's adjacent farmland, and a large fire in 1877 destroyed many valuable buildings. In 1880 the population was a mere 130.

With the increased activity of the early eighties, however, a new interest was shown in Pomona, as evidenced by the formation of a second development company, headed by Dr. Cyrus T. Mills and Moses L. Wicks. This organization called itself the Pomona Land and Water Company and attempted to revive the dying town. It proceeded to buy out many landowners and acquired appurtenant water rights. The timely arrival of the great boom in 1886 aided tremendously. From then onward Pomona had a pleasanter history, and optimism was reflected in newspaper accounts. "A large number of Eastern people," observed a reporter, "are seen daily on our streets with smiling faces that seem to say Pomona is a charming place in which to make a home, with its wealth of fruits and flowers and hospitable people."[1] Realty values climbed daily, and one December day saw $40,000 in property change hands, a single real-estate firm being responsible for more than half of the amount. Hotels were crowded, and, as in Santa Ana, visitors overflowed into private homes. "Everything bids fair," said a reporter, "to give Pomona a most prosperous winter."[2] The winter was prosperous beyond the wildest expectations. Not only easterners, but also investors from Los Angeles, Pasadena, and Monrovia became interested in Pomona land. "The real estate dealers are happy," newspapers proclaimed. "With our new suburban towns [Palomares,

[1] *Los Angeles Tribune*, Dec. 16, 1886.

[2] *Ibid.*, Dec. 20, 1886.

Lordsburg, etc.] they have all they can do, and almost at any
time you can see carriage loads headed toward the new burgs.
It does not seem to affect sales in town and vicinity; they are
as brisk as ever."[3] Several new land companies were incorporated, one of them managed by a woman agent, and the
prospect of construction of the Pomona and Elsinore Railroad had a stimulating effect upon land prices. In May
Pomona was "still at the front," and reporters announced that
more property had changed hands in the past few months
than at any time in the town's history.[4] Adjacent areas profited
in consequence. As a counterpoise to Pomona's monopoly of
Southern Pacific traffic, a new townsite, called Palomares, was
platted a few miles north, as a terminus for the Santa Fe, but
was never overly successful. San Dimas was another Wicks
venture which had close affiliations with the Santa Fe Railroad.

Near by, on the borders of the sandy flats which later became large grape vineyards, George and William Benjamin
Chaffey started their two colonies which played such an important part in the history of southern-California irrigation.
George Chaffey was a Canadian engineer, and his was the
guiding spirit of the California enterprises. The first colony
established by the Chaffeys was Etiwanda (named after a
Michigan Indian chief), platted on a 1,500-acre tract fourteen miles west of San Bernardino. The basis of the town was
a water company organized by Chaffey and L. M. Holt in
1882, and the settlement developed into a small agricultural
community. The town on which the Chaffeys lavished their
best attention, however, was Ontario, named after their own
Canadian province. Land of the Rancho Cucamonga, originally belonging to the Tapia family, passed to George
Chaffey in 1882 for $60,000. The parcel included 6,216 acres

[3]*Ibid.*, Apr. 8, 1887.
[4]*Ibid.*, May 2, 1887.

with water rights in San Antonio Canyon. The colony was later augmented in size by the addition of railway, government, and private acreages. The Chaffeys paid about twelve dollars per acre for their property. A town was laid out on 640 acres, of which one-half was deeded to form a foundation for the projected Chaffey Agricultural College. The mutual water system, to be described later,[5] was set in operation, with 15,000 shares. No saloons were permitted in Ontario, and this provision was enforced by a reversion clause in the title deeds. The Chaffeys employed typical boom methods as early as 1883, sponsoring excursions and supervised sales of colony property. Lots yielded $125 apiece, "villa acres" brought $250, and "horticultural lots" commanded $200 each. On Saint Patrick's Day in 1883 a railway excursion brought visitors from Los Angeles and Colton for the ceremony of laying the foundation stone of the agricultural college. Euclid Avenue was platted 200 feet wide, and a gravity railway was built which later became one of the unique sights of Ontario; mules drew the car up the long, gentle grade, then solemnly mounted the rear platform and rode downhill. So well did the Chaffeys manage their holdings that by 1884 the assessed valuation of the colony land was $93,200, and the figure rose in 1886, the last year of the Chaffey regime, to $350,000.

In 1886 George Chaffey sailed for Australia, there to begin his ill-starred irrigation projects, and his brother was left alone to conclude their business in California. William, over-eager to join his brother, sold out one year too soon. If he had waited for 1887 boom prices, there is little doubt, says his biographer, that he would have obtained $500,000 for their interests. Instead, they received only about $150 per acre. Even without the guiding hand of the Chaffeys, Ontario proved an outstanding success, the most publicized addition

[5]See below, Chapter XVI.

being a tract known as South Ontario, adjacent to the original town area. The plans of the Chaffeys were carried out in detail. The agricultural college, begun by a 100,000-dollar gift from George Chaffey, was operated as a branch of the University of Southern California until 1901, when it became a high school; and recently it has developed into one of the region's outstanding junior colleges, dutifully emphasizing the agricultural studies which Chaffey contemplated.

About three miles north of Ontario on the route of the gravity railway was Upland, another typical boom town. Founded as Magnolia Villa by the Bedford brothers in 1887, it profited by its position as a way station between Los Angeles and San Bernardino. An auction managed by Ben Ward on May 6 resulted in sales aggregating $50,000. One train came from Los Angeles and óne from San Bernardino, bringing about 500 visitors to add to 300 already there. Fifty teams of horses drove the excursionists up Euclid Avenue to the townsite. "This sale," Ward had advertised a few days previously, "will be an auction sale, conducted on the old-style method, wherein the public, not the owners, place the price on the property"; and apparently the method met with popular favor. One hundred and sixty lots were sold in 165 minutes; the highest price paid was $300, and the lowest, $150. "No Band!" Ward proclaimed. "No Circus! But a Plain Business Deal." And, considering the amount involved, business was obviously the keynote of the day.[6]

Claremont, on the lands of the Rancho San José, was laid out on 365 acres purchased by the Pacific Land and Improvement Company from the Pomona promoters, plus an additional sixty-five acres bought direct from a neighboring landowner. The Santa Fe extension from San Bernardino stimulated its growth, and the townsite was fortunate in having an

[6]*Los Angeles Tribune*, May 2, 3, 7, 1887; Netz, in Hist. Soc. of Sou. Calif. *Annual Publications, 1915-16*, X, 63.

efficient sales manager. He was Frank A. Miller, of Wisconsin, who came to California in 1872 to become a ranch superintendent and later started the Glenwood Tavern in Riverside which evolved into the famous Mission Inn. Development began in 1887 with enthusiastic promotion and wordy advertisements. The *Pomona Progress* of March 10, 1887, rhapsodized as follows:

Claremont is the name of the new town on the San Bernardino and Los Angeles Railroad. . . . The townsite is beautifully located on a mesa, some 1200 feet above the level of the sea, and at present is covered with a vast grove of sycamores. . . .
  A large gang of brush cutters are at work cleaning the land of all the undergrowth and trees which will be in the way of streets, avenues and parks. . . . All avenues are to center in a grand plaza. The prospects are that before the railroad shall get to Claremont from San Bernardino that a large sized town will be in existence there. A hotel, bank and newspaper are already promised. Claremont springs into existence with a fine "back country" already thickly settled with an intelligent set of thrifty fruit-growers who are pleased to have a shipping point on a transcontinental railroad at their very doors.[7]

Residence lots were platted 50 by 150 feet in size, but business lots conformed to boom practice in having a mere twenty-foot frontage. "Claremont the Beautiful" boasted perhaps the most flowery advertisements of all the boom towns. It was described in a series of "essays," which were serially numbered, presumably for the benefit of possible collectors. An excerpt from "Essay Number 2" runs as follows: "The newspapers are the enlightening influence of this age—the greatest age the world has ever experienced. They state that the Star of Bethlehem is about to appear. They also state that Claremont is the beautiful home site of all the town sites." And with similar roundabout euphuisms the fact was driven home

[7]Quoted in *This Is Claremont*, ed. Harold H. Davis (1941), pp. 4-5.

that Claremont was not only an artistic but a commercial success.[8] A display of the town plat for only two days resulted
in $100,000 in sales, most of which were probably paper
transactions. The collapse of the boom dealt Claremont a hard
blow, but recovery, though slow, was certain, and today
Claremont is one of the outstanding college towns in southern
California.

Of the smaller communities in the vicinity, Cucamonga and
Chino were born during the boom and still exist as small
towns somewhat overshadowed by their larger neighbors.
The Cucamonga Fruit Land Company and two water companies were organized in 1887 to develop the district east of
Upland. They platted a town and embarked upon the regular
process of promotion—in this case not productive of overwhelming results. Chino, ten miles to the south, owed its
development to its chief patron, Richard Gird. Gird was an
interesting character, having migrated from New York to the
California gold fields at the age of seventeen, thereafter work-
ing with Harry Meiggs (picturesque railway builder of the
Andes), and later prospecting in the Tombstone region. Gird
platted 23,000 acres into ten-acre farm lots in 1887 and designed a townsite one mile square. A narrow-gauge railroad
was built from Ontario; a newspaper, the *Chino Valley Cham-
pion*, was begun; and the incorporation of the Pomona and
Elsinore line in 1888 was expected to do great things for the
town. An attempt to build up an industrial district by the
establishment of iron mills (the Chino Valley Manufacturing
Company) failed with the boom's collapse, and Chino has
remained off the chief traffic routes for many years. In 1891
the Oxnard brothers revived its prospects somewhat by the
construction of a sugar-beet mill, and this served to re-
emphasize the agricultural basis of Chino's economy.

[8]*Los Angeles Tribune*, May 1, 1887.

To the south, nearer Los Angeles, Whittier was another colony that profited from the boom. Acquilla H. Pickering, a midwestern Quaker, organized a land company in 1886 which purchased the Thomas Ranch on May 3 of the following year. The company platted a town, named it after their sect's most famous poet, and held the first lot sale in May. Town lots were marketed at one hundred and two hundred dollars each, and five-acre suburban plots brought a thousand dollars. In July a trainload of colonists arrived from Iowa and were transported to Whittier by spring wagon. That the town was a successful venture is shown by the fact that seventeen plats were recorded for the year 1887. The boom in the country east and southeast of Los Angeles thus centered in two places: Pomona, and the smaller agricultural colonies near by. The flurry actually built Pomona; from a stagnant failure, the town rapidly acquired 3,500 citizens, an incorporated status, and 286 new buildings in the one year 1887. The outstanding smaller colonies were those planned by the Chaffey brothers as irrigation developments, while the Quaker colony of Whittier was unique. The boom was spreading to every community which had even a slight reason for attracting capital; and on its way thither it endowed the intervening spaces, which had no such attractions, with a little of the prosperity of their more fortunate neighbors.

CHAPTER X

Creation of a County:
The Boom in the Santa
Ana Valley

IN THE Santa Ana Valley the boom operated largely on established communities. Of all the towns in the region which were laid out during the period, Fullerton is the only one which has since justified its promoters' hopes. Most realty men of what is now Orange County contented themselves with new tracts, subdivisions, and additions in older municipalities.

The oldest town in the valley was Anaheim. This German-American settlement was founded in the fifties by a group of San Franciscans who were interested in grape culture. They organized the Los Angeles Vineyard Company, and bought 1,200 acres of the Rancho San Juan Cajón de Santa Ana at approximately two dollars per acre. Each member of the colony purchased a 750-dollar share and received in return a twenty-acre farm lot with water privileges. As each twenty-acre tract was soon made subject to further assessments, the average cost of settlement to each colonist amounted to about

$1,200. Here again the lot-drawing method of land distribution found favor; the farm plats were evaluated according to their soil and location from $600 to $1,400, and as each member drew a piece of property, he would either pay or receive the difference between the assessed valuation of his lot and the price he had paid to join the colony. The name of the project was derived from the "Ana" of Santa Ana and the German word for "home." Benjamin Dreyfus, later significantly active in valley affairs, built the first house, in 1857, and Anaheim's first hotel was erected in 1865. The boom struck the town in 1886. In December the local correspondent of a Los Angeles newspaper announced that the realty transactions of the past month amounted to $200,000. Arrival of the Santa Fe in 1887 intensified activity, and many of the early vineyards were subdivided into lots. The excursion method found favor with local promoters, and as early as January a huge excursion and auction attracted 700 prospects, who were given a free lunch and in return spent $38,000 for about 200 lots. The excursionists drew up a resolution of thanks to the promoters, expressing their appreciation for the efficient way in which the affair was managed. Their satisfaction was even greater when Anaheim merchants announced they would not take pay for any small purchases the excursionists made in their stores. Whether or not the merchants were reimbursed by the board of trade is not stated.

The city of Orange, a few miles east, had been platted about 1870 by Alfred Chapman, owner of the San Rafael property. The town consisted of forty acres divided into eight five-acre blocks and included a plaza which is still an attractive part of the little community. The settlement was first called Richland, but, as the Post Office Department refused to validate that choice because there were other postal stations bearing the same name, "Orange" was finally selected. During the boom Orange unfortunately incurred Santa Ana's jealousy.

✑ The Boom of the Eighties ✒

This happened, of course, before the formation of Orange County, while Anaheim, Orange, and Santa Ana were competing strongly for the privilege of possessing the prospective county offices. In April, 1887, the Santa Ana correspondent became suavely vitriolic:

On paper, large real estate transactions have recently been reported [in Orange]. . . . While Santa Ana rejoices in the prosperity with which she is blest, she prefers to move along quietly but surely, and to read of the prosperity of her sister towns in preference to boasting of what she is doing. "Deep waters run quietly and smoothly."[1]

But despite Santa Ana's claims and wishful thinking, the boom in Orange was a vigorous reality. In January, 1887, building activity became so great that a lumber shortage developed; a hotel, the Palmyra, was under construction, and the city fathers had voted to erect a large fountain in the plaza. Orange's biggest excursion party came in April; it was an invitational affair and attracted 150 persons. The sale was partially managed by a hotel owner, who invited the visitors to lunch in his establishment, and they later expressed their appreciation in the approved manner of excursionists—that is, by a vote of thanks. This expedition resulted in the disposal of thirty lots for $15,000. Realty sales for the week totaled $100,000, and the activity was characterized by the *Tribune* as a "boomlet." Most of the buyers were easterners who, according to one promoter, intended to reside on their new land; his statement may, however, be questioned, for news columns mentioned altogether too many such "easterners" who intended to "reside" on their property to warrant the acceptance of all similar claims at face value.

The town which eventually grew into the metropolis of the region was Santa Ana. Not essentially a boom product, it

[1] *Los Angeles Tribune*, Apr. 8, 1887.

owed much of its later expansion to stimulus received during 1887 and 1888. The town had been founded by a Kentucky Argonaut, William H. Spurgeon, who platted his lands into a twenty-four-block village in December, 1870. He exerted every effort to place Santa Ana on the chief traffic lanes of the region, and by a program of judicious road building and by offering certain inducements he persuaded the San Diego stage line to locate its station there. In 1887 the Southern Pacific Railroad built an extension to Santa Ana, and this resulted in the platting of the town's first large addition, known as Santa Ana East. The new tract, despite its builders' hopes, failed to change the location of Santa Ana's business center, although a concession to the railway had been made by laying the addition's streets, not according to the four cardinal directions as they were in Santa Ana, but parallel to the railway tracks. Despite a severe financial blow that had befallen Santa Ana in the early eighties, when a dishonest banking venture swindled depositors of $130,000, the growth of the city was steady, and it was incorporated on June 1, 1886, before the boom reached a climax. Santa Ana's persistent progress was due largely to the adjacency of rich agricultural lands, especially those lying between the town and the ocean and known as Gospel Swamp. Two thousand persons lived in Santa Ana in 1886.

The boom was well under way by the end of 1886, notwithstanding the poor fruit yield of that year. One of the first auctions was held on December 7, by the Los Angeles and Santa Ana Land Bureau and was pronounced a striking success. Seventy-four lots were on sale, and advertisements promised excursionists a warm dinner, a carriage ride around the valley, and music by a brass band. Lodgings were scarce, and hotels were obliged to rent rooms in private homes throughout the city, in order to house their many guests; it was commonly said that buildings were rented as soon as

The Boom of the Eighties

foundations were laid. Gas mains, street lamps, and a local interurban line were completed in 1886.[2] The Santa Fe's arrival in 1887, and, before it came, the mere prospect of its approach, boosted already advancing land values. At an auction held in January five railway cars brought 486 prospective buyers, and the ninety-one lots on sale were transferred for $18,005; most of their purchasers were Los Angeles speculators, but eastern colonists were also present. In April began a building flurry, during which a new hotel, five large business blocks, and a 20,000-dollar schoolhouse were planned, while residential construction was hindered by a shortage of lumber. The local correspondent of a Los Angeles paper announced that, "The building boom has received a new impetus . . . and a better class of houses is being erected here than heretofore."[3] Labor was very scarce; Santa Fe Railroad contractors offered a bonus of one dollar to anyone bringing a laborer to work on the new line. Santa Ana was encouraged by the railroad surveys which accompanied the boom and hopefully awaited a rate war upon completion of the Santa Fe extension, but the boom ended before railway competition could play a great part in it. Acreage in farm property was not neglected; large areas were sold, including among the biggest of them the San Joaquin Ranch, south of the city, which was bought by a Riverside syndicate for $250,000. Agriculture and horticulture were always emphasized, and in May the valley towns held a floral festival in Santa Ana, in emulation of the larger affair held in Los Angeles. That the boundaries of Santa Ana were greatly extended by the boom is shown by the number of new tracts and additions recorded during 1886 and 1887. The former year saw the filing of twenty new plats, while 1887 was responsible for fifty-three,

[2]The Santa Ana, Orange, and Tustin Street Railway.

[3]*Los Angeles Tribune*, Apr. 8, 1887.

proving that Santa Ana was one of the older towns affected most actively by the upsurge in values.

The chief boom town of the valley—that is, the largest community laid out during boom years—was Fullerton. This prosperous city was platted by the Pacific Land and Improvement Company in 1887. The heads of the organization were the Amerige brothers, Edward and George, who sold out a grain business in Boston to establish a town on 430 acres of land north of Santa Ana. They negotiated with the Santa Fe Railroad to assure themselves that the tracks would touch their development and persuaded George H. Fuller, a director of the railway, to join them in their project. Fuller became president of the land company, and the town was named after him, although a temporary revulsion of feeling upon his resignation resulted in rechristening the town La Habra. While the Santa Fe greatly encouraged the Amerige project, the town was never able to take full advantage of the railway's arrival, for the first train did not come until the fall of 1888, when the flurry was in its decline. Under the circumstances, the community experienced a rather slow growth and has seen most of its expansion in more recent years, thanks largely to near-by oil fields and Valencia-orange groves.

Of the smaller valley towns, Tustin was another established community which profited from the expected arrival of the Santa Fe. A branch of the Southern Pacific was built there in 1887, and some rather large land sales were recorded. Buena Park, thirteen miles north of Santa Ana, was platted in 1887; it lay on the Southern Pacific line and was consequently expected to be a railway junction from which the Santa Fe would build to the eastward. That hope was not realized. Neither Buena Park nor Tustin ever experienced a large-scale boom, although they became centers for their respective agricultural districts.

Perhaps the greatest effect the boom had on the Santa Ana Valley was to inspire the formation of a new county—the present Orange County. The project had been discussed as early as 1869, when an interesting citizen of Anaheim, Maj. Max Strobel, described as "a soldier of fortune and a Machiavel in politics . . . always on the losing side,"[4] enlisted the aid of surrounding rancheros in a county-division scheme. All three of the principal towns in the region east of Coyote Creek wanted to be the county seat, and, as a result, when Santa Ana seemed likely to win the struggle, Anaheim's leaders began a furious campaign to secure extension of the proposed boundary line farther west in order to give the German settlement a more central location in the new district. When this effort failed, citizens of Anaheim abandoned the idea, and the plan was carried through without their support. The bill was passed in March, 1889, at the instigation of a powerful lobby led by James McFadden, developer of Newport Beach, and William Spurgeon, founder of Santa Ana. The emissaries' mission met with success largely because of Los Angeles' penuriousness in refusing to finance an opposing lobby and because of San Francisco's gleeful willingness to decrease Los Angeles' size and prestige. The new county was given 780 square miles, about 40 miles of coast line, and some of the best citrus land in southern California.[5]

The chief characteristic of the boom in the lower Santa Ana Valley was its preference for established communities, although the one important example of new-town platting, Fullerton, has flourished. The Santa Fe Railroad arrived too late to stimulate the flurry directly, but prospects of its arrival had very nearly as much effect. The consequent rapid growth of the region encouraged a separatist sentiment which finally resulted in the carving of Orange County from Los Angeles' southeastern coastal lands.

[4]Guinn, *Southern California*, pp. 184 ff.

[5]*The Statutes of California and Amendments to the Codes passed at the Twenty-eighth Session of the Legislature, 1889* (1889), p. 123.

CHAPTER XI

The San Bernardino

County Flurry

T HE towns of San Bernardino County can, like the towns of most southern counties, be divided into two main groups: those founded before the boom and influenced by it, and those established during boom years, later to prosper or to die. Of first importance among the former was the city of San Bernardino itself, the principal settlement in the county and its population focus. Of the latter, Corona, or South Riverside, was an outstanding example.

San Bernardino had been founded in 1851 by a group of Mormon immigrants interested in building a community to emulate Salt Lake City. Though the Mormons departed, the town, already firmly established during the upswing of the early seventies, was staid and venerable by the time of the great boom. During the earlier period land prices had remained fairly reasonable. Berry of Pasadena, for instance, reported that outlying acreage could be bought for prices ranging from two to five dollars per unit; in October of 1873 he described in some detail a section of government land which could be obtained for two and one-half dollars per acre, and also a thirty-five-acre piece closer to the city limits, planted with grapes, oranges, walnuts, and other fruits, which could be had for $12,500. Building costs were reasonable in proportion. However, with the work of enthusiasts like L. M. Holt and Scipio Craig, newspapermen of the vicinity, land values began to rise, and by 1887 San Bernardino was experiencing a building and buying flurry almost as intense as that in Pasadena. The Fairbanks, Everts, Owens, and Christy additions and the Urbita, St. Elmo, Daley, and Hart tracts appeared. In April Maj. George Bonebrake of Los Angeles invested heavily in adjacent ranch lands, purchasing more than 50,000 acres north and west of the city. "If he owns the water he is reported as owning," remarked a Los Angeles newspaper, "an era of development will commence in the neighborhood, at the door of San Bernardino, which will throw all previous colonizing projects far into the shade."[1] The San Bernardino Valley Railroad began track-laying in April, and proposals for extending the existing Colton-San Bernardino motor line to Arrowhead were broached. The Santa Fe Railway's connection with Los Angeles was completed during the same month, and the first train ran on May 14. By May realty transfers amounted to $200,000 per week. In general, coupled with large transfers of land and the platting of several new additions to the city, the boom in San Bernardino reflected itself largely in local railway extensions and in a sharp rise in prices and property values. City assessments rose, for example, from $3,680,745 in 1880 to $11,-189,842 in 1885, and that figure was doubled by 1887. Like other established towns, San Bernardino benefited far more than it suffered from the boom.

[1]*Los Angeles Tribune*, Apr. 8, 1887.

◄§ *The San Bernardino County Flurry* §►

It was in the smaller towns that the boom took its greatest toll in broken hopes and shattered bank accounts. Colton, three miles south of San Bernardino, originated as the Slover Mountain Colony in 1873 and owed its later prominence to the fact that it agreed to grant to the Southern Pacific the subsidy which San Bernardino refused. One newspaper, in an article after the boom, grew reminiscent over that incident:

Speaking of side-tracking, it seems a little odd now to recall the fact that in 1878 or 1879 the people of this city were much concerned over a report that Los Angeles was to be cut off the main transcontinental line of the Southern Pacific and its place taken by Colton. The theory was that the railroad proposed to construct a line from Mojave to Colton, thus saving a few miles, and run an occasional local to Los Angeles as it does now to Calabasas. . . . A few years later the boom came along and the absurdity of a possible rival in Colton was as plain to the alarmists as it had been to the wise ones from the start.[2]

Colton received a San Diego railway connection in 1882, with the arrival of the California Southern line, but once again the Big Four blocked a San Bernardino extension—this time by refusing to permit the California Southern to cross Southern Pacific tracks. Their opposition was finally beaten down in 1883, after a lawsuit. In 1886 the boom arrived and stimulated the subdivision of 300 acres north of the town by P. A. Raynor, and the purchase by a Los Angeles syndicate of 400 lots in town for the sum of $20,000; the November prediction in the *Tribune* was that boom prospects were good and that a new industrial emphasis was to be expected in the vicinity. The *Colton Daily Semi-Tropic* began publication during the same year. In 1887 a small German colony was founded on a 300-acre plat near by, and the Southern Pacific Railroad bought most of the unused lots in town for railway

[2]Luther A. Ingersoll, *Ingersoll's Century Annals of San Bernardino County* (1904), pp. 553-54.

yards and investment. In July Colton was incorporated as a city of the sixth class, and in November a franchise for a motor railway to San Bernardino was granted. Streets were paved in 1888, and other civic improvements followed. To-day, the community is notable chiefly as a cement-manufacturing center. In 1887, Rialto, Fontana and Bloomington, all west of San Bernardino, were laid out by the Semi-Tropic Land and Water Company, headed by George Bonebrake and a Los Angeles banker, F. C. Howes.

The town of Redlands, a short distance southeast of San Bernardino, also owes its early development to railway facilities—the California Southern line, which built north to join the Santa Fe in 1885—although settlers, enthusiastic but few in number, had occupied the region since 1881. The town was platted and put on the market March 10, 1887, and the first auction was held twenty days later. This sale transferred some 200 lots at $200 each, and was so successful that 200 more were immediately offered with a fifty-dollar rise in price. The *Citrograph*, the "largest, neatest, and most enterprising weekly paper in the county, or in the state, for that matter," appeared in July under the editorship of Scipio Craig.[3] During 1887 building went on apace. Business lots were sold under the stipulation that brick blocks be constructed immediately, and no wooden "shacks" were permitted. By September more than a dozen brick buildings had been erected, and a 20,000-dollar hotel was in course of construction. Cement sidewalks were laid, and business land rose from $100 per lot in February to $125 per front foot in September. The East San Bernardino Valley Railway was being graded, and the school district without dissent voted $15,000 in bonds. The Citizens' Stage Line, running Concord coaches, operated between Redlands and Brookside, Lugonia, Crafton, and San Bernardino, and various realty tracts, known euphoniously as Terracina, Residence, Mound City, and

Gladysta, were platted and placed on sale. The Chicago Colony Colonization Society, which had been organized in May of the previous year to start a settlement in Redlands, now boasted sixty families. As early as April, 1887, residence property was selling at the rate of more than forty lots per week, and gross realty transactions were totaling from $500,000 to $800,000 per month.

Agricultural advantages of the Redlands region were stressed vigorously. Old settlers boasted that danger from frost did not exist, and that oranges bore after only four years. It was possible, said one reporter, to clear more than one hundred dollars per acre from a three-year-old vineyard or a grove of equally young apricot trees. One acre produced almost twelve tons of alfalfa, and water from Bear Valley Reservoir was abundant. Land values rose from $100 per acre in 1886 to $1,000 in 1887, although without water rights. In December of 1887 the *Citrograph* was able to say with just pride: "Nine months ago the ground on which the business portion of Redlands stands was a barren waste. Today there is a town on this land of 200 good, substantial buildings and every line of business is represented." The article added that the town then had five restaurants and two brickyards, and was planning a Masonic lodge.[4] Realty assessments had risen from $110,990 in 1886 to $329,055 in 1887—an increase of 196 per cent. The school population grew more than sixfold in the two years 1886-88; and building improvements worth more than $450,000 were erected during the year and a half starting January 1, 1887, in addition to public improvements costing $200,000. The collapse of the boom found Redlands well started. The town was incorporated in November, 1888, and a fruitgrowers' association was established the following

[3]*Ibid.*, p. 449.

[4]*Ibid.*, p. 453.

year. An Improvement Association of 1888 grew into a board of trade which advertised the region, and the women of the Chicago Colony formed an organization known as the United Workers for Public Improvements. Building construction during 1889 was valued at less than half the 1887 figure, but during the next decade a gradual rise culminated in renewed prosperity. Realty assessments reached almost $2,000,000 in 1889, and were well past that mark four years later. Like San Bernardino, Redlands owed much to the great boom.

Lugonia, three miles east of Redlands, was one of the few boom towns in the San Bernardino region which did not flourish. It was platted in the shape of a rectangle and advertised 300 business lots. Auctions were held during 1887 under the auspices of the Los Angeles Land Bureau, the promoters charging two dollars and a half for the train trip and lunch. Redlands made an attempt to engulf Lugonia within its city limits in November, 1887. The Lugonia *Southern Californian* treated the matter with fitting irony:

The people of Redlands love Lugonia. They say so themselves. However they may have felt in the past they love us now. Whether Lugonia has grown more charming or Redlands more susceptible—it is our purpose to learn. A Redlands man got us by the arm this week and overwhelmed us with . . . words! And he held our attention while he drew a little picture that he called "Incorporation." It had Crafton in it. And Lugonia and Redlands and Barton's and Brookside and old San Bernardino. And it was fenced with boxes labeled Miramonte oranges, and it had brick blocks without number and postoffices—N.,E.,S. and W. Miramonte! . . . Well! When Redlands courts Lugonia, there's a colored gentleman within the woodpile. Before we marry the blushing maid we want to ask a few questions.[5]

The near-by town of Riverside was started as a colony by J. W. North, of Knoxville and New York, in 1870. North

[5]*Ibid.*, p. 455.

bought several thousand acres of land from the Silk Center Association, which had settled on the Rubidoux and Jurupa ranches and had failed to convert southern California into a world silk center. He organized the Southern California Colony Association, built a nine-mile irrigation canal to the Santa Ana River, and laid out a town one mile square. The California Immigrant Union advertised the land, with due exaggeration, as embracing 30,000 acres—North's actual purchase had been less than 10,000 acres—suitable for agriculture, stock raising, grain, afalfa, and fruit. The circular added that the town had a population in 1871 of nearly fifty families, that a school, stores, and a hotel had been built, and that the community made a practice of donating land to church organizations. Agricultural land was sold at twenty dollars per acre, and prospective settlers could obtain special railroad rates. In 1874 North was bought out by Samuel C. Evans, an Ohio banker, and W. T. Sayward, a San Francisco businessman who had invested in an adjacent 8,600 acres in the Arlington district. They had first called their acquisition the New England Colony, but after buying North's land they formed the Riverside Land and Irrigation Company. The town was incorporated in 1883.

The boom raised prices for town land for which North had paid about three dollars per acre to more than $200 per block, and, with the establishment of an advertising agency in Los Angeles in November, 1886, prices went up still more. Interest in real estate became so intense that local agriculturists, busy at home, neglected to attend a fruitgrowers' convention held at Riverside in April of 1887. Auctions were highly successful. The Tibbetts Tract at the head of Magnolia Avenue was completely sold at its first auction, in April, bringing more than $26,000 at an average price of over $300 per lot. Among the public improvements enthusiastically planned in May were a 50,000-dollar school and a 250,000-

dollar hotel; later there was difficulty in paying for some of these construction projects.

Corona, in the southern part of the valley, acquired that name with its incorporation in 1896; it had previously been known as South Riverside and was the most important boom town of the vicinity. In 1886 the South Riverside Land and Water Company, headed by R. B. Taylor of Iowa, purchased 12,000 acres of the Yorba-ranch property in the Temescal Valley. The settlement was nicknamed the "Queen Colony," and a town was platted which featured a "grand circular boulevard," one mile in diameter, surrounding it. Inside this periphery, streets ran north and south with logical precision, but outside, suburban lanes radiated from the city center like spokes of a wheel. Water rights were included with realty purchases, and 10,000 acres of the colony were advertised as "choice, cultivable land."[6] In 1887 a pipe line was built twelve miles east to Temescal Canyon, and by May the town was adorned with more than a hundred buildings, including a three-story, verandaed hotel described as "Gothic," and supposedly capable of doing "credit to a town of 3000 population."[7] The boom in South Riverside was aided by the tendency of speculators to move southward as the available land closer to Los Angeles was occupied, by well-managed auction sales which resulted in single-day profits of $50,000, and by high hopes regarding the future of the Pomona and Elsinore Railroad, an abortive venture which started from Corona and went only as far as Hoag's Canyon. The railroad was touted greatly, and prominent businessmen, like Richard Gird of Chino and George Fuller of the Santa Fe, were on its managing board.

Another stimulus to the boom, and one reason for its per-

[6]*Los Angeles Tribune*, May 2, 1887.

[7]*Ibid.*

sistence in the Corona district after its collapse in other areas, was the development in the near-by San Jacinto hills of a body of tin ore, first exploited by Abel Stearns in the early sixties. Edward F. Beale, United States Surveyor-General for California, and others connected with the federal land office became interested in the mines. The title was not cleared until 1888, and work was begun in 1890 by an English organization, the California Mining and Smelting Company. A brief but significant flurry followed. The British directors were lavish with their funds and spent nearly $2,000,000 in improving the property. Their extravagance, coupled with certain obscure causes, was responsible for the closing of the mines in 1892. During two years of operation, however, the mines produced 136 tons of metallic tin—enough to cause a temporary reduction in the English market price. This was the first time that tin pigs had been exported from the United States.

Even the fertile fringes of the desert were made subjects of boom promotion. Beaumont, formerly a tiny hamlet known as San Gorgonio, obtained its real start as a boom venture. Its backers were known as the Southern California Investment Company, and promotion began in 1886. The company purchased the water supply of Cherry Valley, the Edgar Ranch, and Edgar and Noble canyons, sponsored a newspaper, the *Sentinel*, and built a 40,000-dollar hotel in 1887. Picnics and excursions followed, and as many as three trainloads at a time took advantage of the typical free lunches and sight-seeing rides. Land values rose from thirty dollars per acre to $200 in eight months. But the collapse of the boom left Beaumont without well-developed agricultural resources to maintain prosperity. Frantic attempts were made by one of the promoters, H. C. Sigler, to obtain a loan to tide the town over the days of adversity, but he was unsuccessful, and the German Savings and Loan Bank of San Francisco was finally forced, by hard times, to abandon its liberal policy and fore-close. Beaumont then stagnated until a new development company revitalized the region in 1907. Banning, next door to Beaumont, apparently was not affected by the boom, and boasted of this fact. "There has never been a 'boom' at Banning," said one writer, "and the growth has been steady."[8]

Perris and Hemet both owe their births to a combination of realty boom and railway development. The arrival, in 1882, of the California Southern Railroad in the valley doubt-less suggested the development of towns in the rich agricul-tural lands through which it passed, and Perris was named after Fred T. Perris of San Bernardino, chief engineer of the line. The town was platted by George A. Doyle in 1885 and 1886, and its settlement had such a beneficial effect upon the region that every vacant section of near-by government land was taken up very shortly. Perris' chief product was wool, and the extension of the Santa Fe lines improved its market greatly. Subsequent decline of the region, according to local residents, was due, not to the boom's collapse, but to the failure of the Bear Valley water system in the early nineties. Hemet was founded in 1886 by a syndicate which purchased 7,000 acres of land east of Perris, including the site of Lake Hemet and its dam, which was constructed in 1890.

San Jacinto, east of Hemet, was established many years earlier as a Mexican settlement on the Rancho San Jacinto Viejo. The town was surrounded by fruit and grain lands, and was stimulated by the boom and by railway construction in the eighties, to the extent that it was incorporated on April 9, 1888.

Still another result of the boom in the upper Santa Ana Valley was the formation of a new county, Riverside, with the town of that name as its headquarters. Although the actual

[8]Elmer Wallace Holmes (*et al.*), *History of Riverside County, California* (1912), p. 193.

THE LAND OF SOUTHERN CALIFORNIA—RIVERSIDE FROM MOUNT RUBIDOUX, 1890

bill to create the county was not passed by the legislature until March, 1893, the upsurge of the eighties was initially responsible for the concentration of population in the region. Riverside County was given 6,044 square miles of territory formerly belonging to San Diego County, and 590 square miles previously the possession of San Bernardino County; its total area is nearly equal to that of Massachusetts.[9]

As is evident from the foregoing discussion, the boom had six nuclei in the region around Los Angeles. Each of these had its own unique causes for realty promotion. The coast utilized harbor hopes and resort advantages, and built around two population centers, that of Santa Monica and that of the Long Beach-San Pedro area. The San Gabriel Valley upsurge rested on a firm foundation of railway competion and an outstandingly successful colony project, Pasadena. The boom in the San Fernando Valley was not so intense as elsewhere, but its effects, in so far as they were felt, centered around the Southern Pacific Railroad and Maclay's town of San Fernando. Pomona acted as the catalyst for the San José ranch lands, and the locality was further publicized by the notable successes of the Chaffeys in developing irrigation. The Santa Ana Valley possessed three well-established centers from which to expand—Anaheim, Orange, and Santa Ana—and artificial stimulation was applied by various railway surveys for a San Diego route which passed through the farmlands watered by the lower reaches of the Santa Ana River. The Mormons in San Bernardino and Judge North in Riverside laid the groundwork for the boom in that vicinity, and the fact that their region straddled the best routes to the desert and to the East increased its significance.

Thus, to generalize too widely about boom causes is to fall into error. The boom was not simply the result of railway

[9]*The Statutes of California and Amendments to the Code, Passed at the Thirtieth Session of the Legislature, 1893,* p. 159.

competition alone or of effective advertising; other factors, too, played a large part everywhere. Local influences were sometimes equally important. Most boom towns, for instance, were glad to see neighboring communities spring up, as is witnessed by Pomona's attitude toward her satellites. Such municipal growth served to benefit the area as a whole, and high values in one locality were often reflected throughout the region. Along the coast, however, competition was less welcome. Santa Monica, for example, was extremely unhappy over the Santa Fe's decision to promote Ballona Slough rather than South Santa Monica, and a virulent feud took place in the nineties over the respective merits of Wilmington and Santa Monica for harbor development. There could logically be only a single principal harbor for Los Angeles, and the early-day struggle was intense.

Notwithstanding the rivalries which ensued, the boom in the Los Angeles region was far more a co-operative project than is apparent on the surface. It was the day of the seller, not the buyer. A realtor's task during boom years was not so much to compete with his rivals as to time his presentations to absorb as large a share of the easy profits as he could. The absence of local loyalties among the more prominent promoters is evidence of this fact. The ubiquitous Moses L. Wicks was interested in almost every worth-while project in the Los Angeles district. Alfred B. Chapman indiscriminately promoted lands all the way from the Santa Ana River to the Rancho San Rafael. John D. Bicknell was as intricately involved with the fortunes of Azusa as he was with those of Monrovia. There was much provincialism, but there were broader sentiments as well, particularly among those leaders who had the future of southern California at heart.

The boom outside Los Angeles, if not so concentrated in its intensity, was just as significant as the boom in the city itself. For not only did the undeveloped areas bring out their promoters' abstruse skills, but the boom's effects were more easily seen. Los Angeles was a progressive city; fresh developments largely were overshadowed by its own normal rate of growth. But in the suburbs, where previously had been only isolated and scattered settlements, cities now blossomed forth, and the intervening spaces were thickly crosshatched by the pen of the subdivider. Southern California was attaining one of the goals so strongly emphasized by its early advertisers— it was becoming a region of suburban homes whose dwellers were prepared to take advantage of its semitropical climate. The great boom was of course not wholly responsible, but by opening new lands, whether or not they were immediately settled, and by strengthening the established population centers, it brought nearer to reality the ideal of ample living space in a salubrious land.

CHAPTER XII

"Bay 'n Climate": The

Boom in the San Diego Area

C ALIFORNIA'S harbor towns seem fated to struggle for their rights. When Drake sailed northward on his sixteenth-century odyssey, he chose an obscure cove for his landing place rather than the magnificent harbor of San Francisco, and the Spaniards were reluctant to recognize that the Golden Gate was the portal to a more logical spot for settlement than the storm-lashed shores of Monterey Bay. When Los Angeles groped westward for a harbor, city fathers alternated between Santa Monica's open roadstead and Point Fermin's marshes, ignoring completely the more distant but ideal lagoon at Newport-Balboa. In the same manner, San Diego, possessed of the most excellent landlocked bay on the southern coast, found itself deserted by the railroads and forced to resort to high-pressure tactics to assure itself even a branch line.

Perhaps no town in southern California was so eager for a boom as San Diego, and, clearly, no other town realized so well that a railway would help bring prosperity. Not less than three times before the railway boom actually occurred, did San Diego experience a transportation flurry. In 1854 the San Diego and Gila, Southern Pacific and Atlantic Railway was organized with the purpose of utilizing the convenient southern route to the East and South, but the Civil War and inadequate finances ended this hopeful project. In 1869 the abortive Memphis, El Paso, and Pacific, controlled partially by John C. Frémont, started another minor boom and served to consolidate the growing prosperity of New Town. Two years later, Colonel Thomas Scott raised San Diego's hopes sky-high with his Texas and Pacific franchise, but the panic of 1873 blasted that dream. Not until 1880 did a group of San Diego citizens, headed by Frank and Warren Kimball of National City, obtain sufficient encouragement from Santa Fe interests to start a railway of their own, the California Southern line.

Meantime, there had arrived a newcomer who proceeded to prove to San Diego that a railway was not a *sine qua non* of development. Alonzo Erastus Horton, though not a participant in the boom of the eighties, was nevertheless an outstanding example of town promoter. Before his arrival in 1867 San Diego, the present Old Town, had "crawled along for years like a starved dwarf, wandering among trees laden with fruit beyond his reach."[1] There had been one previous attempt to make a metropolis of San Diego, when, shortly before the Civil War, William Heath Davis, Miguel Pedrorena, and others tried to plat an addition and establish the nucleus of a more modern city. Hostilities ended this effort, however, and not until Horton came were their ideas brought to fruition.

Horton, a San Francisco furniture dealer, had had previous

[1] Hubert Howe Bancroft, *Chronicles of the Builders* (1892), VII, 394.

133

experience in town platting in Wisconsin, and he brought with him intense zeal and vitality. He stirred sleepy officials of Old Town to hold a public auction, at which he proceeded to buy 900 acres at twenty-six cents per acre, locating his holdings on the sloping shores of the bay, south of the existing settlement. A firm believer in publicity, Horton knew better than to conduct his own sale from the premises. Instead, he went back to San Francisco, interested prominent citizens like General Rosecrans in his project, and established a land office there. A few months later he turned down an offer of $250,000 for his San Diego holdings. The city developed slowly at first. Returns for 1867 were a mere $3,000, and Horton was obliged to offer inducements to purchasers. He gave lots outright to those promising immediate improvement, and sold others on easy terms. In 1869 he built a 700-foot wharf and sold blocks at prices varying from $2,000 to $6,000. The Memphis, El Paso, and Pacific Railroad flurry aided Horton's advertising, and by 1870 San Diego had 800 buildings and a population of 3,000. Despite Horton's undiminished enthusiasm and his prodigious labors for his protégé, the failure of the Texas and Pacific scheme dealt a heavy blow to San Diego's prospects, and "in 1875 the population had dwindled down to about 1,500, and these were living largely on faith, hope, and climate."[2] Although there was an early decline, Horton's boom was responsible for starting the modern city. He was unsparing in the use of his personal fortune to embellish the town; he built the Horton House, outstanding hostelry of the southern coast until the erection of the Hotel Coronado and the U. S. Grant Hotel. He also built Horton Hall and several business blocks, and was instrumental in the transfer of the post office, courthouse, and county records from Old Town to Horton's Addition.

[2]James M. Guinn, *A History of California and . . . Its Southern Coast Counties* (1907), I, 281.

Horton's work was so effective that David M. Berry on his arrival in California was greatly impressed with the southern city's prospects:

The harbor of S.D. is a beauty. . . . The largest vessels can come here except perhaps the Great Eastern and the Vanderbilt when heavily loaded. The Panama steamers usually draw from 10 ft. to 15 ft. water. The largest of them have been five miles up the harbor and could have gone further. . . . Some persons who came here and plunged in wildly buying real estate at fancy prices are anxious to sell. The original owners seem to be unconcerned and hold their land with a steady, and confident hope in the future of the city.[3]

Despite the nation-wide panic, San Diego realty prices were relatively higher in the seventies than comparable prices in Los Angeles. "Real estate is ten years ahead of commerce,"[4] Berry said. "The lying of the San Diego papers is something awful to think of and worse to experience."[5] When the Texas and Pacific collapsed, the results were sharp and disconcerting. Berry told the tale of an investor who sold at a loss of seventy-five per cent and went disgustedly to Los Angeles, where the situation was calmer.[6] In October, 1874, Berry concluded: "San Diego is bankrupt. Horton is busted and property nearly worthless."[7] Despite his later lack of enthusiasm regarding San Diego, Berry was once greatly interested in the near-by Cajón Ranch, which, he said, could be bought for five dollars an acre. The ranch, he added, "could supply two cities like Indianapolis with fruit and food."[8]

[3]David M. Berry to Thomas Balch Elliott, Aug. 31, 1873.

[4]*Idem*, Sept. 19, 1873.

[5]David M. Berry to Helen Elliott, Oct. 1, 1873.

[6]*Idem*, Nov. 7, 1873.

[7]David M. Berry to Thomas Balch Elliott, Oct. 14, 1874.

[8]*Idem*, Aug. 30, 1873.

⊷§ The Boom of the Eighties §⊷

The turning point in San Diego's history came in 1879, when Frank Kimball of National City, on behalf of a few public-spirited citizens, went East to interest one of the transcontinental railroads in San Diego as a Pacific terminus. He finally decided that the Santa Fe offered the best opportunity and conferred for some months with Thomas Nickerson, the president; in September they reached an agreement which provided that the Santa Fe, in return for a subsidy of $10,000 and 10,000 acres from the Kimballs' National Rancho, would build a railroad forty miles eastward within eight months. Surveys were immediately begun, but the Santa Fe soon changed its plans and stated its intention of using a more northerly pass, as a result of its merger with the Atlantic and Pacific, which already possessed a franchise for crossing the Colorado at Needles. Kimball returned hastily to the East and had more conferences with Nickerson, resulting in the formation of a syndicate composed largely of officials of the. Santa Fe system. The syndicate agreed to build a railway northeast from San Diego, with a terminus at National City, to connect with the Santa Fe main line at Colton. The Kimball brothers donated 16,000 acres of land and sold the syndicate 9,000 additional acres for $100,000, obtaining for themselves a one-sixth interest in the 25,410-dollar subsidy, 17,355 acres of land, and 485 platted lots. An understanding was arranged with the Texas and Pacific, whereby the subsidy formerly granted to that railroad was turned over to a trustee, to be used for railway development. Construction was begun in June, 1881, and in November of the following year the first trains of the California Southern reached Colton. A year later, in September, 1883, an extension was completed to San Bernardino.

Then a series of disasters struck the enterprise. In February, 1884, violent storms and floods washed out a large portion of the track in the Temécula Valley, and for nine months

San Diego was without rail communication. The Temécula
Canyon route was eventually abandoned, and a new line, following the coast to San Juan Capistrano and running to Los
Angeles by way of Santa Ana, was constructed. When the
Southern Pacific bought an interest in the Atlantic and Pacific
and built a line from Mojave to Needles, the California
Southern grew fearful, for, unless Santa Fe trains reached
San Bernardino, the San Diego line would be compelled to
build an expensive desert spur—a project which it could not
afford. The Santa Fe's lease of the Mojave-Needles division
came as a timely relief to this threat. Finally, in 1889, the
Santa Fe itself hurled the final bolt by its decision to move
its shops and general offices from San Diego to Los Angeles.
San Diego succumbed to the railway's arguments—especially
the one to the effect that a basic purpose of the railroad in
moving its offices was to shunt Los Angeles' sea trade to
San Diego—and the shift was completed to the detriment
of the bay city.

However, with the achievement of a certain amount of
rail communication and the promise of more, with the activities of vigorous enthusiasts like Horton and his followers,
and, most of all, with the stimulus of the Los Angeles boom
before it, San Diego was enjoying a realty flurry by 1886.
In October of that year a Los Angeles realtor, who preferred
to remain anonymous, admitted that the southern city was
livelier than Los Angeles, and the activity increased with San
Diego's appointment of a Los Angeles agent. The early progress of the boom is disclosed by a succession of "firsts" in
local improvement: the first transcontinental train from the
East arrived in San Diego November 21, 1885; the first
horsecars and electric lights came in 1886; the first electric-
streetcar line started in 1887; and the first modern dam, the
Sweetwater, was built in 1888. San Diego's correspondent to
the *Los Angeles Tribune* prophesied in April, 1887: "Now

137

look out for us because we are going to begin to boom down here. . . . Up to the present time we have only been getting ready for it. In fact we are not entirely ready for it yet."[9] The San Diego Real Estate Exchange was organized in March, 1887, featuring the multiple-listing plan of modern brokers. "The exchange," said the *Union*, "has already become one of the active factors in building up San Diego, having given $500 to the exhibition at St. Louis, and $500 to defray the expenses of the band boys, and hundreds of dollars in various other directions, and contemplates soon the erection of an Exchange building which will be an ornament and a credit to the city."[10]

The San Diego boom was characterized by much speculation and by several flamboyant, highly publicized enterprises. Business lots in the city proper rose from $25 to $2,500 per front foot, small stores rented for $300 to $500 per month, and if cut into stalls brought $1,000 or more. Poorly furnished rooms rented for $25 to $50 per month. Wages were correspondingly high: carpenters received $5 to $6 a day, bricklayers, $6 to $8, and printers $50 to $60 per week. Once during the flurry the population was estimated at 50,000, and a realty firm in a euphuistic advertisement summed up the matter by stating: "In fact, we may say that San Diego has a population of 150,000 people, only they are not all here yet."[11]

It was reported that residence sales maintained a high average, amounting in some cases to $43,000 per day, and in October, 1887, came the statement that business blocks had almost doubled in number during the preceding year. Realtors felt that business expansion had nearly reached its peak, and strongly recommended that investors consider suburban property or new districts which might eventually develop into

[9]*Los Angeles Tribune*, Apr. 4, 1887.

[10]*San Diego Union*, Oct. 1, 1887.

[11]*Ibid.*, Oct. 1, 2, 1887.

business areas. Suburban land was bringing about $500 per acre, and lots in near-by boom towns were selling at more than $100 each. Total realty transactions recorded in San Diego County offices during the final months of 1887 varied from twenty to sixty every twenty-four hours, and totaled in some instances more than $200,000 per day. There were many large sales of surrounding ranch property to syndicates and individual purchasers, for the purpose of subdivision. As in Los Angeles and Pasadena, the tenacious optimism of the inhabitants, judiciously stimulated by promoters, disclaimed that the boom was an abnormal development. The Combination Land Company, successors to Howard and Lyons, one of the most enterprising realty firms in operation during the flurry, did its part to maintain unbroken enthusiasm:

Oh! generation of Carkers and unbelievers, neither you nor we shall see that day [of reckoning]. This is no mining boom, based upon ledges that can be pinched out or worked out. This is no oil boom, based upon a product the supply of which can readily exceed the demand. This is no boom based upon wheat deals, or pork corners, or financial deadfalls, or railway combinations, or other devices of man. This boom is based upon the simple fact that hereabouts the good Lord has created conditions of climate and health and beauty such as can be found nowhere else, in this land or any land, and until every acre of this earthly paradise is occupied, the influx will continue.[12]

Editors were incensed at the critical attitude of Los Angeles. "There is," angrily asserted the *San Diego Union*, "only one construction to be placed on this senseless and spiteful howl. The press of Los Angeles is becoming alarmed at the rapid rate at which this 'burg' is forging to the fore."[13]

As in other sections of the southland, the boom was on the

[12]*Ibid.*
[13]*Ibid.*

139

wane by the end of 1887, and promoters and local businessmen were forced to gloss over the effects of the collapse. A
wordy supplement which accompanied the *San Diego Golden
Era* in 1888 did a masterful job of obscuring the economic
decline. "San Diego," it claimed, "bears the same relation to
California that California does to the United States, being a
land of climates within a land of climates." There was, even
after the boom, $3,000,000 on deposit in local banks, and "no
stringency in money matters" existed. Three hundred real-
estate agents still depended on San Diego for their living, and
a hundred more operated within the county. The president
of the real-estate exchange boasted of their high standards:
"We believe that there is not one instance in the history of
the present excitement in real estate transactions that there
has been a complaint of false representation." Construction
proceeded apace; more than 1,000 buildings were then reported being erected. "The streets of San Diego," the supplement said, "have for the past year been blockaded by the
improvements under way. There is a new block on almost
every corner, and homes, churches, schools, and stables have
sprung up like magic." More than 18,000,000 feet of lumber
arrived in November, 1887, and Coronado at the end of
the year possessed building contracts totaling more than
$1,500,000. Rents were lower, now varying from $15 to $200
for business buildings, and from $25 to $35 for residences.
Wages, too, were lower, but maintained a comparatively high
level. The claim was made that the cost of living was cheaper
in San Diego than elsewhere in California. Farm land was
bringing from $10 to $150 per acre, and the hill country back
of town was described as "the surest land in the world for
crops."[14] Statistically, San Diego's progress during the boom's
height appears spectacular. In 1868 county realty assessments
were only $600,000; in 1886 they reached $13,838,030; in

[14]*San Diego Golden Era*, supplement, 1888.

1887, $19,542,864. Total assessments (city and county) shot up to more than $40,000,000 in 1888, but dropped back to $26,800,000 in 1890. The population of the county was about 8,600 in 1880; the boom was said to have increased it approximately 480 per cent. During 1887, alone, the population rose 188 per cent. "Hundreds of men," said the *Golden Era*, "have reaped the rich rewards of their faith in the future of San Diego, and there are thousands of chances yet. . . . There will be no backward eddies in the stream of progress."[15]

But boom-time enthusiasm was a stimulant which produced deadening after-effects. By April of 1888, realty advertisements were few and far between in the newspapers. Some suburban property was still being listed, and there were occasional auctions featuring more cash and fewer instalment purchases. But by December all pretense of preserving boom enthusiasm had disappeared. One realtor confessed his changed status in the following manner:

HO! THE LATEST!
Books Burned
All of my last year's prices for-
gotten, and I have burned my books of last year.
NO MORE BOOM! All my prices reduced to
BEDROCK. No more property considered at Boom prices.[16]

Despite the crumbling of the rococo and gingerbread, the boom left a substantial edifice in San Diego. The flurry, Guinn concluded, was "a blessing in disguise."[17] The *Sun* listed improvements that had been acquired; they included the construction of railways ($350,000 in motor railways alone), hotels, cable roads, three schools, a public library, a new opera house, dam and flume improvement, fifteen business blocks,

[15]*Ibid.*

[16]*San Diego Bee*, Dec. 23, 1888.

[17]Guinn, *History of . . . Southern Coast Counties*, I, 283.

several churches, and the Spreckels Wharf and coal bunkers. All of the main business streets had been paved, a million dollars in gold had been extracted from near-by mines, water had been made available at very low rates, more than half a million fruit trees planted in the back country, and investment in the region was reckoned to total $10,000,000. The *Bee* in December, 1888, stated that both Los Angeles and San Diego were growing steadily,

despite the real estate silence. The feverish game of throwing lots back and forth . . . does not necessarily mean growth, but if, after the play is over, there still looms up from the result of it material sufficiently alluring to tempt wise heads to great ventures we may be surely confident there is no danger ahead.

Southern California can't go backward. Apparently we may commit here all the follies in the calendar, and it still seems the one spot on earth where nature almost forgets to mete out to men according to their transgressions.[18]

Occasional disasters quite naturally followed in the wake of the crash, but they were exceptionally few in number. The northern part of San Diego County was more severely affected than the area nearer the coast—in consequence doubtless of overhasty expansion of investment in the Temécula Valley during construction of the California Southern and the subsequent depression, when the railroad moved to the seashore. This particular section "would have been more fortunate," comments one writer, "had it not been exploited by the great real-estate boom."[19] The formation of Riverside County in 1893 might be accounted a disaster by San Diego citizens, for it engulfed over 6,000 square miles and nearly $4,000,000 worth of their property, including the settlements of Temécula, Elsinore, Murrieta, San Jacinto, and Winchester; but

[18]*San Diego Bee*, Dec. 23, 1888.

[19]Joseph J. Hill, *History of Warner's Ranch and Its Environs* (1927), p. 170.

there were still 8,551 square miles left in San Diego County, and what was removed had been hardest hit by the railway's failure. In fact, San Diego, like the rest of southern California, suffered much less than it deserved for the part it played in the boom. Recovery was rapid, and, despite the panic of the nineties, the assessed valuation of "greater San Diego" by 1897 amounted to $16,000,000, and a population of 25,000 lived in the metropolitan area.

As railroads began the boom in San Diego, so the boom started railroads. Among them were the National City and Otay Motor Road, connecting the bay with Tia Juana, the San Diego and Ensenada line, and the abortive San Diego and Elsinore Railway. Local railroads, especially those connected with the Coronado transportation system, also flourished, and projected shorter enterprises were legion. Rebuilding of the California Southern, the coast railway that launched the San Diego boom, was completed in 1888.

The southern boom centered, of course, in San Diego itself, but

the excitement was not confined to San Diego city. It spread over the county. New towns were founded. The founder in selecting a location was governed more by the revenue that might accrue from his speculation than by the resources that would build up his inchoate metropolis. It might be platted on an inaccesible mesa, where view was the principal resource, or it might be a hyphenated city-by-the-sea, where the investor might while away his time listening to what the wild waves were saying and subsist on climate.

It is said that two town sites extended out over the bay like Mark Twain's tunnel that was bored through the hill and a hundred and fifty feet in the air. When the fever of speculation was at its height, it mattered little where the town was located. A tastefully lithographed map with a health-giving sanatorium in one corner, tourist hotel in the other, palms lining the streets, and orange trees in the distance (add to these picturesque attractions a glib-tongued agent, untrammeled by conscience and unacquainted with truth) and the town was successfully founded. Purchasers did not buy to hold, but with hope of making a quick turn at an advance, while the excitement was on. Very few had confidence in the permanency of high prices, but everyone expected to unload before the crash came.[20]

Besides subdivisions in the city proper, which included among others New Town, Middletown, and Horton's, Culverwell's, Caruther's, Helphingstone's, Sherman's, Taggert's and Manassee's additions, there were about twenty towns founded during the boom. These dotted the coast line, the bay area, and Point Loma, extended to the inland valleys, and reached as far north as the San Jacinto River. Like their contemporaries in the north, some of them maintained a prosperous existence after the boom, some merely persisted in bucolic stagnation, and others disappeared entirely.

The outstanding boom project in the San Diego area was, by all odds, Coronado. The peninsula which shelters San Diego Bay from the sea is a narrow strip of land culminating at its northern extremity in an enlarged sandy platform. This area was covered with brush and was unutilized until 1885, when Elisha S. Babcock, the most vigorous local promoter, assumed the responsibility of transforming the peninsula into a seaside resort. Babcock arrived in 1884, inspected the region, and determined to build a million-dollar hotel. He obtained the help of Illinois capital, organized a syndicate, purchased 7,000 acres of land for $110,000, and embarked on a conspicuously noisy advertising campaign. Babcock spent thousands in spreading Coronado's name over the nation; nearly every post office had a placard describing the plat. The property was listed with the Pacific Coast Land Bureau, and suitable inducements were offered to those improving their property rapidly: to anyone who spent $1,000 on his land, the company promised water free of charge for one year and

[20]Guinn, *History of . . . Southern Coast Counties*, I, 282.

HOTEL CORONADO, SAN DIEGO (ABOUT 1888)

120 single-trip tickets per month on the San Diego Electric
Railway, the Coronado Ferry, and the Coronado Railway.
Each additional thousand dollars expended by the property
owner for improvements would be rewarded by an added
year of these services. For wage-earners who did not possess
much cash an additional year's services were to be granted
for each $500 invested after the initial $1,000. Free lots were
distributed, and an auction was scheduled for November 13,
1886.

The first auction was described everywhere as a great
success, but some criticism existed as to methods employed.
Netz said that the crowd had to be enticed into bidding by
fraudulent statements, such as fictitious announcements that
prominent citizens had invested and that colossal improvements were scheduled for immediate construction. These
ruses proved so alluring that about 300 lots were sold for an
aggregate of $110,000, and in the following March lots were
still selling at the rate of approximately $16,000 per day. By
May, 1887, $1,250,000 in lots had been marketed, and the
complete boom transactions totaled well over $2,000,000. A
list[21] of the monthly sales figures from the tract's opening to
the middle of 1887 shows what a golden harvest the promoters reaped:

November, 1886	$182,182.93
December	106,189.25
January, 1887	139,932.50
February	145,824.00
March	438,160.50
April	236,024.50

Coronado was hailed as "The Best Advertised Property in the
United States."[22] Bulletins and descriptive eulogies stressed

[21]*Los Angeles Tribune*, May 1, 1887.
[22]*Ibid.*

that the Santa Fe Railroad printed a Coronado advertisement
in its timecard folder and distributed 75,000 copies. "The
result of this thorough work must necessarily be an influx of
immigration heretofore unknown, and a corresponding en-
hancement of values."[23] The daily papers printed the names of
lot purchasers, with a tacit invitation to consult them about
the worth of their investments. Other circulars described the
sewage system; the water supply, piped under San Diego
Bay; the low-cost transportation including a twenty-minute
ferry schedule; the absence of saloons; the discounts on building material and fuel; the cheapness of living costs; and the
mammoth hotel, formally opened in February, 1888. Excursions were held, one in May, 1887, where lots were offered
at $340 to $2,800 each. Babcock employed between 400 and
1,200 persons, according to the season of the year, in his
Coronado enterprises. Later, he was able to interest John D.
Spreckels, San Diego's foremost citizen, in the venture, and in
mid-1887 Spreckels bought Babcock's shares. Spreckels was a
sugar refiner and steamship magnate who had arrived during
the boom and invested heavily in San Diego ventures; he rose
to be the chief figure in local realty, irrigation, transportation,
and commercial enterprises.

Coronado became such an institution in the bay region that
it soon graduated out of the satellite class and acquired suburbs
of its own. In October, 1887, both Coronado Heights and
South Coronado were offered by the syndicate. The former
was denominated the "Pasadena of San Diego," and the latter
claimed to be only five miles from San Diego by way of the
Coronado transportation system. But Coronado, despite its
pretensions to being a city, has remained primarily a resort,
although more recently a permanent population has been
built up.

Of the other boom settlements close to San Diego's city

[23]*Ibid.*

limits, two were advertised rather extensively. East San Diego
and Nob Hill were located ten minutes from the business
district, in the hills north of town, and featured a twelve-acre
park. A grand hotel and sanitarium (as usual) were planned,
and lots 25 by 140 feet were offered for $150 each. These
presentations were made by the Pacific Coast Land Bureau.
"Don't forget," the advertisements concluded, "that this
property will be advanced from week to week and month to
month, without further notice."[24] South San Diego was
located on the southeastern shore of the bay, and was destined,
according to its backers, to be "the largest suburban town in
Southern California. . . . The whole product of the valleys
leading out from the head of the bay will be marketed, canned,
preserved, and prepared here for distribution over the whole
world."[25] A motor line was being built, and a Santa Fe branch
line was contemplated. The tract featured a "Grand Hotel,
Sanitarium, College, Driving Park, Boulevard Drives, Park
and Artificial Lake," most of which existed, of course, only
on paper.[26]

In 1869 Frank A. and Warren Kimball bought the Rancho
de la Nación, consisting of 27,000 acres near the southern end
of the bay. They subdivided their land, built a wharf, and laid
out a town about four miles south of San Diego. Despite the
necessity of competing with Horton's New Town development, they managed, by the use of adequate promotion methods, to build National City into a flourishing settlement. In
1873, when Berry was searching for lands for the Indiana
Colony, the Kimballs offered him twenty acres without
charge, if colony members would guarantee to improve the
land. The grant was to be in the form of three or four dozen
lots, alternating with lots belonging to the Kimballs. When

[24]*San Diego Union*, Oct. 1, 1887.
[25]*Ibid.*
[26]*Ibid.*

Berry did not seem too favorably impressed, they offered 1,000 acres, undivided, at fifty dollars per acre. "I made no offer," said Berry astutely, "but think they will take less."[27] The Kimballs' efforts to locate National City on a railway line have already been related; clearly, the Santa Fe's decision to use the more northerly route was disastrous to their hopes. National City could prosper only if the Yuma route were chosen. The attempt to salvage part of the scheme by locating the Santa Fe shops in National City was only temporarily successful, and, when the general offices went, National City subsided into the status of a San Diego suburb.

Two miles south on the bay shore was the boom town of Chula Vista. This was a presentation of the San Diego Land and Town Company, controlled by the Santa Fe Railroad, which owned much south bay acreage. The tract consisted of 5,000 acres divided into five-acre plats for suburban homes. Water was plentiful, streets were graded, and the steam railroad, which Coronado interests built to circle the bay, went directly through the town. The end of the boom saw it still a small settlement; its relatively sedate growth could be attributed to the sales methods of the Land and Town Company, which refused to sell land unless the purchaser pledged immediate improvement to the amount of $2,000. Southeast of Chula Vista lay Otay, terminus of the National City and Otay Motor Railway. The auction system was used here fairly effectively; advertisements were succinct and pithy. "Think. You have judgment. Use it,"[28] realtors advised. Free lunches were an additional attraction for Otay prospects.

Of the boom towns along the coast, Oceanside was one of the most successful. It obtained an early start in 1884 and profited greatly from the shift of the California Southern

[27]David M. Berry to Thomas Balch Elliott, Sept. 2, 1873.

[28]*San Diego Union*, Oct. 1, 1887.

Railway to its coastal route in the following year. The town was located forty miles north of San Diego and was the junction point for a California Southern branch which ran to Fallbrook. Southern Pacific surveying crews added to local excitement by running their lines through Oceanside, and the commencement of construction of a wharf enhanced property values. The village enjoyed a boom-time population of 700, and had three hotels. An advertisement stated glibly that it was "destined to be the Cape May and Long Branch of the Coast."[29] During the boom, Oceanside boasted several additions, the most prominent being McNeil's, Hosmer and Dearborn's (consisting of seventy lots in McNeil's subdivision), Bryan's (on the hills back of town), Horne's, the Townsite, and Reece's. The last-named tract was advertised extensively in Los Angeles newspapers, promoters at one time offering 230 lots at $150 each, and listing nine prizes, consisting of houses valued from $500 to $1,000.

Encinitas (sometimes spelled Encinitos) was located fourteen miles south of Oceanside, on the coast, and was advertised largely during mid-1887. Sorrento can be classified as a coastal town despite its location two and one-half miles inland. It was situated on the plateau just south of the Torrey Pines grade and lay on the new route of the California Southern line. Lots were priced at $100 each, and acreage between $100 and $150 per unit. Sorrento was described as having land that would "grow anything in the world with or without irrigation."[30] Here, again, a coastal location made irrigation improvements relatively unimportant. La Jolla, sometimes called La Jolla Park, was offered by the Pacific Coast Land Bureau; it featured piped mountain water, a scenic shore-cliff environment, and a graded wagon road which led to the California Southern depot a mile inland. The Cottage Hotel cared for

[29]*Los Angeles Times*, June 5, 1887.
[30]*San Diego Union*, Oct. 1, 1887.

early visitors, and a larger structure was planned for completion in the early months of 1888. Because of La Jolla's picturesque surroundings, it soon became an artists' colony, with its future assured.

North of San Diego there lies a salt-water lagoon, some three miles in diameter, which has had various names; during boom years it was best-known as False Bay, and at present is commonly called Mission Bay. The lagoon proved a convenient nucleus for boom resorts, and several dotted its shores. On its north side, about two and a half miles from the ocean, lay the vigorous settlement of Pacific Beach, founded in the summer of 1887. Pacific Beach was prosperous; a single auction, in December, 1887, brought $200,000 to the promoters. Educational opportunities were stressed and were partially realized with the opening of the San Diego College of Letters, whose history is reserved for another chapter. The college failed after the boom, but Pacific Beach remains a popular seaside resort. Ocean Beach lay at the southern tip of False Bay, where it opened into the ocean. Here, again, "bay 'n' climate" proved successful attractions, and advertisements stated that 2,500 lots were sold in three days, even before the completion of surveys. The land on which Ocean Beach was platted rose in value fivefold during the first year of the boom, and there were four more appreciations in assessed value before the boom's end. Long advertisements, headed by large steel engravings of a projected hotel, kept Ocean Beach before San Diego purchasers. Lot prices were raised ten per cent on the first of each month, and by October, 1887, they had attained the relatively high figure, for suburban property, of $302.50 each. Improvements to the amount of $100,000 were scheduled; their featured attraction was the Cliff Hotel, completed in 1887. A motor line from Old Town was promised, and water was said to be plentiful. Excursions were planned, but 2,000 lots were sold "without a cent's expense for advertising."

"The locality of Eden," promoters concluded, "was lost to the world, until Carlson and Higgins discovered Ocean Beach."[31]

Ever since Horton had developed his addition to the south of it, Old Town had resented its relegation to suburban status. The boom gave it an opportunity to retrieve part of its lost fortunes, and the abortive expansion scheme of William Heath Davis in the fifties was resurrected and used to advertise Old Town property. Davis and his partners, promoters stated, had "used judgment, and selected the best natural site on the bay for a commercial city."[32] The Santa Fe built a station in 1887, and financed construction of a wharf, which produced much enthusiasm. Half lots (this was one of the few instances in which a twenty-five-foot piece was described as a "half" portion during the boom) sold for $3,000, one-third payable at the time of purchase. Promoters were falsely optimistic about the tract's prospects; they entitled it New San Diego, and claimed that sales were slow because incumbent property owners realized the town's future and refused to sell. "Has New San Diego had a boom yet?" they asked themselves. "Well, no, but it will soon."[33] The hoped-for upsurge never arrived, however, and Horton's judgment still held good.

The southward-jutting peninsula culminating in Point Loma was the scene of several settlements. The most widely advertised was Roseville, on the northern shore of the bay. Begun by Louis Rose in the sixties, it was later acquired by the San Diego Mutual Land Association. Steamboat excursions carried hundreds of interested visitors to the peninsula: "lots will be cheap and scarce at $1,000 per twenty-five foot front," promoters claimed in 1887.[34] Free lots were distributed to persons contracting to improve their property within three

[31]*Ibid.*

[32]*Ibid.*, Oct. 2, 1887.

[33]*Ibid.*

[34]*San Diego Union*, Oct. 1, 1887.

months, and a standing offer of a complete block, two hundred by three hundred feet, was made to anyone who would build a hotel. A motor road was graded to Roseville, and the town still exists, though in attenuated form. The other two settlements on Point Loma did not live to remember their former glory; they belong, therefore, in the category of ghost towns.

Although the formation of Riverside County subtracted several of the Temécula Valley settlements from San Diego County, the California Southern line, San Diego's chief railway venture, was responsible for starting most of them. Therefore, they may fittingly be considered in connection with other San Diego enterprises, particularly as they were still included in San Diego County during the boom. Five towns in this northern region owe their existence largely to boom promotion. Elsinore was located on the northeastern shore of the lake of that name, and resulted from the activity of a syndicate, formed in 1884, which bought some of the Laguna Ranch lands. The region was acclaimed for its hot springs and its consequent suitability as a health resort, and also, paradoxically, for its industrial possibilities, made evident by the discovery of a coal vein, three to nine feet thick, covering some 4,000 acres, according to promotion literature. Other mineral deposits promised to make Elsinore a factory town; potter's clay and terra cotta, iron outcrops, marble, and limestone were discovered. For a time the coal was used for firing the kilns of a pipe-making establishment, which utilized the clay deposits; in January, 1888, the first carload of coal was shipped to South Pasadena. "It is the initial car," said a newspaper article, "of many to follow and marks an important era as the beginning of a new industry in Southern California."[35] Despite local enthusiasm and the construction of a manufacturing plant whose raw materials would be the local

[35]*Commercial Bulletin of Southern California*, Jan. 28, 1888.

stores of clay and terra cotta, Elsinore has never realized the high ambitions of its founders, but has remained primarily a quiet lake resort, somewhat off the beaten track.

Seven miles south of Elsinore lay Wildomar, also on the railroad. This town was backed by the same persons who promoted Elsinore, and remained a small settlement.[36] Murrieta, five miles nearer San Diego, was platted in 1886. It originally constituted part of the Temécula Ranch lands, some 14,000 acres of which had been purchased by the Temécula Land and Water Company and subdivided in the fall of 1884. Murrieta boasted hot springs, a genial climate, and a fair production of hay and grain from the surrounding country. Land could be purchased, at the height of the boom, for six dollars per acre and upward, in "tracts to suit."[37] Temécula was situated just north of the future county line, and for a time after the floods of 1884 formed the southern terminus of the railroad. Chicago capital built a small hotel, but the shifting of the railroad left Temécula to a purely pastoral existence. Fallbrook was located eight miles southwest of Temécula, almost due west of Palomar Mountain. Of the northern settlements, it was destined to rank second only to Elsinore in importance, although it never became a large town. Its promoters were oversanguine; Fallbrook, they claimed, "was not created by a 'boom.' The 'boom' was caused by it, and a few similar places."[38] The country, they said, would grow anything that could be grown anywhere else in southern California, and glowing descriptions were given of the abundant timber on the near-by hills, and the joys of hunting the small game and deer which abounded there.

[36]The name "Wildomar" came from the first syllables of given names of certain members of the syndicate: William Collier and Donald and Margaret Graham, the original purchasers of the Laguna grant.

[37]*Los Angeles Tribune*, Apr. 4, 1887.

[38]*San Diego Union*, Oct. 1, 1887.

ᴇ⳹ The Boom of the Eighties ⳼ᴇ

The most important inland town north of San Diego was Escondido, laid out in 1885 by a syndicate composed of San Diego and Los Angeles capitalists. Lots were sold rapidly, and several business blocks, a hotel, and a bank were built during the boom. The early arrangements for irrigation were unsatisfactory, and not until 1905 were financial difficulties solved. Lakeside, near San Diego River in the El Cajón Valley, was publicized extensively during the final months of 1887, and a hotel was promised. About twelve miles southwest of Lakeside, La Mesa was platted by the San Diego Development Company, which, with Howard and Lyons, helped to immortalize southern boom literature. In February, 1888, a lengthy advertisement notified the world that La Mesa auctions were successful, that a hundred "solid men" had already invested in villa tracts there, and that the town was destined to be the Pasadena of San Diego. "What the Los Angeles 'prize suburb' is to that city, La Mesa will inevitably be to this, with all the difference in merit in favor of La Mesa." This effusion was climaxed by the following verse:

> The shades of night were falling fast,
> When up through San Diego passed
> One hundred men whose shrewd advice,
> Free given, without cost or price
>   Was "Buy La Mesa! Buy La Mesa!"[39]

Despite such activity, certain realtors admitted that the El Cajón Valley never experienced the full force of the boom, and the settlements, although widely advertised, failed to attain importance.

To omit consideration of the boom's effect upon the lands of Lower California and Mexico would be to neglect a most interesting aspect. During the boom the border town of Tia Juana was nicknamed the "El Paso of California," and ex-

[39]*San Diego Free Press*, Feb. 2, 1888.

perienced a flurry of building and buying activity. Tia Juana was said to have "the ONLY commercial importance of any suburb around the great city and future metropolis of Southern California—San Diego."[40] Local hot springs were proclaimed equal to those of Arkansas, and transportation improvements were pushed rapidly. Farther south, beginning at a line fifteen miles below San Diego and including a 300-mile strip of the peninsula from gulf to ocean, lay the 18,000,000 acres of the International Company of Mexico. The International Company had been organized to take advantage of the liberal terms offered by the Mexican colonization act of 1883. Its guiding genius was a Michigan lawyer named George Sisson, and the company's purpose was to colonize Lower California. Lands were advertised in San Diego and Los Angeles newspapers, and several towns were started. Farm land could be bought for five dollars per acre and up, and the assertion was made that the Mexican grants were ideal for the "man of small means."[41] One subsidiary of this scheme was the San Quintín Land and Town Company, organized by Sisson in 1887 to develop the town of that name on the Pacific shore about 150 miles south of the border.

Another Mexican project which received wide publicity in Los Angeles newspapers was the Tobolobampo Colony of Sinaloa. This had originated in a grant made by the Mexican government to the Texas, Tobolobampo, and Pacific Railroad on condition that a town be established near Tobolobampo Bay. A co-operative colony known as the Crédit Foncier of Sinaloa was formed. Several colonists migrated to Sinaloa, but some of them were not of the highest moral caliber, and by 1887 reports of disaffection began filtering northward. Alvan Brock, promoter of the Palos Verdes Ranch lands, was a

[40]*San Diego Union*, Oct. 1, 1887.

[41]*San Diego Bee*, supplement, Dec. 23, 1888.

director of the company, and he accused the general manager, a Colonel Owen, of peculation. A number of the colonists returned to southern California to give reporters lurid accounts of happenings in the colony, and the project was never a great success. The chief significance of these Mexican ventures lay in the fact that they profited by the enthusiasm reflected from the southern California boom—even to the extent of stimulating the subdivision of certain sections of Mexico City.

The boom in the San Diego region was therefore a lively and widespread phenomenon. Using the bay as a nucleus, realty activity expanded with railway construction, first into the Temécula Valley, then along the coast toward San Juan Capistrano. Promoters tried manfully to carry the excitement into the back country immediately east of the bay, but the lag in irrigation development precluded any immediate growth of this area. The boom was also used as an excuse to colonize the barren lands of Lower California and northern Mexico. The bay, however, remained the chief center of activity; San Diego and Coronado were the flurry's outstanding achievements, and settlements on the bay shore mushroomed as a result of transportation improvements, vigorous public interest, and eager, if temporarily futile, attempts to construct adequate irrigation facilities.

CHAPTER XIII

The Rural Boom in the North: Santa Barbara and Ventura Counties

T HE influence of the boom on Santa Barbara and Ventura counties was modified by their smaller population and slower agricultural and commercial development. Thus, although the flurry assumed very nearly the same form as its counterparts in Los Angeles and San Diego, the excitement was not so intense, and generally less capital was involved. One very evident reason for the difference was the fact that neither Santa Barbara nor Ventura could hope to compete as a terminus for a transcontinental railway. The mountain barrier, which hugs the coast closely north of the Tehachapi transversal, defined the railway situation immediately: the only transportation boom that could strike the northern counties would be the result of a San Francisco-Los Angeles coast line—which the railroads hesitated to build, both because of construction difficulties and because of the existence of the parallel San Joaquin Valley route.

The first Santa Barbara boom took place in the late sixties

and early seventies, and resulted in the construction of the
Hotel Arlington and the platting of several suburban properties. "Santa Barbara," says one local historian, "should have
been case-hardened after its experience of the previous decade,
but remembrance of the depression that had followed the former swift rise and swifter fall in values was not enough to stay
the prevailing hysteria."[1] Like all other southern counties,
Santa Barbara realized that its best selling points were climate
and agriculture. The district's chief products were grain, in
the form of barley and wheat, mustard, and beans. The Carpintería area was especially prolific in legume crops, and it
was said that "beans have removed mortgages from many . . .
fertile ranches" there.[2] Even the growing of sugar cane was
discussed as a possible large-scale enterprise, while Lompoc
and Santa Ynez valleys had notable grain yields. Nonagricul-
tural resources were also becoming evident. Berry, writing in
1873 from a cabin on the steamboat "Orizaba," remarked:
"Near Santa Barbara vast quantities of petroleum rise to the
surface of the sea and overspread and perfume a large area.
Our recollections of good Saint Barbara will be that she was
a messenger of peace pouring oil upon the troubled waters."[3]
The littoral fields which Berry mentioned were doubtless
those near Summerland, whose wells now are built on piers
over the waters of a cove.

But, like other southern counties, Santa Barbara was un-
willing to await the steady and slow development which
would result from exploitation of natural resources. She
wanted a boom, and the best way to start one, according to
those with experience elsewhere, was to acquire a railroad.
Even before there were any real hopes of doing so, Santa
Barbara was busily lobbying in the offices of the various trans-

[1]Owen H. O'Neill, *History of Santa Barbara County* (1939), p. 281.
[2]*Santa Barbara Weekly Independent*, Sept. 18, 1886.
[3]David M. Berry to *Inter-Ocean*, Sept. 1, 1873.

continental lines. Local editors concluded that a railroad was "certain, but delayed."[4] Much of the delay was occasioned by the expense of construction over coastal mountains, some by competition among various way points that demanded stations on the main line. Prospects simmered down to three: a Southern Pacific coast route, which was a fair possibility; a more tenuous contemplated extension by Santa Fe interests; and a proposed narrow-gauge line, backed by former Governor George C. Perkins, which would tap the northern valleys near Paso Robles and San Luis Obispo.

The railroad which eventually arrived in Santa Barbara was the Southern Pacific, building north from Los Angeles. Construction was begun in 1886, and a flurry of realty activity along the prospective route followed immediately. "The extension," said the *Santa Barbara Weekly Independent*, "of the Southern Pacific down the coast has aroused some of the sleepy centers of the region between Soledad and Newhall to new life and activity."[5] By January, 1887, there was agitation in Santa Barbara for a street railway, and in April property owners were further excited by the Atlantic and Pacific's purchase of the Pacific Coast Railway, which held a franchise for a coast line through San Luis Obispo, Los Alamos, and Gaviota Pass. In May, however, the intention of the Southern Pacific to buy out all competition became clear, for the Big Four's surveying crews were at work in the pass; on August 17 the first trains arrived in Santa Barbara. The advent of rail communication was made the occasion for a typical Santa Barbara fiesta, with a civic celebration, a banquet, and a ball commemorating the day's achievements. The railway stopped building almost at once, and Santa Barbara remained the terminus for several years, partially accounting for the early

[4]*Santa Barbara Weekly Independent*, Apr. 24, 1886.

[5]*Ibid.*, Oct. 23, 1886.

collapse of the region's boom. There was talk of Santa Fe competition, and some surveys were made, but the company failed to act. Editors urged shippers to offer inducements. The Santa Fe Railroad, one writer said, had made many Los Angeles suburbs "what they are today."

> Our people should offer them some encouragement to build into our county. . . . When you go East, buy your ticket on the Santa Fe. When you ship your freight, see that it is marked via the Santa Fe fast freight line. Demonstrate to the company that Santa Barbara County has business to give them, and they will be very apt to come after it with their own line.[6]

Such an attitude showed lack of appreciation for what the Southern Pacific had done to stimulate the area, especially since that railroad had reduced freight charges in September.

The great boom started in March, 1886, with the recording, in one week, of twenty property transfers, and from that time on there was a steady increase in activity. The block facing the Arlington Hotel was put on the market, and five units of this new tract sold on the first day for eighty dollars per front foot. One hundred and thirty-seven deeds were filed in September, 1886, as compared with only thirty-six for the previous September. By November the city's brick supply had been exhausted, and a shipload of 597,446 feet of lumber—the largest ever imported by Santa Barbara—was landed. The 1886 boom was noteworthy enough to stimulate half-hearted publicity in Los Angeles newspapers. The *Tribune* reported in October that the prospect of the railroad had caused a fivefold increase in city realty activity, including a San Francisco investor's purchase for the large sum of $65,000 of 185 acres of hill land north of town. The article ended with a qualifying statement to the effect that, in spite of the so-called boom, times were relatively dull, and the

[6]*Ibid.*, Oct. 29, 1887.

county was not so attractive as Los Angeles. By January, however, Los Angeles newspapers had lost some of their jealousy and were featuring long descriptive articles about other southern-California communities. On January 31, Santa Barbara was eulogized by the *Tribune*, and subsequent issues did much to counteract the earlier selfish attitude. Santa Barbara journals were effusive from the start. In October the *Weekly Independent* described the results of the 1886 boom: "A tidal wave of enthusiasm, destined to sweep away forever the lethargy hitherto so characteristic of our town, has indeed set in and at the crest of it are those energetic members of our community who have already done a large share of their work in these vast improvements."[7] Residence building gave way to business-block construction during the final weeks of the year. A railway to the northern foothills was planned, and a syndicate bought 500 additional acres there for the purpose of subdividing.

The great year of the boom, 1887, began auspiciously with renewed enthusiasm for residence property. A newspaper article was headlined: "New Homes. Rapid Rise in Value of Homesites; Fine Residences now Being Built; Money and Art Used with Effect."[8] "Roofs are no longer monotonous," the article exulted, "but break into pleasing angles. . . . Palisades no longer surround gardens, as though each householder must be prepared to withstand a siege of murderous Indians. . . . green lawns spread unobstructed to the sidewalk, evidence that the lowing herds are winding over some other lea."[9] Such was the effect of the boom on the architecture of the "cow counties."

The hotel shortage was acute throughout the entire year.

[7]*Ibid.*, Oct. 16, 1886.

[8]*Ibid.*, Jan. 1, 1887.

[9]*Ibid.*

In February there were four hostelries: the Arlington, a triumph of the previous flurry; the San Marcos, which occupied the abandoned classrooms of an old college building; the Commercial, and the Morris House—the last two relatively unpretentious and unsuited for resort purposes. The Arlington and San Marcos both belonged to the estate of William Wells Hollister, an Ohio Argonaut of 1852 and chief ranchero of the county, whose lengthy list of realty holdings as enumerated in his will was virtually a catalogue of improved property in the district. The Arlington, Santa Barbara's pride, with the Raymond of Pasadena and the Coronado of San Diego was one of the "Del Montes of the Southland." But even those who praised the Arlington's elegance realized that it did not solve the problem of housing the city's transients. "Perfect as Santa Barbara is," said the *Independent* on March 13, 1886, "we need somewhat to make our city capable of supporting the army of tourists and travellers even now on their way. Our hotels are as fine as can be, but we need more of them." The inadequacy of accommodations became even more apparent in August of 1887, when Ben Ward, the Los Angeles auctioneer, arranged for a Masonic excursion to Santa Barbara. Although the Masons were adequately entertained, city fathers frantically organized a "Citizens' Hotel Committee," with the object of building an inn by subscription. "There are many men among us," said an enthusiast, "who have made from $50,000 to $200,000 within the last few months, solely from the unprecedented rise in real estate, and who have large landed interests still. It would advantage them, from a purely business point of view, to come forward and help put up a hotel such as the times require."[10] The citizens' committee failed to achieve its immediate objective, but it did serve to attract public attention sufficiently to stimulate projects like the Burton Mound campaign, designed to build a

[10]*Ibid.*, July 30, 1887.

hotel on the beach, and the Hope Ranch development, which included plans for a railroad-owned hostelry in the suburbs.

The boom also centered attention on other improvements. Santa Barbara Bay's open roadstead needed a mole, although loyal citizens insisted that the cove was safer than any other harbor in southern California except San Diego's. New business enterprises largely devoted to construction supply were organized, and real estate companies sprang up by dozens. Two examples of the latter were the Santa Barbara Improvement Company and the Santa Barbara Development Company, both of which engaged in platting and developing the hilly districts north of town. The Development Company spent $25,000 in improving its tract, which featured 50-, 100-, and 200-foot lots, each 200 feet deep and fronting on two streets. Streets were paved—$180,000 was spent on paving State Street for two miles—and sidewalks laid.

Few of the urban Santa Barbara tracts were advertised with a vim equal to that displayed by Los Angeles sales campaigns. Scattered instances will suffice. The Oak Park Tract, managed by the Los Angeles Land Bureau, was stressed during the early months of 1888. This subdivision consisted of 200 residence lots, 40 by 140, 50 by 150, and 46 by 140 feet. The Eddy Tract, controlled by the Southern California Land and Immigration Company, occupied much newspaper space, and in January, 1888, an excursion by special train came from Los Angeles. Mission Heights, in the foothills to the north of the mission, consisted of seventy-one acres of rolling land, located "in a direct line with the city's growth."[11] Villa sites of two to six acres were offered with special inducements to purchasers making improvements costing at least $3,000. Many of the tracts were small, like the West End Tract (including Anacapa, Anapumú, and Mission Streets), which consisted of only two and one-half blocks. The Riviera, another foot-

[11]*Santa Barbara Morning Press*, Jan. 1, 1887.

hill tract, was promoted by W. N. Hawley to such good effect that land formerly worth $200 per acre sold during the boom for $20 a front foot.

Enthusiasm was rife, as in other localities, until the spring of 1888, when the looming depression became evident even to the most sanguine. At the boom's outset a local editor has told an eastern visitor: "We are not boosting California for *all* she's worth, because, sir, no man knows what she's worth."[12] Later prophets were not so cautious, but, as elsewhere, optimistic prognostications were insufficient to sustain the excitement. Because of their previous experience, Santa Barbarans were quick to take a philosophic attitude. "There is nothing new in the southern situation," the *Morning Press* commented on April 26, 1888. "Throughout the history of this State local booms have been periodical. . . . They have always acted in precisely the same way." Although the accuracy of the last sentence might be questioned, the statement in general was true. Newspapers protested the reluctance of citizens to resume normal occupations after a taste of boom profits. One editorial in the *Morning Press* was entitled "Go To Work," and included the following admonition: "There are too many men in California waiting for something to turn up. The lively times of the past few years have spoiled many a good mechanic, many a farmer, and many of our best tradesmen. . . . People cannot live on climate alone."[13] Realty prices suffered most from the collapse; land which had sold at eighty dollars per front foot now was offered for twenty, and found no buyers. Arlington Heights held out to builders the bait of a discount of ten per cent on lumber. But these inducements were insufficient. The boom was gone, and after a brief and tantalizing taste of its succulent profits Santa Barbara

[12]O'Neill, p. 282.

[13]*Santa Barbara Morning Press*, Apr. 26, 1888.

relapsed into a state of lethargy, which differed from previous interims of apathy in that the ranchos had been broken up and more people than ever before were living in the town and on the small farms surrounding it.

Statistically, the boom in Santa Barbara was not nearly so striking as in other localities. Only about forty plats were filed during 1887 and 1888 for city property. Recorded sales during seven months at the height of the flurry amounted to $5,000,000, and the total of boom transactions probably did not exceed $7,000,000. Beneficial results, however, were numerous. A "Year's Review" was published by the *Morning Press* on New Year's Day of 1888. "The year, which closed at midnight, was the most memorable in the history of Santa Barbara, and marked the transition of the place from a quiet country village, to a bustling and progressive little city with unlimited possibilities before it,"[14] said the article. Among improvements and activities that had helped to transform the city were an electric-lighting system, a Young Men's Christian Association and a kindergarten, a 150,000-dollar lumber company, which built the State Street Wharf and planned a general shipping business in addition to its construction activities, a Building and Loan Association, an annex to the Arlington, improved street-railway facilities, the discovery of new artesian wells and the consequent organization of the De La Guerra Gardens Spring Water Company, and a flower festival which further advertised the town. Other aspects and achievements of the boom included the organization of a humane society, the construction of a new post-office building, the opening of a race track by the Santa Barbara Land and Improvement Company, and the formation of a·yacht club. The year 1887 saw the spending altogether of $1,000,000 in building improvements and witnessed a large population increase. The "crowning event" was the arrival of the railroad.

[14]*Ibid.*, Jan. 1, 1888.

The Boom of the Eighties

An interesting phase of the flurry was the press war waged between the *Press* and *Independent*—somewhat on the order of the controversy between the Los Angles *Times* and the *Tribune*. The Santa Barbara situation, however, was complicated by the intrusion of a third element, the *Herald,* which busied itself with sharp criticism of the *Independent's* policies.

There were relatively few boom towns in Santa Barbara County. The city itself monopolized most of the activity, and the residue was taken up by a number of villages which had for the most part obtained their start in the seventies. Summerland, however, was an exception. Located five miles east of Santa Barbara, on the beach, Summerland was originally platted by H. L. Williams in 1888, "after the subsidence of the boom."[15] Williams bought 1,050 acres of the Ortega Ranch, subdivided 160 acres, and established on the seashore a "spiritualist colony," which resembled for a time the theosophical center on Point Loma and the later Rosicrucian settlement at Oceanside. The sale was opened in November, 1888, and within three years there were sixty houses in the colony. During the first period of enthusiasm about 1,450 lots were sold, a newspaper, the *Reconstructor*, was started, a library built, and natural-gas pockets discovered.

The flurry affected neighboring communities with varying degrees of intensity. Ballard, in the Santa Ynez Valley thirty miles northwest of Santa Barbara, had been platted in 1881 by George W. Lewis, and depended on surrounding wheat farms for its economic support. The boom affected it mildly. Los Alamos, fifteen miles north of Ballard, was promoted enthusiastically. It was dubbed the "chief town in the northern part of Santa Barbara County," and the "coming county seat of the to be Los Alamos County."[16] Auctions were held

[15]Yda Addis Storke, *A Memorial and Biographical History of the Counties of Santa Barbara, San Luis Obispo, and Ventura, California* (1891),p. 94.

[16]*Los Angeles Express*, Feb. 29, 1888.

166

in the early months of 1888, ocean and rail excursions on boats of the Pacific Coast Steamship Lines and trains of the Southern Pacific were advertised, and a persistent sales campaign was supervised by the Los Angeles Land Bureau. The town's advantages were the possession of dairy, fruit, vine, and farm lands, in pieces ranging from 25 to 4,000 acres in size; 50 small farms of 2½ to 25 acres each; and 200 residence lots. In all, 14,000 acres were subdivided. Los Alamos' chief disadvantage (transformed by promoters into a selling point) was its location between the relatively populous centers of San Luis Obispo and Santa Barbara; the newer town's benefits were not such as to overshadow the advantages of these more securely-established communities, and the halfway point never caught up with its rivals. Santa Maria, on the county's northern border, had seven new plats recorded in 1887 and four in 1888. Montecito boasted five plats and additions in 1887, and the Rincón area, on the coast three miles east of Carpintería, two. Los Olivos, between Los Alamos and Santa Ynez, was platted by the Los Angeles Land Association, and filed a map in September, 1887. Other communities encouraged by the boom were Santa Ynez, Carpintería, and Goleta.

The most spectacular aspect of the Santa Barbara County boom was the flurry in undeveloped ranch property. H. I. Weiley, for example, bought 10,000 acres of the Rancho San Carlos de Jonata from R. T. Buell; and 21,000 acres of the great College Ranch were sold for $210,000. One of the promoters interested in this latter piece was a General Willey, who projected a new town called Wilmington, designed to compete with Los Olivos. The Los Alamos Ranch was sold in April, 1887, to a Santa Cruz buyer for $350,000; the transaction involved 14,000 acres. The Santa Ynez Land and Improvement Company devoted itself to the subdivision of the College and Jonata grants. Isolated from the main arteries of California's transportation, Santa Barbara County maintained its pastoral aspect longer than other sections of the state. Not until the boom of the eighties was the process of disintegration of the large ranchos, which had been achieved earlier in the districts farther south, completed.

The Ventura County boom surmounted many obstacles. Ventura was the smallest and least populous of the southern counties, and it suffered from Santa Barbara's chief malady— the inability to compete with a transcontinental-railway terminus. Nevertheless, the boom was no less vigorous in the Ventura region than in any of the northern coastal valleys; from the town of Ventura as a nucleus, the realty upheaval spread out and extended from Simi to Rincón and from Hueneme to Ojai. Agriculturally, Ventura County was in a favorable position. Barley, wheat, corn, wool, and honey were produced in large quantities by the middle eighties. The brownstone of Sespe, the vegetables from the truck gardens of Hueneme, and the brandies, wines, and fruits of Camulos, Ramona's home, gave Ventura a reputation for prosperity which the promoters did not need to exaggerate. Two products which gave the region a special fame were oil, only then becoming important, and flower seeds. The Theodosia B. Shepard Seed and Plant Company was established in 1886, and an article describing the founding of the organization asserted, "the flowers here have a much finer color" than in Los Angeles County.[17]

The city of Ventura was greatly expanded by the boom. Eight plats in 1886, ten in 1887, and eight more in 1888 added to its boundaries. Population was nearly doubled. In 1887 was organized a development association that included such large landowners as Leonard Rose, Charles Barnard, and Dr. J. H. Reppy; property improvement shifted "uptown" so rapidly that a group of "downtown" businessmen strove to obstruct the movement by building the Anacapa Hotel. The

[17] *Ventura Free Press*, Aug. 15, 1887.

Hotel Rose, costing $75,000, was erected by Leonard Rose in 1887; a theater was built; streets were graded, and sewer bonds to the amount of $20,000 were projected. The feverish building boom resulted in a lumber shortage. Improved land sold from $1,250 to $5,000 per unit, comparing favorably with Los Angeles prices, while rural land was on the market for $6 to $150 per acre.

The construction of the railway to Santa Barbara in 1887 stimulated Ventura promoters to further effort, and, as a result, land prices rose sharply in April. A station was built immediately, and vigorous attempts were made to squeeze every possible type of profit from way traffic to Santa Barbara. On August 21, 1887, a group of excursionists traveling by train to the northern city were halted in Ventura and greeted by a welcoming committee. "Polite gentlemen and ladies" presented the excursionists with baskets of fruit and flowers.[18] Because of this cordiality, several of the tourists stopped in Ventura on their return, and local realtors were gratified to hear experts from Los Angeles and San Francisco appraise Santa Clara Valley lands at $1,000 per acre. Sea traffic was also encouraged. In 1886, before the boom had really started, 173 ships landed at Hueneme, the county's chief port, and citizens hoped that, if Ventura could not become a railway center, it would at least develop a flourishing sea trade.

Of the four small valleys in the county—Ojai, Santa Clara, Simi, and Conejo—only the northernmost three were affected strongly by the boom, and the realty activity centered largely along the Santa Clara River and on the coastal plain east of the town of Ventura. Ojai, although it cannot be accurately classified as a boom town, boasted eight additions to its preboom area. Matilija Hot Springs, near by, was advertised enthusiastically in 1888. Fillmore City, on the Santa Clara

[18]*Ibid.*, Aug. 22, 1887.

River eleven miles from the Los Angeles County line, was recorded by the Sespe Land and Water Company in 1888, although it existed as a tract before that time. Fillmore consisted of 66.57 acres, and the ranch lands surrounding the settlement comprised 3,270 acres divided into five-, ten-, twenty-, and forty-acre plats. Efforts were made to attract colonists, and auctions, barbecues, and fruit displays lauded the productivity of Sespe Ranch lands. Bardsdale was laid out by R. G. Surdam, founder, in the sixties, of the town of Nordhoff, and Thomas Bard, sheep rancher and organizer of the Union Oil Company. The town lay two and one-half miles from Fillmore, on the south side of the river; its plat was filed in 1887. Picnics and barbecues featured its sales campaign, but Fillmore City eventually overwhelmed it. Sespe City was located on the railroad two miles west of Fillmore, but never developed greatly.

Santa Paula, fifteen miles east of Ventura and on the Santa Clara River, was not a boom town, but was one of the most prosperous settlements in the county. "Although," said its correspondent to the *Tribune* in April, 1887, "we cannot claim as great a boom as can our friends of Los Angeles County, there is a continued, healthy march all along the line." Oil development encouraged Santa Paula, and for a time it was the terminus of the Southern Pacific Railroad, which gave it temporary fame. Lots, priced lower than in Ventura, were listed at $75 to $150 each; surrounding acreage in rich valley lands sold from $75 to $3,000 per unit. Where the river broke into the coastal plain, the town of Saticoy was platted in 1887 by W. D. F. Richards, a local rancher. Advertised extensively in the spring of 1887, Saticoy consisted of 132 lots priced from $200 to $250 each, a college site, and Richards' estate. A "family hotel" was projected in May.[19] Montalvo,

[19]*Los Angeles Tribune*, May 2, 1887.

six miles closer to the ocean, was recorded in January, 1888; a hotel and university were among the ambitious projects scheduled.

The sale of the Simi Rancho in May, 1887, to a syndicate including Thomas Bard, L. T. Garnsey, and Dan McFarland was hailed by the *Los Angeles Tribune* as the "largest individual transaction . . . consummated in this county since the boom began."[20] The ranch consisted of 96,000 acres, including rich valley lands suitable for agriculture and 17,000 acres of grazing pasture. In early 1888 the tract was subdivided for sale at ten to one hundred dollars an acre: "less than half the prices asked anywhere else in Southern California for lands of the same quality"[21]—a claim made with varying degrees of reliability from Tia Juana to Paso Robles. Although the Simi Valley has since gained a reputation for agricultural wealth and rural prosperity, the town of Simi is still small and relatively undeveloped.

Hueneme, on the seashore, was the county's port and enjoyed a period of prosperity as the result of the incorporation of the Los Angeles, San Fernando, and Hueneme Railroad in August, 1887. Although that project was supported by such sturdy promoters as Thomas Bard and his associates, it later failed. A more profitable venture, and one which embodied a note of prophecy, was the oil pipe line constructed from Santa Paula to Hueneme in July, 1887. A letter from the Hueneme correspondent to the *Ventura Daily Free Press* complained the following month: "The boom has struck our town but not in the way we wished for, another saloon to deal out poison to poor weak humanity, and two restaurants have been started."

The Ventura boom—to sum up—was largely an agricul-

20*Ibid.*, May 16, 1887.

21*Los Angeles Express*, Jan. 17, 1888.

tural and rural one. The county was advertised as "a land flowing with milk and honey, oil and wine, and teeming with the richness of tropical and semi-tropical fruits."[22] There was a fair amount of urban activity, as evidenced by the investment of $617,000 in city and town lots during the boom's climax; the remainder of the county's real estate was assessed at $4,007,906. Of the smaller towns, Ojai profited most, and there was much excitement over abortive ventures, many of which depended upon newly platted ranch lands for support. Despite its smaller scale, the boom was real; state and county taxes rose from $75,336 in 1884 to $127,766 in 1887. As in Los Angeles, the decline was not overly severe; in 1889 the county tax had gone down only $22,000 from its inflated 1887 figure.

As the boom in the San Diego zone extended its tentacles over the border and into old Mexico, so the boom in the northern counties reached across the mountain barriers and stimulated areas in the San Joaquin Valley and along the coast. Both Paso Robles (then called El Paso de Robles) and San Luis Obispo received publicity in Los Angeles newspapers during the boom. The former was noted for its mineral springs and baths and the cheapness of its land, priced from sixteen to thirty dollars per acre. San Luis Obispo was described as the center of "the great butter and cheese belt of Southern California."[23] Land here was also moderately priced, at eighteen to twenty-five dollars per acre. There were in April, 1887, between 3,000 and 4,000 inhabitants in the region, and land values rose sharply. San Luis Obispo boasted that it possessed more than 2,000,000 acres of prosperous back country, one-half of which was cultivable.

The boom in the San Joaquin Valley centered in Tulare.

[22]*Ventura Daily Free Press*, July 8, 1887.

[23]*Los Angeles Tribune*, Apr. 12, 1887.

As early as December, 1886, the Sunset Colony, consisting of 5,000 acres, was advertised in Los Angeles. It comprised good raisin and grape land, according to promoters. Tulare County was "the place for men of moderate means to buy homes"[24]— the same appeal used in describing lands of Lower California and Mexico: the farther from Los Angeles, the boom's nucleus, the lower the prices. Numerous sales were made in the spring of 1887, and prices tripled in value—although land never rose much above one hundred dollars per acre. Appeals were not limited to small purchasers; an advertisement in April, 1887, was addressed "To Capitalists!" and offered the Tulare Ranch (presumably undivided) near Porterville.[25]

The boom in the northern counties of the southland was never, therefore, so noisy, so intense, or so widespread as in Los Angeles and San Diego. The conformation of the land, which obviated the possibility of making either Santa Barbara or Ventura into a transcontinental-railway terminus, was largely responsible for the flurry's gentle character. Its absence of vigor in the San Joaquin was due to the lack of the mild climate which constituted the chief selling point of southern promoters. Both Santa Barbara and Ventura were foci for spurts of activity in their respective counties, but neither was affected so greatly as the established towns farther south. In other respects, however, the boom here followed the same pattern. Cities prospered, tracts were platted and filed, feeble suburban villages gained new strength, ghost towns were born and died. There seemed to be fewer fly-by-night promoters in these areas; land sales were largely the work of their older settlers who saw a new and interesting way to make money from their holdings. Because of this relative absence of a floating boom population and the con-

[24]*Ibid.*, May 15, 1887.

[25]*Ibid.*, Apr. 4, 1887.

sequent elimination of many of the tragic aspects of the
collapse, the boom was proportionately more beneficial in the
northern counties than in areas where it was wilder and less
controlled.

CHAPTER XIV

Ghost Towns

O F MORE than one hundred towns platted from 1884 to 1888 in Los Angeles County, sixty-two no longer exist except as stunted country corners, farm acreage, or suburbs. These defunct municipalities, some of which, like Port Ballona and Lordsburg, were later revived under different names, are here classified under the title of "ghost towns." Often these villages were platted near an already flourishing city, with the hope that the infant would profit by close association with its more mature neighbor and assume a relationship comparable to that between Pasadena and Los Angeles. But usually they were not content with satellite potentialities; more often they aspired to be centers of agricultural regions and to flourish in their own right. Los Angeles County was not alone in its possession of such indices of boom enthusiasm; San Bernardino, San Diego, Santa Barbara, and Ventura counties also had their share—generally in less proportion, because of the smaller amount of capital available.

175

❧ The Boom of the Eighties ❧

The area between Los Angeles and the seacoast was the scene of at least twenty abortive enterprises. In 1886 Alamitos Beach was platted on the Rancho Los Alamitos, near the marshy inlet southeast of Long Beach. Although the district is at present a crowded settlement of summer homes, it never developed the civic responsibilities which its owners predicted. The great majority of ghost towns in this area had their inception during 1887. Sunset, recorded November 26, was platted by the Los Angeles and Santa Monica Land and Water Company, which had purchased the Wolfskill Ranch for $440,000. A townsite, surrounded by ten-acre farm tracts, was laid out, water was developed, a hotel partially completed, and a newspaper begun. Transportation facilities were emphasized: a "foothill" interurban railway was to cross the townsite, and a "grand boulevard" was to form the main thoroughfare between Los Angeles and Santa Monica. Sunset, however, was doomed from the start. Its promoters began late, and the speculation's height was past before the venture was well under way. Sunset's hotel was later used as a hay barn, until it burned down some years afterward. Another near-by community, Morocco, never developed sufficiently to be officially recorded, but it was included in Rowan's tract map of Los Angeles County.

Hyde Park, two miles northeast of Centinela Springs, was platted in February, 1887, by Moses L. Wicks. It was advertised as being seven and a half miles from Los Angeles, on the Los Angeles and Santa Monica Railroad, which was part of the California Central system being extended to Ballona Harbor. Lots were sixty by a hundred feet and cost one hundred dollars, two-fifths down. Five- and ten-acre villa lots were also available, and Wicks ran daily excursions in May. Hyde Park was dubbed a "midway town between the city and the harbor,"[1] and was the subject of extensive publicity. Nadeau

[1] *Los Angeles Tribune*, May 13, 1887.

176

Park, eight miles east, on the junction of the Southern Pacific and California Central, was recorded in August; Vernondale and New Vernon were started near by as hopeful suburbs. South Arlington, on the Rancho Las Ciénegas, and Arlington Heights were also recorded during this year. Six miles south of Los Angeles, on Vermont Avenue, Rosecrans began with a projected hotel, a narrow-gauge railroad, and a promoter's promise that prices would rise 500 per cent. The town was laid out in 3,000 lots, averaging 50 by 140 feet, and priced at fifty dollars each. When the hotel and railroad were well under way, the extravagant promise was in a fair way of coming true, for lot prices were raised to $240. Promoters advertised extensively and ran flatcar excursions on Sundays. So successful were these tactics that Rosecrans doubled in size as a result of "public demand."[2]

A few miles north of the Palos Verdes hills, the townsite of Walteria and its adjoining colony project of Meadow Park received wide publicity. There were excursions from Wilmington to both places. Walteria, a part of the Meadow Park Tract of the Rancho Palos Verdes, was subdivided in May, and lots were offered at fifty dollars apiece. The adjoining Meadow Park colony consisted of 700 acres in plats of five, ten, and twenty acres each. Ten thousand fruit trees were planted, and water was said to be plentiful at shallow depths. A typical auction-excursion was held on May 10, when a special train made the round trip from Los Angeles for a fare of seventy-five cents. Instalment payments were the rule, with ten per cent "at the fall of the hammer." A similar near-coastal settlement was Clearwater, a project of the California Co-operative Colony near Long Beach. Of the ghost towns founded in 1887 on the seashore, La Ballona has been discussed in a previous chapter, while Seabright, between San

2*Los Angeles Times*, Jan. 1, June 3, 1887.

Pedro and Wilmington, was founded by George W. King on September 17.

Fewer ghost towns were platted in this district in 1888. The most ambitious was Cahuenga, in modern Hollywood, between Sunset and Fountain avenues. Cahuenga was recorded in November and boasted one of the most decorative plats of any boom town. The survey featured four traffic circles, or plazas, as nuclei for an attractive residential section. Later city fathers thought such a design too complex for increased traffic, and Cahuenga's ambitions were lost in the growth of Hollywood. Also on the western outskirts of Los Angeles, at the end of the Temple Street cable line, lay the town of Waterloo. It comprised seven acres and was put on the market in July, 1887, although the record was not filed until the following year. A new attitude toward publicity was shown in Waterloo advertisements, of which the following is an example:

NOTICE

In putting the Waterloo Tract upon the market, the owners have decided:
To use a little printer's ink, and a great deal of cement sidewalk.
A few locals, but many shade trees.
A brass band only in the distance, but water very near, and in front of each lot.
Auctioneer? Not any! And our

GRAND FREE LUNCH
is composed mainly of. prices that the most chronic dyspeptic can easily digest.[3]

In the San Gabriel Valley, spirited center of boom enthusiasm, more than a dozen ghost towns were platted.

[3]*Ibid.*, July 11, 1887.

Bethune, a suburb of South Pasadena, was characterized as the "Best Investment on the Market Today."[4] It was put on sale by Russell, Cox, and Company, and enjoyed a very short life. The town of Raymond began as a suburb, but one could detect in its publicity the promoters' hidden hope that the tract would blossom into a self-sufficient municipality. Raymond was located south of Pasadena, and was developed by M. T. Scott. Scott and his associates paid $600,000 for one hundred acres, with the stated purpose of obtaining a hundred per cent profit. Raymond, lying as it did on the lines of the California Central, was expected to be the "greatest railroad center in the county,"[5] outside of Los Angeles, for connection was available with the Southern Pacific and the main lines of the Santa Fe. Additions were made from time to time, their backers hoping to profit from the "Raymond land bonanza." A typical addition consisted of 184 acres of Shorb pasture land, subdivided in the late spring of 1887.

South of Alhambra lay the flourishing settlement of Ramona, on the lands of J. De Barth Shorb. The project consisted of 500 acres on the line of the Southern Pacific, about six miles from Los Angeles, and for a time Ramona had the distinction of being the first stop east of the city. Advertisements boasted that Ramona had the largest rainfall in the valley and was only four miles from the Raymond Hotel. By January, 1887, six blocks of the town had been sold—embracing a total of 215 lots; in addition, a 300,000-gallon water reservoir had been completed, and a hotel was under discussion. The Southern Pacific was said to have purchased five complete blocks with the object of locating railroad shops there. "Contracts have been let for several houses," said the *Tribune*, "and there is every indication that the boom has

[4]*Los Angeles Tribune*, May 18, 1887.

[5]*Ibid.*, May 16, 1887.

reached Ramona."[6] Savannah, between San Gabriel and El
Monte on the Southern Pacific, lay in the center of a hay-
and-grain area and was further distinguished by being the
site of Leonard J. Rose's trotting stables. The boom apparently never struck Savannah with much intensity, and publicity emphasized the sedateness of its progress.

Huntington, midway between Pasadena and Monrovia on
the proposed Southern Pacific extension, was financed largely
by outside capital. It was described as "without any exception, the garden-spot of the far-famed San Gabriel valley,"[7]
and advertised its prohibition of saloons as an incentive to the
highest type of citizenry. A reservoir was planned, and the
vigorous Abbot Kinney interested himself in the town's water
supply from Sierra Madre canyons. The plat was located near
the Sierra Madre Villa hotel, and consisted of 120 acres subdivided into five-acre farm tracts costing $750 each. A credit
sale in April, 1887, saw fully half of the townsite change
owners. Broadacres, near by, was subdivided by Frank Mc-
Coye, a pioneer Los Angeles realtor, in May, 1887. Other
towns in the Pasadena area which have not survived as independent entities were Edgemont, South Pasadena Highlands,
and Fairoaks.

Alosta was situated across the railway tracks from Glendora, and was recorded the day after Glendora's map was
filed (September 22, 1887). Rivalry between the two did not
persist, however, for Alosta was swallowed up by post-boom
deflation. Another spirited competition between two communities was begun when Lewis L. Bradbury founded West
Duarte on the tracks of the California Central, shortly after
the platting of Monrovia. Bradbury sponsored the erection of
a hotel, two stores, a livery stable, and an office building,

[6]*Ibid.*, Jan. 26, 1887.

[7]*Ibid.*, Apr. 19, 1887.

but the town did not thrive. Monrovia resented West Duarte's existence, because rail travelers to Monrovia had to alight at the West Duarte station. Bradbury later bowed to the inevitable and changed its name to Monrovia, the title already informally bestowed upon it by irate Monrovia citizens. Most of West Duarte's buildings were later transported to Monrovia.

Perhaps the most extravagant boom-town scheme in the San Gabriel Valley was that of Chicago Park. This plat was located on part of the San Francisquito ranch lands and consisted of a rectangular town plot some two and one-half blocks long by five blocks wide. Less than half of the town was marked off into lots on the first plat, but three additional maps were filed during subsequent months, showing that lots sold as readily here as in more desirable subdivisions. Most of the lots were small—25 by 133.4 feet, except for a few at the eastern end of the plat. The town was recorded on March 15, 1888, and street names, such as State and Dearborn, recalled the promoters' affinity for the Windy City. Chicago Park was an especially remarkable boom achievement because it was platted in the sandy bed of the San Gabriel River. Its nearness to Monrovia gave it a reflected popularity, and the village was often known as "South Monrovia." It was characterized, however, as a "flagrant fraud,"[8] and critics claimed that posters showing steamers on their way up the rippling waters of the San Gabriel were used to advertise the town. Only a Californian can appreciate the joke, for the San Gabriel River consists largely of underground flow, and its surface waters never rise more than a few inches, except during brief floods. Chicago Park was therefore an extreme example of the speculative character of boom prosperity; the fact that lots were sold at all in such a ridiculous location showed that people

[8]Wiley, *History of Monrovia*, pp. 54 f.

cared little what they bought, so long as they could sell to someone else at a profit.

Near the foothills, Altamont maintained a brief, feverish, and largely imaginative existence. It was an agricultural community, consisting chiefly of farm plats. An attempt was made to construct a 4,000-dollar town hall, and a hotel was "demanded," but the town never developed.

The oustanding example of southern-California boom town was first brought to the attention of newspaper readers in Los Angeles by a half-page advertisement[9] which contained merely one striking word:

x

x   x

GLADSTONE

x   x

x

This was followed by the boom period's largest realty advertisements, which explained (for the first time on April 16, 1887) that Gladstone was a new town near Azusa, possessing the best prospects of any boom community in the southern counties. The Gladstone plat was a combination of nineteen different properties, amounting in all to 525 acres; there was a fixed schedule of prices, and lots would be sold on the basis of ten per cent down, one-third of the balance in ten days, and the remainder in six and twelve months, at ten per cent. "The lands purchased for Gladstone," newspapers stated, "possess a more valuable water right than those of any other part of the State. The source is the San Gabriel River, which is constant in its flow, whether the season is wet or dry."[10]

The land on which Gladstone was situated had been sold in 1882 for $150 per acre. In 1887 Henry H. Boyce, the

[9]*Los Angeles Tribune*, Apr. 10, 1887.
[10]*Ibid.*, Apr. 16, 1887.

town's chief promoter, paid $372,661 for the land—a price which, in Netz's opinion, was too high even in those days of lush prosperity.[11] There was good reason for Gladstone's superior propaganda campaign—the fact that Boyce was an experienced newspaper man, one of the owners of the *Los Angeles Tribune*. There was also good reason for the town's failure: lack of direct railroad connection with either of the major lines running through the valley. Promoters of Glendora and Azusa maintained a close relationship with the railroads; Gladstone's builders apparently neglected to do so. "Whether or not these facts affected the route," speculates Baker, "when the junction of the two roads [the Santa Fe and the Los Angeles and San Gabriel Valley Railroad] was effected, Glendora and Azusa had a railroad, while Gladstone, which lay between them, was left two miles south of it."[12] The town was named after the British prime minister, who at that time was enjoying a period of popularity in the United States. An article in the *Tribune* on April 25, 1887, stated that the "Rt. Hon. Wm. Ewart Gladstone, The Premier Statesman of the World, will be presented with the title deeds to a lot in the new town of Gladstone, In the Heart of the Azusa. Other people can buy them of Frank McCoye, No. 23 North Spring Street."

Despite its eventual failure, Gladstone enjoyed a brief period of prosperity upon the completion of the Santa Fe line into Los Angeles in April, 1887. The first excursions were run on April 19, 20, and 21, and there were others on the two following days. A sale was planned for Saturday, April 23, and advertising crescendoed to an unequaled burst of enthusiasm. Gladstone was dubbed the "Business Center of the Valley." Water and power were declared to be abundant

[11]Netz, in Hist. Soc. of Sou. Calif. *Annual Publications, 1915-16*, X, 65-66.

[12]Charles C. Baker, "The Rise and Fall of the City of Gladstone," in Hist. Soc. of Sou. Calif. *Annual Publications, 1914*, IX, 188.

from inexhaustible sources in Sawpit Canyon. "Mountains of marble" existed in Cajón Pass and, with the aid of the Santa Fe, could be laid down in Gladstone "cheaper than brick." Visitors coming by railway admittedly had to alight in a rocky, desolate spot, but that inconvenience was only temporary—the planned extension had not been finished. A chief attraction was eighty-foot Citrus Avenue, nine miles long; a "granite bank" and a newspaper were promised immediately. The climate was said to be perfect. A near-by rancher was quoted to the effect that "nowhere else in Southern California can oranges be grown with such a perfect combination of flavor and color, the latter being a bright cherry." Already, on April 18, there was a "good-sized village" consisting of four schoolhouses, three churches, four stores, several shops, a winery, and a livery stable. The company was capitalized at $1,000,000, five of the six founders having contributed $166,660, and Boyce the remainder. This masterpiece of boom advertising ended with the intriguing statement: "There is another advantage the place has, or rather will have, which cannot yet be made public."[13]

The Los Angeles sale of Gladstone properties, which took place on April 25, 1887, was by later estimates not a great success. People proved more eager to attend than to buy, and the excitement at the auctions was a typical result of promotional psychology. At one sale, four loaded railway cars, each with white-canvas signs lettered in red and black, "GLADSTONE," departed from Los Angeles for Azusa, where the train made a brief stop. Lunch was served at the tract, and afterward Colonel Boyce "mounted a dry-goods box, and explained the terms of sale." Another colonel, named Weller, was auctioneer. A man with the suggestive name of Welsher obtained first choice of two lots for his fifty-dollar bid. "So

[13]*Los Angeles Tribune*, Apr. 18, 1887.

eager were the purchasers," ran the *Tribune*'s version of the sale, "that 150 of them missed the train to this city."[14]

Among the accouterments of boom promotion was the "card of thanks," often issued by a group of excursionists after partaking of a realty company's cheer, good will, and free lunch. It would be unkind, but probably true, to suggest that many of these signed resolutions were planned by agents of the company as an excuse for additional column-inches of publicity, but the fact remains that some, doubtless, were spontaneous and sincere. The Gladstone version was presented after the Sunday train trip of April 24, and read as follows:

We, the late Gladstone excursionists, take this opportunity of expressing our sincere thanks to the management for their kind care of us throughout the trip. Especially are thanks due to Colonel Boyce for fatherly care of us during our stay at Monrovia, and we feel that with such a man at the head, Gladstone is on a firm basis, and is certain to have a bright future.[15]

Litigation was a natural result of the haste which characterized property transactions of the period, and Gladstone had its share. The tract became involved in two lawsuits which were given wide and scurrilous publicity in Los Angeles, the virulence of the quarrels highly intensified by the rivalry between the *Times* and Boyce's paper, the *Tribune*. In April, just as the town was getting started, Boyce and his partner, Clarence J. Richards, organizer of the Cahuenga Land and Water Company, were sued by an attorney, James Damron, who claimed that they had swindled him out of his one-third share of the Gladstone property. The land had previously been owned by H. C. Luce and Joseph Sartori, the banker, and Damron claimed he had acquired the land from them

[14]*Ibid.*, Apr. 24, 1887.

[15]*Ibid.*, Apr. 26, 1887.

185

with the understanding that he was to keep one-third and turn the remainder over to Boyce's organization. Boyce denied that any such three-cornered arrangement had ever existed; he said that Damron was merely his agent, and that he had dealt directly with Luce and Sartori for the whole property. The squabble immediately cast a cloud over the tract's title, and effects on land sales were quickly felt. By long, front-page articles in the *Tribune*, Boyce tried manfully to mitigate these unhappy consequences of the suit, while the *Times* gleefully publicized Damron's views. One of Boyce's stories was headed:

IT IS NOT GLADSTONE
The Pretty New Town Not Involved in a Law-Suit
The Dougherty Tract is Not in the Town
Proper, Nor Does it Involve the Title of
Any Property Belonging to the Gladstone
Improvement Company[16]

This article went on to say that Boyce had been served with papers just as he entered the train on sale day (April 23), but that, despite misfortune, lots to the amount of more than $100,000 had been marketed. The fact was emphasized that only fifty-six acres were involved in the litigation, and that title to the whole property was by no means in question. Boyce and Richards expressed their willingness to deed Damron the third he claimed—if he would purchase it on the regular terms; but, they said, he was able to make only part of the required cash payment. At the same time, they reasserted that Damron's name had not been mentioned in the transaction, and they implied that the only purpose of their offer was to avoid trouble and expense. "Even if the 56 1-10 acres had formed a portion of Gladstone, it would be a very small affair as compared with the whole superb tract, and it

[16]*Ibid.*, Apr. 25, 1887.

is not probable that the lawsuit will have very much effect upon the boom in the Azusa country," the article concluded.

Damron finally withdrew his charges on April 23, admitting that the affair was settled, and that it had never involved the entire tract. The *Tribune* made much of his acknowledgments and also of the next suit which was filed—that of Boyce against the *Times* for the sum of $50,000 for defamation of character. Boyce's associates joined him, and together they demanded $200,000 from the rival journal. Gladstone's promoters apparently considered that they could profit just as much from a successfully prosecuted lawsuit as they could from land sales, and thenceforth the *Tribune* reversed its policy and no longer attempted to hush the effects of litigation on Gladstone's prosperity. An article on May 6 admitted that, although 70,000 dollars' worth of Gladstone property had been sold before the *Times* put forth its claim that Boyce's title was not clear, buyers had refused to make their second payments, and no further sales had been made. Boyce continued the fight with such enthusiasm that by the middle of May the *Times* was forced to yield. The *Tribune* asserted that the *Times* tried to quiet the issue by a ruse on May 16, whereby one copy of the paper was printed with a retraction, and shown to Boyce, who thereupon agreed to withdraw the suit. But, when the trick was discovered, charges were resumed. How much of this is true cannot easily be determined, but the *Times* did print a retraction on May 18, and the *Tribune* gleefully hailed it as "The Dish of Crow the 'Times' Agreed to Eat."[17]

Returning from the San Gabriel Valley to the lands of the Rancho San Rafael, the boom-time traveler passed through three embryo cities, none of which managed to survive in the form its promoters intended. Rockdale was recorded November 12, 1886, and Minneapolis, near the rancho's southern

[17]*Ibid.*, May 4, 6, 17, 19, 1887.

boundary, on December 8, 1887—the latter by Ben Ward. Ivanhoe was situated on the Los Feliz Rancho, comprising the eastern portion of the Lick Tract; it was recorded June 2, 1887, and consisted of 700 acres divided into 1,300 lots, ranging in size from one-hundred-foot frontages to five acres and in price from $150 to $750. A free carriage went to the tract daily. Near the line of the Southern Pacific running northwest from Glendale and Burbank were two ghost towns. One of them, Dundee, recorded October 12, 1887, was a mile south of modern Roscoe. The other, Monte Vista, first platted in 1885, was in the La Cañada Valley beyond Dundee, and sixteen miles from Los Angeles. In 1886 Monte Vista's hotel accommodations were proclaimed inadequate, and a new building was started; a church was planned on a lot donated by the Monte Vista Land and Water Company, and the town was described as an excellent sanitarium site. Another attraction was Tujunga Park, filled with live-oak trees. Land sold from $200 to $400 per acre.

Three boom communities of the northern desert were publicized widely, and two of them were immortalized by Guinn as comparable to Chicago Park in their glaring fraudulence. Maynard, in the Antelope Valley, was advertised as a region of cheap land, adequate rainfall, and easy settlement. Border City and Manchester clung precariously to desert hillsides. They were the brain children of Simon Hamburg, a boom genius more interested in profits than in ethics, who made, in some cases, 1,000 per cent on his investments by carefully limiting his sales to customers so far away they could not investigate what they were buying. Border City, says Guinn, "was most easily accessible by means of balloon, and was as secure from hostile invasion as the homes of the cliff dwellers. Its principal resource . . . was view—a view of the Mojave desert. . . . Manchester was a city of greater resources than Border City. Being located higher up on the mountain, it had a more extended view of the desert."[18] These townsites, filed in 1887, were too inaccessible to survey. Hamburg had bought two quarter sections at ten cents per acre, and he sold them for one dollar to $250 per acre. His profits probably amounted to $50,000. So many of his deeds were filed for record that the county recorder was said to have a special book of his holdings—with 380 pages made out in blank. Hesperia, on the desert north of Antelope Valley, was supposedly backed by Robert M. Widney, but in later years it surrendered to Victorville and Barstow its pretensions to being a desert railway center. Three miles east of Palm Springs, a 160-acre town was platted under the name of Palm Dale. A hundred acres near by were planted to orange trees, but they promptly died, and grape culture was tried as an alternative. A narrow-gauge spur from the Southern Pacific line through Beaumont failed to resuscitate the feeble village. Palm Dale—and $100,000 of its investors' funds— eventually vanished.

The Pomona area had three communities which disappeared after the boom. One of them, Lordsburg, was revived under another name, and is now the small college town of La Verne. It was platted by a Pasadena realtor, I. W. Lord, in 1887 and was made the subject of a publicity campaign second only to Gladstone's. Large advertisements with the town's name blazoned in huge letters appeared in newspapers of the day; long descriptive articles and advertisements explained in detail the advantages of Lordsburg investment. The town consisted of a 600-acre tract on the Santa Fe line, four miles northwest of Pomona, and the development was said to be "under the especial patronage of the Santa Fe people, and unquestionably intended by them to be their rival to Pomona, on the South-

[18]James M. Guinn, *Historical and Biographical Record of Los Angeles and Vicinity* (1901) p. 141.

ern Pacific."[19] Lordsburg was further destined to become the
junction point with the Elsinore branch of the Santa Fe. Like
most boom towns, it was designed, not for business development, but for "Eden-like homes."[20] An auction on May 25,
1887, brought 2,500 persons to the tract and resulted in lot
sales aggregating $200,000. A brass band had canvassed the
city the previous day, and thirty railroad cars were reserved
to carry the eager buyers from Los Angeles, while special
trains also left Riverside, San Bernardino, and other towns
about the same time. The affair was described as probably
"the largest auction in Southern California."[21] Lot prices were
high, ranging from $400 to $800. Three auctioneers and two
sets of recording clerks insured efficiency, while three brass
bands entertained the crowd as it consumed the "mammoth"
lunch. Probably nothing did more to relegate the Lordsburg
auction to a deserved oblivion than the "poem" which com-
memorated it:

> What is this day
> That seems to say
> We're going to stay
>   In Lordsburg?
>
> The train to-day
> One dollar to-day
> Great sale to-day
>   In Lordsburg.
>
> Don't pass it by
> At least do try
> To go and buy
>   In Lordsburg.[22]

[19]*Los Angeles Tribune*, May 17, 1887.

[20]*Ibid.*

[21]*Ibid.*, May 25, 1887.

[22]*Ibid.*

Another town which attempted to be the chief Santa Fe depot for the Pomona region was Palomares, recorded April 7, 1887. The Los Angeles Land Bureau, in charge of its sales, guaranteed that the Santa Fe was "under contract to stop every passenger train" at the townsite.[23] A Congregational college was endowed with $200,000 in land and money, but the denomination finally centered its efforts in near-by Claremont. The same enthusiastic churchmen, under the direction of Charles B. Sumner, were responsible for laying out the third ghost town of the district—Piedmont, whose lands composed the endowment for the future Claremont Colleges. Piedmont was recorded November 3, 1888—too late to profit from the boom.

There were nearly a dozen ghost towns in the lower Santa Ana Valley, in what is now Orange County. McPherson, two miles east of Orange on the Tustin branch of the Southern Pacific, was named after a raisin-packing concern, and prospered temporarily, but was finally eclipsed by Orange. The flatlands at the mouth of the lower Santa Ana Canyon were the site of several town failures. St. James, recorded in 1887, was located near the canyon's mouth, five miles from Orange; sales were managed by the Pacific Land and Improvement Company, whose work was so effective that opening-day cash sales totaled $8,000. There is now no sign of St. James on the map. Carlton, a mile south of the outlet of Carbon Canyon, was another town whose chief advantage was view. It was situated too high above the flats to have a usable water supply, but ambitious publicity resulted in a flurry of sales which raised prices to $500 for corner lots. So intense was the excitement that a single realtor disposed of 3,000 pieces of Carlton land, and the town had a population of 400 in 1887. Richfield and Yorba were located on the north bank of the Santa Ana River; both of them were platted in 1888.

[23]*Ibid.*, May 18, 1887.

The Boom of the Eighties

Less than two miles from the railway joining Santa Ana and Newport Beach was the town of Fairview, promoted by a development company which sold hundreds of lots and started a newspaper, a hotel, and a bathhouse featuring sulphurated artesian water. The venture began auspiciously in December, 1887, backed by middle-western as well as local capital. The company bought more than 1,700 acres for $297,500, projected a fifty-acre town, and cut up the remainder into small farm tracts. Plans were made to develop a natural-gas flow near by, and to build a hundred-foot highway from Santa Ana to Newport, which would connect Fairview with both the bay and the inland city. The Santa Ana Valley and Pacific Railroad was incorporated and began laying track in the spring of 1888—about the same time, in fact, that suits for nonpayment of instalments on Fairview property were begun by promoters. A newspaper, the *Fairview Register*, appeared in May, 1888, and lasted a year, while the first excursion on the new railroad was run in June. Both company and town were ruined by the 1889 collapse, and went into receivership the following year.

Two ghost towns lay between the Santa Ana settlements and Los Angeles. One, Rivera, on the Santa Fe Railroad three miles west of Whittier, straddled the boundary between the ranchos Santa Gertrudes and Paso de Bartolo. The second, Carmenita, was located on the Los Coyotes ranch lands three miles east of Norwalk, and hoped vainly that the Southern Pacific line would bring it prosperity.

About eighteen ghost towns rose in the San Bernardino area during the boom years 1887 and 1888. Ten of them were in the immediate vicinity of San Bernardino and Riverside, and the others were scattered between the San Jacinto Valley and the desert north of Cajón Pass. Redlands proved to be the nucleus for a cluster of settlements, like Terracina and Gladysta, which failed to achieve more than suburban status.

Harlem, recorded in 1888, was on Base Line Street between San Bernardino and Highlands; Urbita, filed in 1886, between Colton and San Bernardino; and Mound City, another product of the last year of the boom, bordered Colton on the south. Even the suburbs had their satellites in turn: a West Highlands and a North Rialto were founded in 1887; Riverside Heights lay to the north of the parent city, and Box Springs nestled in the eastern hills. Alessandro was platted near the present location of March Field, on the road to Perris. It was recorded in July, 1887, and utilized its position as a station on the California Southern as a chief attraction. Temescal, twelve miles northwest of Lake Elsinore, on Temescal Wash, was also a product of 1887.

Rincón, on the bank of the Santa Ana River, west of South Riverside, was filed in 1888. The town was platted and advertised during the preceding year, however, lots having been sold as early as May. Rincón was to be a station on the projected Riverside, Santa Ana, and Los Angeles Railroad, and constituted what its promoters called a "natural trade center." Six hundred acres were subdivided by the Rincón Land and Town Company; seventy of them formed town lots, and the company donated to the school district a lot supposedly worth $2,400. "All this," said the article advertising the first sale, "indicates that within the next sixty days Rincón is to develop into a stirring town, and that there is to be a good deal of business done here from the start."[24] Electric lighting was promised, and other improvements were listed. As a result of these efforts nearly 80,000 dollars' worth of land was sold in a few days. Irvington, Oro Grande, Auburndale, and Greendale were other San Bernardino County communities that failed to survive the flurry.

The ghost towns of San Diego County were more numer-

[24]*Ibid.*, May 5, 1887.

ous in the bay region and in stream valleys east of the city
than in the back country or along the northern coast. There
were, however, scattered examples in the north, and at least
one of the projects there, Linda Rosa, was the subject of an
advertising campaign equal to the boom's loudest.

The southward-jutting peninsula culminating in Point
Loma had always been a favorite site for realty promotion.
During San Diego's first boom following Horton's development projects, two cities had been platted near the point.
One of them, La Playa, was a typical ghost town, consisting
chiefly of newspaper publicity and a 400-foot wharf. Benjamin Truman, writing in 1869, said: "Owners of lots of this
metropolis (on paper) are the singular possessors of more
money than brains."[25] Roseville, two miles farther up the bay,
managed to exist as a San Diego suburb but later degenerated
into a launch landing and the home of professional fishermen.
The great boom saw the establishment of Hyde Park here—a
namesake of the Los Angeles suburb. View appeared the chief
benefit of residence in this plat, and notices stressed the varied
scenes which lay before the home owner in the new town.
The entire southern-California landscape from Coronado to
Mount San Antonio was visible from the site, according to
one promoter, and, he added, one-third of Hyde Park itself
could be seen "with the assistance of a field glass,"[26] from the
streets of San Diego. Motor lines and a ferry service were
planned, but these projects, so far as Hyde Park was concerned, died with the town.

The river valleys opening on the bay mothered a host of
ghost towns. Englewood, in the Sweetwater Valley, boasted,
"No fog, no frosts, no alkali, no adobe"—and, one might add,
within a few months there was no town. Englewood's 700

[25]Guinn, *History of . . . Southern Coast Counties*, p. 272.

[26]*San Diego Free Press*, Feb. 2, 1888.

acres of citrus land were located fifteen miles from San Diego, and its backers were not particular why their customers purchased: "Buy a home. . . . Invest. . . . or Speculate. . . . and double your money in six months."[27] The country watered by the San Diego River and El Cajón Creek was dotted with ghost towns. One of these, Barona, "The Promised Land," was on the Rancho Canyada de San Vicente y Mesa del Padre Barona and consisted of more than 13,000 acres devoted to agriculture. T. J. Daley, owner of the ranch, built a school and church for settlers on his property, distributed cattle for home use, free of charge, and furnished fruit trees, farming implements, and teams at cost. Daley emphasized that Barona was not for speculators, and priced his land from $50 to $100 per acre. Near by, Helix and Waterville were platted in 1888, and Teralta was offered by the energetic Combination Land Company.

Farther south, Richland lay east of National City and offered its farm lands for $175 per acre; Oneonta, thirteen miles south of San Diego, prided itself on having a two-story hotel, a good beach on the bay shore, and "no saloons, fist, or bull fights."[28] The False Bay region entered the competition with Morena, expected to profit from its position as a way station on the Santa Fe. Seven miles east of Encinitas, up the coast from San Diego, was Glen-Barham. "What is the matter with Glen-Barham?" asked its promoters. "Nothing," they replied. "This is God's own arrangement for the consumptive, the dyspeptic, and the broken down."[29]

Inland, near the early line of the California Southern, four communities failed to outlive the boom. Lucerne, at the head of Lake Elsinore, was financed largely by San Diego capital.

[27]*Ibid.*

[28]*San Diego Union*, May 3, 1888; *Southern California Independent*, Nov. 10, 1888.

[29]*San Diego Union*, Oct. 2, 1887.

Linda Rosa, two miles southeast of Murrieta on the railroad, was acclaimed as the "future manufacturing center and metropolis of San Diego's back country."[30] Platted on the sloping foothills of the Rancho Santa Rosa, the town was surrounded by 200,000 acres of land suited for fruit culture. A 5,000-dollar railway station was finished by early 1888, and a hotel projected. Industry had already arrived in the form of the New York and Linda Rosa Canning and Fruit Packing Company, which planned to cultivate a thousand acres to feed its preserving machinery and keep busy its thousand employees. The Santa Rosa Land and Improvement Company, backers of the town, offered to finance the price of lots for one year, at low interest, for those intending to make immediate improvements on their property. The company made a "free donation" of $800 with every twentieth lot sold, and the twenty purchasers were to decide among themselves how to distribute the money. Prices ranged from $50 to $400 per lot but rises were threatened. South of Escondido, in the Poway Valley, the town of Peermont was platted, and Agua Tibia lay on the California Southern line.

Ventura and Santa Barbara counties were less prolific in the production of ghost towns, because the boom as a whole struck these areas with less intensity. There were, however, a few widely advertised communities which failed to mature. In Santa Barbara County many boom tracts were located, logically, near the county seat. Tarragona, recorded in 1888, was one of these, and Verona, "twenty minutes ride" from town, another.[31] La Serena was a village that perhaps owed its failure to the late date of its promotion—October, 1888. Naples was platted by the Southern Pacific Railroad on its projected extension, fifteen miles northwest of Santa Barbara.

[30]*San Diego Free Press*, Feb. 2, 1888.

[31]*Santa Barbara Morning Press*, Feb. 7, 1888.

Naples was recorded in November, 1887, and a hotel was planned for immediate construction, but the tract never amounted to more than a minor railway stop. It was located "on the Riviera of the Santa Barbara channel," on high, sloping land near Los Pueblos Creek. "This is not a Paper Town!" cried the promoters,[32] but they were unable to argue it into importance. Templeton, between Paso Robles and San Luis Obispo, was not in Santa Barbara County, but because of the vast publicity it received in southern newspapers should be included in the list. The town, located on the Southern Pacific Railroad, was destined to be the community center for various ranch lands surrounding it, which totaled 63,000 acres. Promotion began in December, 1886, and by April of the following year there were three hotels, two livery stables, and three general stores in the village. Templeton Institute was founded by a professor from Missouri. Sales were managed by the West Coast Land Company, directed by C. H. Phillips, of San Luis Obispo, and having on its board the distinguished figure of former Governor George Perkins. The company, after buying surrounding ranchos, divided its land into small farms and sold them for ten to thirty dollars per acre. By April 300,000 dollars' worth of farm lands had been disposed of. Advertisements pointed out that the county's population had more than doubled since 1880, and that irrigation was unnecessary, as the lands were so near the coast. The developers were encouraged by the purchase of 50,000 dollars' worth of farm land by Willard V. Huntington, Collis' nephew, who was a San Francisco real estate broker; Huntington projected a large fruit and vine ranch. Excursionists to Templeton were so numerous that more than a thousand extra cots for their accommodation during the height of the flurry were set up in store buildings. The place is now hardly more than a country village.

[32] *Ventura Free Press*, Nov. 4, 1887.

⤳ The Boom of the Eighties ⤳

In Ventura County, Lexington, Colonia, Oak Glen, and Nordhoff were the outstanding ghost towns, although the last-named was first platted in 1874. Lexington was laid out in February, 1887, at the junction of Lockwood and Piru creeks, near the county's eastern border. Its chief promoter was A. W. Smith, who subdivided 560 acres into farm plats and 25- by 75-foot lots. Smith was apparently interested in mining, for several streets of the town bore names of minerals, such as Silver, Gold, Emerald, and Carbonate. Colonia was located seven miles southeast of Ventura, at the "geographical center of Ventura County."[33] It lay on the south side of the Santa Clara River, on the proposed branch of the Southern Pacific to Hueneme. The tract consisted of 73 acres, and there were 104 town lots. Taylor and Jepson, the subdividers, held a raffle, distributing one ticket with each lot sold; there were three prizes, of $1,500, $1,000, and $500 in gold, and the drawing, to insure fairness, was to be managed by a committee chosen by lot buyers. Jerusalem, also platted by Taylor and Jepson, was also on the south bank of the Santa Clara River, and consisted of one hundred town lots, surrounded by a group of 65-acre tracts. Oak Glen was platted near Ojai, as was Nordhoff, named after Charles Nordhoff, the noted traveler and writer. Nordhoff, twelve miles from Ventura, was acclaimed as a health resort, boasted hot springs, and had two hotels by the beginning of 1887, but gave way in importance to near-by Ojai.

Ghost towns were thus one of the most characteristic of boom products. Founded sometimes with sincere purpose, often with merely a hope of immediate profit, these abortive enterprises were a monument to the risks incident to speculation in rural real estate. The projects usually prospered if care and good judgment attended the choice of the location,

[33] *Ventura Daily Free Press*, July 6, 19, Aug. 11, 1887.

and if there were adequate financing and honest leadership. Otherwise, ghost towns generally resulted from the lack of these benefits. It must be admitted, however, that in some cases failure came despite the most efficient and intelligent management; ill fate seemed to intervene in several otherwise stable projects. Raymond and Ramona might each have been an early San Marino—if purchasers had not simply preferred to invest elsewhere; Ivanhoe might have been another Glendale— if settlers had not bought on the northern, rather than on the southern, slopes of eastern San Fernando Valley. Luck as well as business acumen or the lack of it was a concomitant of success or failure in the great boom; and ghost towns, existing today only on musty maps in county recorders' offices, were the outstanding illustration of that fact.

CHAPTER XV

Men and Methods

REAL-ESTATE booms would be few indeed were it not for
the peculiarities of human psychology which allow
the profit motive to become infected with emotion-
alism. The human element is therefore extremely important.
Several classes of persons contributed to boom fever—among
them the professional promoter, the astute, honest California
man of business interested in steady growth, the dupe who
plunged and lost, the tourist who invested or looked on, and,
finally, the social parasite who accompanies any flurry.

Many promoters had been thoroughly schooled in the
Middle West in boom psychology and methods. Kansas was
called a "hotbed of land speculation."[1] There, railway-land
sales, mass migrations to newly opened grain areas, and homestead activity formed a background which enabled professional promoters to arrive in California as trained experts in
their field. The methods of some of these promoters—or

[1]Brooks, in *Land of Sunshine* (May, 1895), p. 102.

"Escrow Indians," as they were popularly called—elicited highly uncomplimentary opinions. Guinn states that they were, for the most part,

fellows who had left their consciences (that is, if they had any to leave) on the other side of the Rockies. These professionals had learned the tricks of their trade in the boom cities of the west when that great wave of immigration which began moving after the close of the war was sweeping westward from the Mississippi River to the shores of the Pacific. These came here not to build up the country, but to make money, honestly if they could not make it any other way. It is needless to say they made it the other way.[2]

Their confident attitude, their suave talk, and their ingratiating manners made otherwise intelligent people gullible. The *Times* classified the newcomers as "dudes, loafers, paupers, those who expect to astonish the natives, those who are afraid to pull off their coats, cheap politicians, business scrubs, impecunious clerks, lawyers, and doctors."[3] Nefarious practices, such as hanging oranges on Joshua trees and then selling desert lots as citrus groves to "greenhorns," did not add to their popularity.

The boomers hired hackmen, hotel employees, and waiters to seize prospects for them. Sometimes they would spy on legitimate realtors, and, when these honest tradesmen showed interest in certain lots, boomers would buy the property and sell it to them at a handsome profit. The boomers formed syndicates to market their wares. The *Santa Ana Herald* described a group, for instance, which united to develop acreage near Newport Bay: "These gentlemen are of the energetic, pushing kind, and we feel gratified to know that they have

[2]Guinn, *Los Angeles and Vicinity*, p. 260.

[3]From Quiett, *They Built the West*, p. 282.

determined to make their homes with us."[4] Such gentry became so numerous that the demand for real estate offices in Los Angeles exceeded the supply, and new ones had to be built. When foreign promoters outnumbered local realtors who had grown up with the area, the boom quickly became unhealthy and dangerous.

Nevertheless, many efficient promotional organizations and methods were begun largely through the efforts of boom realtors and in some cases permanent beneficial effects upon the growth and development of the southern counties resulted. Among the first institutions to be organized by businessmen interested in publicizing a locality's prospects was the board of trade or chamber of commerce. Practically every full-fledged town made some attempt at founding an organization of that sort, and, although not a few of these earlier bodies proved failures later, the seeds which they planted bore fruit in an intensified civic consciousness and a local patriotism that played an important part in municipal growth. The Pasadena Real Estate Exchange was an example. Organized in August, 1887, at the boom's height, "to devise, encourage, and foster schemes of public improvement and benefit to the city at large,"[5] the exchange subsequently became the Pasadena Realty Board. Los Angeles had both a board of trade and a chamber of commerce, which operated concurrently. In 1871 there had been an unsuccessful attempt to organize the former, and not until twelve years afterward did the board become an actuality. The chamber, first founded in 1873, ceased its activities in 1877 when prospects were dark, but resumed in 1888.

Perhaps the most ambitious type of promotional organiza-

[4]From Blanche Collings, "Fairview, Boom Town," in *Orange County History Series*, II, 68.

[5]Carew, *History of Pasadena*, I, 485.

tion was the state-wide agency that operated under the name of the California Immigrant Union. It was founded in October, 1869, by a group of outstanding citizens, "for the purpose of Encouraging Immigration to the State of California."[6] It maintained an office on California Street in San Francisco and offered itself as a clearing house for information on state lands, showing special interest in the formation and settlement of colony groups. Its leaders included both old and new settlers. There was an honorary committee headed by George Newton Booth and including such men as Leland Stanford and Jesse Livermore, while Mark Hopkins and Peter Spreckels were members of the board; William T. Coleman, of Vigilante fame, was the first president. The Union had a general agent at San Francisco, and others at Copenhagen, Hamburg, and Bremen. There was also a traveling agent in Germany, and a general agent for the eastern states. The Union, in its fight for a grant of state funds, explained the benefits which would accrue to the region by its activities and argued that the "sick tax" which each immigrant paid on entry would, if devoted to the expenses of the Union, completely cover them. Although the Union did not specialize in southern-California lands, it played an important part in disposing of them; men like Stearns and Willmore often listed their realty offerings with the Union, to share in its widespread advertising benefits.

Eastern encouragement for such an organization was not lacking. Two months after its birth, the Union was in receipt of a missive from J. S. Loomis, president of a similar group in Kansas, in which he advised unification and co-operation with eastern bodies. Loomis urged that the proper functions for such a state institution were: first, to sponsor subdivision of large tracts to make investment easy for the less-wealthy immigrant; second, to act as agent for railway and steamship lines; third, to educate prospective immigrants as to economic

[6] *All about California* (1870), p. 41.

advantages and to furnish guides and advisers for their trip;
and, fourth, to feature cheap lands and cheap transportation.
"I believe," Loomis concluded, "we could send you one hundred thousand people within two years if you will unite on a
practical plan."[7]

Often the immigrants themselves organized spontaneous
nonprofit-making promotional groups, in the form of state
societies, that effectively advertised southern California
through correspondence and articles in home-town newspapers. One of the first of these state societies was the Illinois
Association, founded December 18, 1886, with nearly 200
charter members. The somewhat facetious opening resolutions
read, in part, as follows:

Whereas, We, the members of the Illinois Association, having
endured the tortures inseparably connected with life in a region
of ice and snow, and having fled from our beloved State to this
favored land; therefore, be it

Resolved, That we deeply sympathize with our friends and
former fellow-citizens in Illinois who still endure the ills they
have, rather than fly to pleasures that they know not of. . . .

Resolved, That in this grand country we have the tallest mountains, the biggest trees, the crookedest railroads, the dryest rivers,
the loveliest flowers, the smoothest ocean, the finest fruits, the
mildest lives, the softest breezes, the purest air, the heaviest
pumpkins, the best schools, the most numerous stars, the most
bashful real estate agents, the brightest skies and the most genial
sunshine to be found anywhere else in North America. . . .

Resolved, That we heartily welcome other refugees from Illinois, and will do all in our power to make them realize that they
are sojourning in a "City of the Angels" where their hearts will
be irrigated by living waters flowing from the perennial foun-
tains of health, happiness, and longevity.

All of which is respectively submitted in faith, hope, and climate.[8]

[7]*Opinions of the Press . . . on the Value and Importance of Immigration
and the Necessity of State Aid* (1870), p. 26.

[8]*Los Angeles Tribune,* Dec. 19, 1886.

Other bodies of a similar nature were quickly started, and the bases were laid for the present annual picnics in Los Angeles' Sycamore Grove and the now-outworn Iowa anecdotes of Long Beach.

Smaller districts within the state carried on their own promotional ventures largely by means of agents in the cities. The *Tribune* boasted as early as December, 1886, that agents from all parts of California then had offices in Los Angeles. The article added smugly that Los Angeles did not object, because development of any part of California would indirectly boost the southland, and the writer devoted many subsequent editorial inches to praising Los Angeles for this generosity. On December 23 the *Tribune* listed the agents then present; they included men from San Diego County, Riverside, the Santa Ana Valley, and Coronado. The "northern citrus belt" had announced its intention of sending a promoter, and a few days later the *Tribune* boasted with satisfaction that southern California had been so successful in promoting immigration that Sacramento was sending an agent to Los Angeles to find out whether southern publicity methods could not be applied to northern projects. On January 6 there were, besides those mentioned above, agents from Fresno, Santa Barbara, Ventura, and San Bernardino counties, and from the city of Anaheim. "They are all welcome," the *Tribune* graciously concluded. Tulare sent a representative the same month.

Many boom promoters were not undesirable, and often honestly wished to build up the region. Several, in fact, deserve to be remembered, in the annals of the southern counties, for what they contributed in initiative, business honesty, and constructive enthusiasm. To list every respectable citizen who dabbled in real estate during these years is, of course, impossible, but a fair sampling of the more active individuals follows.

There is little doubt that, had it not been for the Chaffey

brothers, the Pomona region would have grown at a much slower pace. Without their contributions to the improvement of irrigation methods, many neighboring communities would have been hampered, and some would not have been founded at all. George Chaffey, as already stated, was a conspicuously able Canadian engineer whose earlier efforts had been largely devoted to designing lake steamers. His brother, William Benjamin, was the businessman of the team. On their departure in 1886 for Australia the Ontario *Record* testified wholeheartedly to the esteem in which they were held by the community: "We say in all sincerity, and we believe it to be the sentiments of the citizens, that no colony in Southern California owes as much to its founders as does Ontario. . . . The plan on which the tract was laid out, the avenue, the water works, the college, are enduring monuments of liberality and foresight."[9] And, again: "In starting Etiwanda and Ontario they did more in advertising the resources of Southern California in the East, in giving a wide circulation to immigration literature than, we think we may safely say, any other colonizers in this part of the State. They did a great work in inducing immigration which benefited not only their own colonies, but all Southern California."[10] George Chaffey later returned from his Australian projects, somewhat discredited by their economic failure but with a long record of honorable effort behind him. He re-entered the field of local irrigation development and re-established his fallen fortunes, in partnership with his son, Andrew. Subsequently, he became interested in Imperial Valley water development. His brother, William Benjamin, remained in Australia.

As George Chaffey was the outstanding promoter of the

[9] J. A. Alexander, *The Life of George Chaffey* (1928), p. 98.

[10] *Ibid.*, p. 100.

Ontario region, so Nathaniel C. Carter was the most picturesque boomer in Sierra Madre. Some of Carter's enthusiasm
was justified, for he gave the California climate credit for
curing him of tuberculosis. Arriving in 1871, he invested in
San Gabriel Valley land, purchasing seventeen acres near
Hugo Reid's ranch. He became one of southern California's
foremost publicists, and his methods were as varied and versatile as his interests. He devised a halftone cut of himself,
which depicted him before and after he was cured of tuberculosis; he titled the picture "Before and After Taking," and,
when asked what remedy he referred to, described at length
the California climate. A "good mixer," Carter was enthusiastic and sincere in his attitude, and became widely known,
not only locally but in the East as well. He was one of the
first to discern the advantages of the planned excursion, and
he attempted to interest Collis Huntington in the idea as early
as 1872. Beginning in 1874 and for twenty-five years thereafter, Carter made annual trips to Massachusetts for the
purpose of advertising California. "He was the pioneer in this
field," says one local historian, "the first California 'booster'
to 'boost' on a big scale. Incidentally he made it pay him
handsome profits."[11] In 1880 Carter became "Lucky" Baldwin's agent, and bought 1,100 acres from him, during the
following year, for twenty-five dollars an acre. Carter subdivided his plat, sponsored a hotel and school, began the sale
of lots, and thus started the town of Sierra Madre.

In Glendale, Capt. Cameron Erskine Thom, a Virginian
who had gained his commission in the Confederate forces and
later entered legal practice in Los Angeles, aided in the development of the eastern part of the San Rafael ranch lands.
He arrived in California in 1849, mined gold on the South

[11]Carew, I, 364. See also the Los Angeles Chamber of Commerce letter,
To the General Managers of the C. P. & U. P. Railroad Companies (1876),
indorsing Nathaniel C. Carter as excursion agent.

Fork of the American River and also in Mormon Island and Amador County, and in the early fifties held several government posts. He was, consecutively, assistant legal agent for the United States Land Commission in San Francisco, the Los Angeles agent for the commission, concurrently city and district attorney for Los Angeles city and county (to fill unexpired terms), and subsequently was thrice elected district attorney of Los Angeles County. He was admitted to the state senate in 1856. Despite these services, he was temporarily barred from practice in Los Angeles on his return from the battlefields of the Civil War, but was afterward pardoned by President Johnson. He then served a term as mayor of Los Angeles, helped found the Farmers and Merchants Bank, and invested in Glendale citrus land. Both he and his nephew, Erskine Ross, contributed much to the growth of the San Rafael area, and Ross's name is perpetuated in a modern subdivision, Rossmoyne.

Another Glendale promoter, who extended his realty activities to Orange County, was Alfred Chapman, a San Gabriel resident. Born in 1829, Chapman graduated from West Point and served in the army before entering the practice of law. In Los Angeles he went into partnership with Andrew Glassell and George H. Smith, the latter a Confederate officer, and became a public figure to the extent of being named, at various times, city attorney, district attorney, and superintendent of schools. In 1879 he devoted himself to citrus ranching, and bought 1,600 acres of the Santa Anita property. By the time of his death he had subdivided and sold 900 acres. Chapman's interest in Glendale real estate has been recounted, as was his founding, with Glassell, of the city of Orange.

Across the hills, Ivar A. Weid, a Danish immigrant, made two purchases of Hollywood real estate which caused him to be dubbed "one of the early landed proprietors of Los Angeles county."[12] His acquisitions included 400 acres between the present Second Street and Santa Monica Boulevard, extending from Western Avenue to the Hollywood Cemetery. Another purchase, of 240 acres, included hillside property around Weid Canyon. Weid had arrived in this country during the Civil War and had immediately joined the Union Army. He was promoted to a captaincy, and after the war entered merchandising in San Francisco. Here he remained until 1871, when he invested in Los Angeles County land. Among his other realty projects was the subdivision of an area four miles west of the courthouse, on Temple Street. Weid also held a government position as United States revenue gauger.

John D. Bicknell, another attorney, was one of the most successful boom realtors. He was born in Vermont in 1838, graduated from the University of Wisconsin, and became, at various times, a teacher, captain of a western emigrant train, prospector, and lawyer. His legal business in Los Angeles involved some of the most famous partnerships of post-Civil War days, including a four-year association with Stephen M. White. Bicknell was vice-president of the First National Bank, president of the Western Union Oil company, and an active clubman. His realty ventures, among which were the markedly successful town developments of Monrovia and Azusa, proved so profitable that he abandoned his legal practice some years before his death in 1911, and his total holdings were appraised at $1,340,000.

Jonathan Sayre Slauson arrived in California in 1868, after practicing law in New York and Nevada. He entered the mining business in the latter state, and participated in politics sufficiently to be elected mayor of Austin. Slauson then went to San Francisco, and eventually arrived in Los Angeles,

[12]James M. Guinn, *A History of California and an Extended History of Los Angeles and Environs* (1915), II, 263.

where he organized the Los Angeles County Bank, was director of the Santa Monica railroad and an investor in several
street railways, became a director of the Southern Pacific
Railroad, and aided in the organization of the Los Angeles
Chamber of Commerce. His philanthropic activities included
support of orphans' homes and the local Young Men's Christian Association. Realty development interested him most,
however, and he was a conspicuously successful boom promoter, purchasing 5,800 acres of the Azusa Ranch in 1885
and adding 7,800 acres of the Rancho San José. Retaining
500 acres of the Azusa land for himself, he sold a part interest
in the remainder to Bicknell, Hellman, and others, and organized, with their help, the Azusa Land and Water Company.
Slauson sold his San José property in 1887, at the boom's
height, but continued to develop his own 500 acres as a citrus
grove. He constructed his own packing and shipping plant,
which he named the Foothill Citrus Company. He owned
other citrus land and much city property. Slauson died in
1905, and an important boulevard bears his name.

Accounts of boom subdivisions, building construction, and
improvement projects mention, time and time again, one of
the most active promoters of Los Angeles—Moses L. Wicks.
One of the younger boomers, Wicks was born in Mississippi
in 1852 and was therefore only thirty-five years of age when
the boom reached its climax. Nevertheless, he managed to
identify himself with realty activity all the way from the
Temécula Valley to Ballona Inlet and to aid in the establishment of numerous large-scale business organizations. "There
are few prominent enterprises in this portion of the state in
which he has not been one of the leading promoters," was
Bancroft's encomium.[13] Wicks's father was a prosperous Tennessee banker and railway man, while Wicks himself took a

[13]Hubert Howe Bancroft, *History of California* (1884-90), VII, 8 n.
Wicks is often confused with his brother, Moye, a Los Angeles attorney.

law course at the University of Virginia and began practice
in Anaheim in 1875. Later moving to Los Angeles, he soon
permitted real estate operations to overshadow his legal work.
In 1882 he invested in Pomona lands and shortly afterward bought a piece of the Dreyfus Tract, a part of the
Rancho San Rafael. He purchased San Bernardino property,
acquired the Dalton portion of the Rancho San José, and was
instrumental in founding most of the land and development
companies required to plat and sell these properties. In addition, he became affiliated with two others: the organization
to develop Ballona Harbor, and the Temécula Land and
Water Company. Wicks was furthermore interested in the
Savings Fund and Building Association of Los Angeles, the
Los Angeles and Santa Monica Railroad, the Abstract and
Title Insurance Company, and the California Bank. Two of
his most picturesque ventures were the Ballona Harbor project
and the development of a water supply in the hill district of
Los Angeles.

Aside from Senator Maclay, the chief promoter of San
Fernando Valley was Col. James B. Lankershim. Coming to
California as a farmer, he supervised a grain warehouse in San
Francisco and managed stock ranches in Fresno and San
Diego counties. He invested in 60,000 acres in San Fernando
Valley in 1872, and subdivided a portion in 1887, selling the
remainder of his holdings, in 1910, to the Lankershim, Van
Nuys Company for subdivision. Other of his activities included the presidency of the Main Street Savings Bank, the
erection of the Lankershim Building in 1890, the organization
of the Los Angeles Farming and Milling Company for the
purpose of utilizing the product of his San Fernando grain-
fields, and the construction of the San Fernando Building in
1908. He was Park Commissioner of Los Angeles, a lieutenant
colonel in the National Guard, a delegate to Washington to
lobby for harbor improvement, and a prominent clubman.

~§ The Boom of the Eighties ⮞

An account of the Santa Monica bay area would be incomplete without mention of Abbot Kinney, one of the most vigorous and enterprising individuals to associate himself with the southern-California boom. A well-to-do New Jerseyan born in 1850, Kinney had the benefit of a European education and much travel, and arrived in California in 1880 with many ideas and superabundant energy. He first became interested in citrus culture in the Sierra Madre region, later was appointed assistant commissioner, with Helen Hunt Jackson, to investigate the California Indian situation, and in 1885 was named chairman of the state forest board. The range of his publications makes him worthy of the title of "universal man" of the southern California realty renaissance; his books include works on sociology, parenthood, the Australian ballot, the reservation system, the tariff, and climatology. He was president of the Southern California Academy of Sciences and a member of the Southern California Forest and Water Association and of the Yosemite Park Commission. In addition, he helped organize the Santa Monica Improvement Company, a civic group devoted to the welfare and progress of the community, assisted in founding the local library, and in all ways endeavored to utilize his wealth in a socially profitable manner.

Kinney's realty developments were original and spectacular. In 1886 he planned to subdivide Santa Monica Canyon, west of the town, and transform it into the "Nob Hill" of the region. The platting was carried out, a railway extension was planned to connect the Southern Pacific with the canyon's mouth, and, to demonstrate Kinney's interest in forestry, a station site on the hills was donated to the state board of which he was a member. The design failed because Kinney was too good a businessman to pass up the Southern Pacific's offer for his property, and he was quite willing to see his project transformed with chameleon-like suddenness from a

Nob Hill to a prospective Battery. His enthusiasm for California real estate did not diminish, however; through his efforts and those of his partner, F. G. Ryan, southern Santa Monica, the present Ocean Park, was developed in 1891. Later, Kinney grasped an opportunity to purchase the salt marshes and sand dunes of the southern bay area and to plan an even more ambitious project—the "Venice of America." The marsh was drained, canals were built, and by 1905 the new town began to take shape. Oil development later spoiled Venice as a beach resort.

Because Pasadena played such an important part in the great boom, and because much information is available about its developers, more space will be given to discussion of its two chief promoters than might seem their due. However, both of them are interesting characters—typical of the leaders of those hordes who migrated to California to seize the western land-bait which dangled so seductively before them.

Benjamin D. Wilson (or "Don Benito," as he was nicknamed) has been dubbed an "average southern Californian."[14] In many respects he was, for he arrived with an emigrant train in the early forties, married into a Spanish family (the Yorbas), and became a respected and venerable gringo landholder, whose Yankee enterprise, coupled with the richness of his possessions, resulted in astonishing local development. Details of his career are well known; his own account and that of a recent investigator have made familiar his adventures in the Micheltorena-Pico war, his capture in the battle of Chino, and his political activities as mayor of Los Angeles, state senator, and Indian agent. His realty activities have also been described, but perhaps they are sufficiently important to bear recapitulation. Wilson's landholdings were vast. He owned the Jurupa Ranch near Riverside, controlled in his

[14]Caughey, in *Huntington Library Quarterly*, II, 285.

wife's name part of the great Rancho Santa Ana, and bought, in partnership with W. T. Sanford, the Rancho San José de Buenos Ayres. Later he added the Huerta de Cuate, a small property of 128 acres purchased from Hugo Reid's widow, which became Lake Vineyard, his home estate. From Manuel Garfías he purchased the Rancho San Pasqual, of which he afterward sold an undivided half interest to Dr. John Griffin;[15] and by several complicated deals he acquired much of the land once belonging to the San Gabriel Mission. In addition to other partnership purchases which are not easy to trace in detail, Wilson owned, with Phineas Banning and associates, 2,400 acres of the Rancho San Pedro.

Wilson used his lands for three purposes: stock raising, vineyard culture, and subdivisions. The droughts of the sixties ended the chief business of the "cow counties," and at the time of Wilson's death, in 1878, the increase of immigration had already forecast the extinction of the vineyards, at least in the Pasadena area—although J. De Barth Shorb, his son-in-law, carried on as a grape grower for several years after Wilson's death. Don Benito's activities as a realtor were largely centered in the operations of the Lake Vineyard Land and Water Company, chiefly engaged in developing Pasadena east of Fairoaks. These activities of his have already been described, and only their significance will be noted. It will be recalled that much of the difficulty regarding the purchase of San Pasqual lands by the San Gabriel Orange Grove Association was due to Wilson's and Griffin's differences of opinion. Whereas Griffin did not wish to be bothered with details of

[15]John Strother Griffin was born in Virginia in 1816, graduated from the University of Pennsylvania, and entered medical practice in Louisville. He joined the army as a medical officer, was with Kearny at Santa Fé and San Pasqual, and then became staff medical officer under General Persifor Smith at Benicia. He resigned from the army in 1854 and came to Los Angeles, where he began the development of land east of the river. He died in 1898.

subdivision, and preferred outright sale to the Association, Wilson refused flatly to sell, and insisted on a division of his holdings so that he could market his lands in his own way. Don Benito thus proved his own adaptability and served as an example of many Californios whose careers included business or the professions, stock ranching, farming, and finally real estate. Wilson is an outstanding illustration of the importance of the human element in the real-estate boom of the eighties. Although he died before the great boom ran its course, he paved the way for its utilization of his lands, and demonstrated the willingness of the Yankee Californio to break through the traditional conservatism of his Latin environment.

The other outstanding Pasadena realty leader was David M. Berry, representative of the San Gabriel Orange Grove Association, and a detailed discussion of his trials and tribulations will serve to illustrate the career of a typical colony agent. Berry arrived in California in 1873 and examined much of the available land in southern California before deciding on San Pasqual. On September 12 of that year he reported to Dr. Elliott, eastern head of the organization (which was still the Indiana Colony), that he had found a tract of 2,800 acres at ten dollars per acre, which could be subdivided and sold at a profit of 1,000 per cent. "There is in all," said Berry, "a tract of 5600 acres but half belongs to Wilson, who is getting $1500 yearly per acre from his orange trees and *he has quit selling land.*"[16] Berry suggested buying, not only the San Pasqual portion, but also the "upper end," of San Fernando Valley, from its Spanish owner; and at another time he favored the purchase from Griffin of the land southeast of the San Pasqual area. He opened an office on Main Street and advertised his firm as follows:

[16]David M. Berry to Thomas Balch Elliott, Sept. 12, 1873.

❧ The Boom of the Eighties ❧

Los Angeles Real Estate Agency
32 Main St.
WILEY & BERRY
Land of Every Description, and City Property for Sale.
Money Loaned, and Colony Lands Selected.[17]

Berry realized very soon that the Indiana Colony was bound to fail, and in October, 1873, he suggested the formation of a syndicate. If the colony still wanted land, he believed he could get some San Bernardino acreage for it.

Wilson caused some difficulties in the pre-sale division of the property. Don Benito objected, in the first place, to Shorb's plan of dividing the water, but apparently gave in, for Berry stated that Wilson usually permitted his son-in-law to "have his own way."[18] Further trouble was encountered when the Association chose the upper half of the lands in question, instead of the lower. This dispossessed several immigrants who had reached an agreement with Wilson regarding settlement on his lands. In November, Berry reported:

We did not make our payment today because Wilson is disappointed because we chose the upper half, and he wants to express his disappointment by trying to coax us to let his North Carolina Pikes remain where they are, and we won't.

He divided the ranch to suit himself, and made *the upper half the best*, and so we chose that. That's what's the matter with Don Benito Wilson.

Griffin is mad and sent word to Benjamin D. Wilson that he had the privilege of a choice and had chosen, but rather than have a "Damned Row" he would give $1000 to get rid of Don Benito's relatives from the Ranch. We wait the result of the cussing of these old and lifelong friends, who seem to love each other better after each damning.[19]

[17]*Idem*, Oct. 6, 1873; July 6, 1874.

[18]*Idem*, Oct. 15, 1873.

[19]*Idem*, Nov. 20, 22, 1873.

The organization of the syndicate which Berry advocated in November, 1873, solved the colony's financial troubles for the time being, but Berry had already experienced many difficulties. One was the basic question of salary, and lengthy and vitriolic were the pleas, threats, and denunciations sent by Berry to the colony through his friend, Dr. Elliott. In October, 1873, he wrote:

I sent you September 22, an account of my expenditures for the colony $176.28. Now if I give six weeks hard work to the colony for nothing, and at least $300 more than I have charged in my expenses it seems quite enough. If they are going to pay it, why not do it? If not, why not say so? I am disgusted and offended at such treatment. It is shameful.[20]

Another hardship which Berry was compelled to undergo was the problem of getting the colony group, 2,500 miles away, to act on his recommendations and to carry out pledges which he made in its name. Colony members were exceedingly loath to contribute toward expenses: Berry requested $500 to bind the San Pasqual deal, and the colony, after suitable delay, sent him $200. He replied angrily: "People here will think I represent a d—— small set of capitalists who can't raise over $200 on a trade of $20,000. Isn't it very thin? I am ashamed."[21] When the panic of 1873 struck the East, the colony project, of course, succumbed. Berry, seeing the long-hoped-for deal in a fair way to vanish, reproached the colonists for not acting during flush times: "It is remarkable how many wanted to join the colony as long as there was no money to pay, but as soon as pay-day came around, they were not to be found! . . . Happy colonists! buying land for nothing!!!"[22]

[20]*Idem*, Oct. 14, 1873.
[21]*Idem*, Oct. 19, 1873.
[22]*Idem*, Nov. 4, 1873.

Even after the formation of the syndicate, details of long-distance business transactions were vexing. On November 26 he complained:

Now just imagine that people are just as well educated here as there and just as honorable, and know how to make conveyances of land in accordance with the law. You can order those drafts honored or we shall fill up the list here without you. I can send a plat, *if it will do any good*, but I have got tired of writing, writing, writing and being misunderstood. Already I have written two hundred letters to you and others about San Pasqual and sometimes a dozen pages a day. Now you know that I cannot afford to do so any longer. It is more than you have a right to ask, and more than I would ask of anybody.[23]

The draft, when it arrived, required the signature of the surveyor, who by this time was on another job, some miles out in the desert. Berry was all but speechless: "If your next remittance comes in the same shape I don't know what we shall do besides getting mad."[24] Toward the end of November Berry was thoroughly disgusted with such practices. "You change your minds so often that we cannot tell what is wanted and when wanted."[25] And in December he abruptly reduced his burden by ceasing to act as colony agent, confining his activities thenceforth to being a local real-estate agent and representative of the San Gabriel Orange Grove Association. But his troubles were not yet over, for he became involved in a plot in which someone distributed anonymous letters accusing Berry and Elliott of being in a "ring" to swindle the Association stockholders. Berry exploded with wrath and resigned both from the Association and from its secretaryship. His resignations were not accepted, and a short time

[23]*Idem*, Nov. 26, 1873.
[24]*Idem*.
[25]*Idem*, Nov. 27, 1873.

later the scheme was exposed and declared to be the work of a "scoundrel" who had failed to sell the colony his lands. Even the realty business was irksome. Berry said that he was "tired out showing land to Eastern scoundrels and liars who only pretend they want land in order to be shown around free. Such wretches are all abroad. . . They haven't brains enough to see that land will advance every year."[26]

Clearly, promoters were not guilty of *all* the mischief. Berry was but one of many sincere enthusiasts who believed intensely in southern California's future and who were convinced that with effective promotion the southland would prove a treasure-trove for publicists and investors alike. And, despite his tribulations, he maintained the unshakable confidence of the true southern-California booster, for, after all his violent missives to Elliott, after all his complaints, pleas, accusations, and disgust, he wrote Elliott again in June of 1874, when the Association scheme was well under way: "Now if you can come and carry out what we have started I will run the ranch and start another colony next winter."[27]

Many amusing tales have been told of less-prominent promoters. Pasadena had its share of these local characters who contributed to boom tradition. Edward C. Webster was one of the more flamboyant:

He was a speculator at all times and would buy a subdivision in the planet Mars if the prospect scanned good. . . . "Ed" could approach a man who had no thought of participating in the proceedings going on about him; in ten minutes have him absorbed in a scheme, and in thirty, drawing his check. He could buy more, for less money, than any other man in town, because he made the seller believe in him, and trust his capacity to pull through any proposition he handled.[28]

[26]*Idem*, Mar. 24, 1874.

[27]*Idem*, June 4, 1874.

[28]John Windell Wood, *Pasadena, California: Historical and Personal* (1917), pp. 160-61.

❦ The Boom of the Eighties ❧

John McDonald, also of Pasadena, was the first to organize moonlight excursions to real estate tracts. He lured so many prospects by this plan that two assistants were needed to help him take in money by aid of lantern light. Typical promoters' ways may be illustrated by the following anecdote: Johnny Mills, another Pasadena realtor, rushed into a drugstore one evening, interrupting the druggist in his preparation of a prescription. Mills showed him a map, announcing that a new tract would be opened the next morning. He said he desired to sell the druggist the first lot. The man at first refused, but, when Mills rushed out of the store to catch a streetcar, the druggist called him back and gave him ten dollars as first payment on a 750-dollar lot. High-pressure informality was the essence of boom psychology.

Perhaps the best of these stories is the following, found in a Santa Barbara boom pamphlet:

A little dapper man, with a mild eye and an Eastern make-up, called upon one of our real live boomers the other day and asked, in the very softest and meekest tone, if he had any land for sale. The great real-estate King, not deigning to lift his eyes from his important business, asked in a loud facetious tone if he wanted a colony, or would a township do him. The little man seemed embarrassed and hoped he would be excused if he had mistaken this for a small retail place, he meant no offense, etc., etc., Then the great magnate thawed out somewhat, and took the small man in his chariot to the *Great Paradise Regained Tract,* where he filled him with a half-hour speech, fairly bestudded with glittering facts and figures, regarding this wonderful piece of land, and hinted, in closing, that that was the kind of North Americans we were out here in the West. When the speaker concluded, for lack of breath, the small, mild-eyed man quietly removed his coat and, rolling up his sleeves, he climbed upon the fence, and, clearing his throat, said: "Now allow me to describe this piece of property in the Eastern tongue." Whew! talk about thoughts that breathe and words that burn!! The manner in which that stranger threshed the atmosphere with his arms and used up the mother tongue was *prodigious.*

When he finished, the magnate asked feebly of the stranger what his business was, and where he had come from. The small man said he had graduated in real-estate booming in Chicago, and had practised in Kansas City, Omaha, and all the principal towns of the West, and, elevating his voice, he stated that he was going to open a real-estate office right in that neighborhood and going to do business, too, and called upon anyone within sound of his voice not to forget it, either. The now vanquished and thoroughly exhausted magnate leaned heavily against the fence and asked, in a voice husky with emotion, and scarcely above a whisper: "Stranger, can I post bills for you?"[29]

Promoters were most successful in rural areas, where entire towns could be laid out. They sold one-hundred-dollar property at $300 to $500 per acre, promising it would yield $1,000 in orange profits; some platted "choice villa" tracts, which were priced at $800 to $1,000 per acre, their value lying largely in view and prospective improvements. The majority of these tracts were "paper towns," although a few were railway stations or agricultural centers. Cash sales were unusual; most customers bought on contract, paying one-third or one-fourth down and the balance in semiannual instalments. As stated before, many of the transactions were never recorded, property being reconveyed at tremendous speed. This suited the boomers, for quick turnover, with minimum cash outlay, was their goal. The recording of transfers was subject to other complications, among them the fact that the record stated the full selling price, which was often not completely paid. Of some records the opposite was true: the transaction was filed "for the consideration of one dollar," and no price value was listed. Real-estate statistics of the boom period must therefore be considered with reservations, absolute accuracy being impossible. They are valuable, however, as indices.

One of the worst features of boom procedure was the method of handling options. As a pure speculation a pro-

[29]E. McD. Johnstone, *By Semi-Tropic Seas* . . . (1888) (lacks pagination).

moter would often take out an option on a lot, for sixty or
ninety days, by payment of a few dollars. Thereby, the property was reserved, and, if prices rose meanwhile, the promoter would profit. If they fell, he lost only the deposit.

The habit of standing in line to wait for the presentation
of a particularly desirable piece of land has already been
referred to in the case of certain San Gabriel Valley towns.
One village was said to have been so enthusiastically welcomed that investors formed a line Sunday night for a
Wednesday sale. The promoter hired a hall, moved the line
into it, and had the enthusiasts sign up in order of precedence.
He thereafter called the roll from time to time, and, if anyone failed to answer, the line moved up. Despite so pro-
pitious a start, the town was a failure, because most of the
attending buyers proved to be tramps and down-at-heel
gentry who did not possess the price of a lot, but who hoped
to profit by selling their positions in line. This story takes its
place among the legends of the boom as an unverifiable incident which might well have been true.

A necessary prerequisite of town platting was the surveying of the property, and here, of course, there was opportunity for dishonesty. Strangely enough, most surveys were
accurate but a notable exception was the platting of the town
of Rosecrans, on the southern slope of a rise known as Howard
Summit. The surveyor failed to plumb his stakes, and as a
result the buyer obtained a forty-nine-foot lot instead of the
advertised fifty-foot one. Some notoriously fraudulent tracts
slipped by with setting block-corner stakes only, and others,
like Sidney Hamburg's protégés, were even more flagrant in
their slipshod mapping.

As in all economic flurries, the easy flow of capital encouraged fraud and corruption. That such methods did not
take firmer root in the fertile soil of California is a tribute to
the boom's personnel. Tricksters soon found themselves en-

tangled with the law; respectable citizens who disdained quackery were as much interested in upholding California business standards as in profiting from the excitement.

The victims of promoters came from many walks of life. They included winter tourists who suddenly discovered that southern California was habitable in the summer as well, businessmen "investigating the situation," invalids, and prospective middle-class settlers, chiefly from farms in the North Central states. The outstanding characteristic of these people was their prosperity. The *San Francisco Call* commented: "The quality of the newcomers is not less noteworthy than their numbers. They are almost invariably persons of American birth, good education, and some means. . . . This is the best American stock; the bone and sinew of the nation; the flower of the American people."[30] The victims, unlike those of other booms, were often intelligent men of property, and sometimes the heaviest losers were the people who carefully kept out of the excitement during its early phases, and then allowed themselves to be drawn in just in time for the crash. Van Dyke protested: "The Californians have been accused of shearing a drove of innocent lambs from the East. If true, this would have been one of the most interesting features of the times; for, as we shall see, the lambs afterward sheared the shearers in charming style. But the sad and homely truth is, that nearly all the innocents were wise and successful men who insisted on being shorn."[31] Not least numerous among the sufferers were the original California landowners, who sold prematurely at moderate prices, and then, when the frenzy reached its height, rebought their property at advanced rates and were caught in the collapse.

The ill-fated investors themselves contributed to the debacle by their unshaken optimism and confidence. Men who should

[30]Quoted in *Ventura Free Press*, Nov. 9, 1887.
[31]Van Dyke, *Millionaires of a Day*, p. 56.

have known better made extravagant statements. Philip D. Armour, at the peak of the flurry, said: "This is merely preliminary to a boom that will outclass the present activity as thunder to the crack of a hickory nut."[32] On September 6, 1887, the *Pasadena Daily Union* published a round robin by local businessmen, entitled "The Outlook." Some of the statements included were the following:

There is not the slightest doubt in my mind that the coming winter will see more people here than have come in all the previous years together. From every avenue of information news comes of thousands, even tens of thousands, who are coming to Southern California for the winter. . . . People do not come to California any more solely on account of the climate. They find that this is the greatest money-making country in the world, as well as a sanitarium, consequently they come from all quarters to invest their wealth in her real estate and products. . . .

The outlook for the coming season seems better to me than it has at any time since I came to Pasadena. . . .

I anticipate a very bright and prosperous winter season for Pasadena, and, more than that, I believe that the prosperity of our beautiful city is going to be permanent.

I look for Southern California to have a bigger boom this season than it ever enjoyed before. It will not be an inflated boom, but a period of genuine prosperity.

Years afterward, such statements and the propaganda of promoters could be justified by pointing to the enhanced property values of southern California. True, the boom was temporary, but the most reckless boosters proved to be more accurate long-time prophets than did the realistic skeptics.

These persons—promoters, respectable citizen-landowners, dupes, and tourists—formed the bulk of the population during boom years. But other groups also entered, giving southern California a conglomerate and none-too-savory populace. Approximately 50,000 people lived in Los Angeles during the

[32]Mayo, *Los Angeles,* p. 88.

boom's climax, and the city jail had, on the average, from 250 to 300 inmates; ten years later, with a population twice as large, the average was only a hundred. Santa Monica hoodlums gained such notoriety that Long Beach smugly aired its own moral superiority in comparison. Said the *Los Angeles Times:*

One of the strongest arguments in favor of incorporation [of Santa Monica] was that the town, if incorporated, would be better able to check the lawlessness of the Los Angeles hoodlums, male and female, who resort thither by the hundred every Sunday. These toughs committed some of the most atrocious outrages against law and decency, both at the beach and on the home-bound train; and their actions were fast scaring off the thousands of respectable people who like to go down from the city every summer Sunday for a few hours by the echoing sea. These riots went on practically unchecked last season and had begun again this year, but the severe examples made by the authorities a month ago did a good deal to check the evil. The Santa Monica authorities, too, got on their muscle, and appointed a lot of deputy marshals—having from six to ten on duty every Sunday. In view of all this the hoodlums have rather fully subsided, and Santa Monica, even on Sunday, is a pretty orderly place.

Another nuisance, hardly less prejudicial to the town, has been the prevalence of gamblers and robbers. These sharks, of every swindling stripe, have infested the place to a remarkable extent, and never a Sunday has gone by without their reaping a more or less rich harvest from the interminable sucker. The shell game is the favorite.[33]

Boom-time San Diego was also troublesome:

Gambling was open and flagrant; games of chance were carried on at the curbstones. . . . the desecration of Sunday was complete, with all drinking and gambling houses open, and with picnics, excursions, fiestas, and bullfights, the latter at the Mexican line, to attract men, women, and boys from religious influence.

[33]*Los Angeles Times,* June 15, 1887.

Theft, murder, incendiarism, carousals, fights, highway robbery, and licentiousness gave to the passing show many of the characteristics of the frontier camp.[34]

The boomers with their flagrant and noisy business methods, the victims with their ready cash and unfailing optimism, and the less respectable hangers-on made the region colorful and lively. Quick action was the watchword, and if anything more was needed to rouse southern California from pastoral lethargy, these newcomers provided it. From 1888 onward, the southern counties were imbued with Anglo-American aggressiveness.

[34]William E. Smythe, *History of San Diego* (1908), II, 428. (Quoted from Walter Gifford Smith, *The Story of San Diego* [1892].)

CHAPTER XVI

Irrigation Improvements

S OUTHERN CALIFORNIA'S history is inextricably involved
with the story of water development. If the region below the Tehachapi had been content to maintain a
"cow county" status, there would have been no need for irrigation, but with the development of horticulture and the
arrival of new citizens whose interests went beyond a pastoral
economy, the search for water became of prime importance.
Before the development of extensive conduit projects, like the
Los Angeles Aqueduct and the Boulder Dam diversion, southern California's water came from two main sources: surface
streams flowing from mountain canyons, and ground water
store in *ciénagas,* or marshy sinks. Water from the former was
obtained by means of diversion dams, tunnels, ditches, and
flumes; from the latter, by wells and the impounding of artesian sources.

In view of the rugged character of the Sierra Madre, the
building of high dams in some of the larger canyons, as has

227

been done in recent years, might have seemed to be the least difficult method of furnishing a steady supply of water. Early opinion, however, felt that these canyons were in general too narrow and steep for storage sites, and that such projects would be overly expensive in proportion to their value. As cost was thus the chief hindrance to irrigation development, the boom, with its easy-flowing capital and ambitious promotion policies, was responsible for many new undertakings in this field. For example, in the foothill belt east of Los Angeles alone, there were fifty-seven irrigation companies organized between 1880 and 1902; of these, thirteen were formed during the rising-price period of the early eighties; twelve were organized during the boom years 1886-88; and the remainder were started largely by the stimulus given their respective areas through boom settlement. Before 1880 scattered ditch companies, with here and there a loose organization of water-right holders, were the only developmental groups in the region, and the first great acceleration of irrigation improvement, not only in the foothill belt but in all southern California, was due to the great boom.

Los Angeles city itself had depended upon various extensions of the old *zanja* (water-ditch) system fed by the spasmodic flow of the Los Angeles River. Irrigation was confined in the seventies to the region close to the river banks, but bond issues, necessary post-flood improvements in 1884, and urbanization of the community gradually expanded the facilities. The boom's chief effect upon local irrigation was to force agriculturists farther away from the city limits, and, by the reduced need for irrigation water in the city itself, to enable the construction of widespread ramifications of the *zanja* system.

The area south and east of Los Angeles had been irrigated in early days by wells and ditches diverting water from the Los Angeles River and from the two streams—the San Gabriel and the Rio Hondo—which cut the Puente Hills at the Paso de Bartolo. The Downey region saw three new water companies organized during the first months of the boom—in each case merely a consolidation of water rights which had existed for many years. Toward the close of 1884 the Los Nietos Irrigation Company was incorporated for the purpose of utilizing irrigation works supposedly started by Pío Pico. In May, 1885, the Agricultural Ditch and Water Company was formed to supply the lands southeast and east of Downey; and, about the same time, the Arroyo Ditch and Water Company united several holders of rights in the San Gabriel River flow. The last-named organization immediately became involved in litigation with fifteen of the original claim holders who refused to join, and also with the Santa Ana Irrigating Company over apportionment of the San Gabriel waters.

Farther north, the Alhambra Addition Water Company obtained a lead over many of its contemporaries, because of the early speculative interest in Alhambra real estate. The company was founded in 1883 to control the flow from El Molino Canyon, east of the dike on which the Raymond Hotel was built, and it later augmented the supply by digging wells. Near the foothills, Elias J. Baldwin obtained water rights in Santa Anita and Little Santa Anita canyons (which he shared with the Sierra Madre Water Company), together with certain *ciénagas* and wells, and part of the supply from the marshes north of the Paso de Bartolo. These he developed, both during and after the boom, until they were irrigating more than 1,200 acres devoted to citrus and deciduous fruits, grapes, and alfalfa. The Sierra Madre concern had been formed in 1882 by that dashing promoter, Nathaniel C. Carter. Four miles northwest of Sierra Madre, local settlers, including Monrovia-founder James F. Crank, organized the Precipice Canyon Water Company in 1887, to divert and use waters of Eaton (Precipice) Canyon. Near by, citizens of

Monrovia were obliged in 1886 to organize a water company for the purpose of buying some of Baldwin's rights in Sawpit Canyon, and they afterward constructed a reservoir and pipe line.

Duarte and Azusa had more complex irrigation histories. Two companies were formed in the early eighties to water Duarte lands: the Duarte Mutual Irrigation and Canal Company, to supply the thousand acres of citrus groves closest to the foothills; and the Beardslee Water Ditch Company, which piped to the 400 acres above the San Gabriel Wash, west and south of the Mutual's district. The two companies apportioned waters of the upper San Gabriel so that the Mutual obtained about two-thirds of the flow. The boom stimulated the construction of new works, which were completed in 1887 and paid for in the ratio of 1,260 parts by the Mutual group to 225 parts by Beardslee.

Disputes between claimants of San Gabriel River water became so intense and complex that a settlement was made in 1889 which effectively resolved their differences. How these various claims were built up is clearly seen in the case of Azusa, which depended upon the San Gabriel for its supply. Three companies complicated the problem here: the Azusa Water Development and Irrigation Company, organized in 1882 and rechristened the Covina Irrigating Company in 1886; the Azusa Irrigating Company, incorporated in 1886; and the Azusa Land and Water Company, formed by Jonathan Slauson in 1887 to supply his new town, and in 1888 given the name, Azusa Agricultural Water Company. These concerns furnished water, respectively, to 1,400 acres, 4,000, and 900. The 1889 agreement solved disputes among the three claimants by permitting them to participate in a division of the San Gabriel flow into 720 parts, placing it under the control of a committee of nine, who thereafter adjudicated the claims.

⊸§ *Irrigation Improvements* §⊷

The career of the Glendora Water Company illustrates how boom enthusiasm caused overexpansion and final disaster. Organized in 1887, the group bought most of the rights in Big Dalton Canyon and proceeded to construct 63,000 dollars' worth of improvements. These excessive expenditures and the boom's slump forced the company to sell out to Chicago financiers. Another case of poor management was the boom-time use of the San Dimas Canyon flow. In 1885 the San Dimas Land and Water Company was organized to build pipe lines connecting the ravine with the mesa lands east of the lower wash, but the San José Ranch Company, formed in 1887, bought the San Dimas Company, added to the rights thus obtained those of a *ciénaga* one mile southeast of San Dimas and those appurtenant to Sycamore Flat Canyon, and agreed to furnish the disbanded company with thirty-five miner's inches of water.[1] Overinvestment in tunnels, conduits, and other improvements, however, coupled with poor management, forced reorganization in 1894.

Pasadena showed interest in water development directly proportionate to its realty activity. In 1874 Wilson organized the Lake Vineyard Land and Water Company, later managed by Shorb, which obtained water from Devil's Gate springs and supplied 2,500 acres. Improvements included a 13,000-foot canal, "the first work of its class in southern California since the days of the padres, but it has been extensively imitated since."[2] The company sold out in 1883, partly to the San Gabriel Orange Grove Association, and partly to a syndicate of twelve residents of Pasadena. The association's water rights were acquired in 1884 by the Pasadena Land and Water Company, and in the same year those of the syndicate were bought by the Pasadena Lake Vineyard Land and Water Company. Complications immediately followed. Some Pasa-

[1] A miner's inch consists of a flow of about nine gallons per minute.

[2] William Hammond Hall, *Irrigation in Southern California* (1888), p. 508.

231

dena water-right holders had refused to join either group, and by merely paying assessments thought to inveigle their way into a position where they could enjoy company improvements without purchasing stock. Difficulties were increased by the rapid expansion of urban Pasadena, which diminished the prospects for a stockholding irrigation concern. A lawsuit between the rival organizations resulted in division of Devil's Gate spring rights, giving seven-tenths to the Pasadena Lake Vineyard group. In 1887 the boom encouraged further improvements, and the two former competitors now amicably joined forces in laying a steel conduit to replace the ditch from the springs. During that year, also, the Arroyo Seco Water Company was formed to protect the claims of those right holders who had refused to participate in the organization of the Pasadena Lake Vineyard company; but the latter was plagued by internal dissension and was disincorporated in 1894. Despite the tumultuous early history of these rivals, order gradually evolved, and in 1904 the Pasadena city engineer estimated the total value of the works at more than $200,000.

Southeastern Pasadena was served by the Marengo Water Company, a firm established in 1884, which derived its supply from springs north of the Raymond dike. The company later constructed wells and tunnels along San Pasqual Wash. Northwestern Pasadena, consisting chiefly of the 1,800-acre Painter and Ball Tract, was served by the North Pasadena Land and Water Company, organized in 1885. This group possessed water rights in the arroyo above Millard Canyon, and acquired the tract as well, reimbursing the original owners with shares of stock. There were also numerous water companies on the outskirts of Pasadena, which owed either their inception or their first real success to the great boom.

Glendale was supplied from the waters of Verdugo Creek, owned jointly by several ranchers of the region. A lawsuit in

1870 apportioned the water into 10,000 shares, and ten years later a time schedule was adopted. The Verdugo Canyon Water Company, whose formal organization in June, 1884, resulted from the increase of boom land sales, furnished four subordinates: the Verdugo Springs Water Company, the Verdugo Pipe and Reservoir Company, the Glendale Reservoir and Pipe Association and the Child's Tract Water Company. Some development occurred in the Glassell and Chapman properties southeast of Glendale, known collectively as Boulevarde Valley. Northwest of Glendale, Tujunga Canyon's mouth was irrigated by a pipe system, and certain of its owners started the Monte Vista Colony in 1886. Here was one case in which water-right holders were responsible for the organization of a colony project, instead of the reverse, as was usually the situation.

There were three water companies in San Fernando Valley before the boom—all of them started as adjuncts to realty development. The San Fernando Land and Water Company owned the low-water flow of Pacoima Canyon and constructed a submerged dam, the "largest work of the kind yet attempted in Southern California."[3] It was built of boulder-filled cement, but despite its pretentiousness was a failure, either because of faulty construction or the lack of sufficient subsurface flow in the canyon sands. The Porter Land and Water Company owned rights in the east and west *ciénagas* near the town of San Fernando, in San Fernando Creek, and a half interest in Aliso Canyon. The San Fernando Valley Water Company was organized in 1888 and derived the bulk of its supply from works in Mormon Canyon, built during that year. The company had an agreement with the San Fernando Valley Improvement Company whereby the former owned the actual water rights and the latter built dams and conduits which it turned over to the water company in ex-

[3]Hall, pp. 525-26.

change for stock. The policy of the firm was to sell water shares independently of land purchases for $1,000 per miner's inch.

The Pomona Land and Water Company, which obtained its supply from San Antonio Canyon and auxiliary wells, organized three subsidiaries during the boom. One was the Irrigation Company of Pomona, formed in 1886, which distributed water rights on the basis of ten shares per acre of land sold; when a majority of the stock had been transferred, the management surrendered its control and sponsored the establishment of a mutual water company, on the order of the Chaffey enterprises. The company's sources of supply were San José Creek and numerous wells. The Del Monte Irrigation Company, begun in 1887, obtained its water from two *ciénagas:* the Del Monte, southeast of Claremont, and the Martín, west of the same town. Artesian wells were bored in 1886. The Palomares Irrigation Company was started about the same time, and depended on artesian wells. In the years of the boom's decline two more Pomona companies appeared. The Consolidated Water Company, dating from May, 1889, served the town by means of artesian wells and tunnels in a near-by *ciénaga* and in San Antonio Wash. The Orange Grove Tract Water Company was established in 1889, and irrigated both the Orange Grove and Vineyard tracts.

The flow from Cucamonga Canyon, not far away, supplied both the Hermosa Water Company and the Cucamonga Development Company. The Hermosa, which obtained in addition some of the Deer Canyon water, was organized in October, 1887, and installed 4,000 dollars' worth of improvements. *Ciénagas* which trapped the subsurface flow from these canyons irrigated more than 8,000 farm and vineyard acres west of San Bernardino; the *ciénagas* were controlled by the Cucamonga Water Company incorporated by owners of the Cucamonga Fruit Land Company, which financed most of the improvements. Between 1888 and 1890, the Fruit Land Company invested nearly $100,000 in waterworks, but subsequent dry years brought lawsuits and reorganization. Some of the *ciénaga* rights were owned by the Cucamonga Vineyard Association. Farther south, Richard Gird, patriarch of Chino, dug a series of wells which yielded nearly 350 inches of water during boom years. His 200,000-dollar investment was rendered useless, however, by dry years following the flurry, and his experience was but a forecast of the later dry seasons which ruined so many boom irrigation enterprises.

The projects of the Chaffey brothers were uniformly successful and efficient, and worthy of note because of the innovations in water-right management which they introduced. Their first enterprise was the Etiwanda Water Company, organized in 1882 with the assistance of L. M. Holt. It supplied 1,200 acres, and has been called the first real mutual water company, because a share of stock was transferred with each acre. The Chaffeys built one and one-half miles of V-shaped wooden flume and laid several miles of pipe to supply their colony. They depended solely on the canyon flow, as the subsoil water was too deep for wells. The Chaffey masterpiece, however, was Ontario, the "Model Colony," whose lands were watered by the flow from the east side of San Antonio Canyon. Despite rivalry, the San Antonio Water Company (organized by the Chaffeys) joined the Pomona Land and Water Company in building a dam in 1882. Their co-operation was short-lived, however, for in 1897 the Pomona organization sold out to Ontario. The San Antonio concern was strictly a mutual water company, with water shares transferred only to owners of colony acreage. George Chaffey's improvements were spectacular. In 1883 he began construction of a 3,000-foot tunnel in the gravel bed of the canyon, to trap the underground flow; it was completed in 1889 at a cost of $50,000. The supply was augmented by an

interest in the Eddy (Cucamonga) Tunnel, a structure built
to tap the water of a western *ciénaga;* the tunnel was 4,000 feet
long and lined by wells. The canyon and the Eddy Tunnel
were sufficient for the colony until 1893, when wells were
deemed necessary; but George Chaffey was relieved of the
responsibility of digging them, for in 1886 his rights passed
to the Ontario Land and Improvement Company, which
carried on his work.

Colony enterprises in the Santa Ana region were irrigated
by water from the lower Santa Ana Canyon, a winding,
rounded valley of the coast range. Anaheim colonists early
solved their water problem by building ditches from the river
to their lands: several companies were organized, but they dis-
puted violently among themselves until 1884, when the
formation of the Anaheim Union Water Company resolved
most of the quibbles. This company operated throughout the
boom, supplying 7,000 acres devoted chiefly to vineyards.
The town of Santa Ana had a less colorful irrigation history,
although the Anaheim Water Company sued Santa Ana's Semi-
Tropic Water Company in 1883 over division of the river's
flow. The Semi-Tropic concern and the Santa Ana Irrigation
Company, begun in 1877, served the city throughout boom
years, and the acreage under irrigation steadily increased from
6,400 in 1879 to 14,000 in 1886 and 15,000 in 1888.

The San Bernardino region was outstanding in its utilization
of boom capital for irrigation improvement, and the area was
further distinguished by the erection of one of the most ambitious irrigation projects in southern California, the Bear
Valley Dam. Although not strictly a boom project—having
been built in 1883-84—nevertheless it owed its financing to
the easing of credit which was a precursor of the great boom,
and owners' profits would have been much less, had it not
been for the numerous boom colonies which leased its waters.
This granite dam, 300 feet long and 64 feet high, was con-

structed at the western end of Bear Valley, a watershed of 45 square miles in the heights of the Sierra Madre. In 1883 a young engineer, F. E. Brown, and his partner, Hiram Barton, bought 3,800 acres in the valley from Los Angeles owners and 700 acres from the Southern Pacific Railroad. They organized the Bear Valley Land and Water Company, selling stock to eleven local subscribers, and the value of the stock rose from $25 in 1884 to $225 in 1887.

Various ditch and water companies in the vicinity of San Bernardino were either reorganized or enlarged during boom years. Among them was the Semi-Tropic Land Company, established in February, 1887, to take over the functions of the Lytle Creek Water Company, whose services had been impeded by chronic litigation. The City Creek Ditch, near San Bernardino, was extended during 1886 and 1887, and the East Twin Creek Ditch was purchased by a Kansas City syndicate in 1887. Legal difficulties halted the work of the latter organization in 1888.

The Riverside area experienced numerous troubles in settling its water problems. Development, under the management of the abortive Silk Center Association, started in 1869, but when this group was replaced by the Southern California Colony Association in 1870, work proceeded more speedily. Disputes began with the purchase of land south of Riverside by Evans and Sayward, and continued in increasing intensity for several years. They were resolved partially in 1875, with the formation of the Riverside Land and Irrigating Company, which gradually acquired the water rights, and with the establishment of the Riverside Canal Company in 1878— merely a second reorganization. Charles Felton, a financier who had sold his shares in the Riverside Colony to Evans and Sayward, still maintained his interest in the canal company. The difficulties largely arose from the diverging attitudes of Felton and the other stockholders. Finally, in 1884, L. M.

Holt proposed a compromise by which the canal company sold out to citizen water users, under the name of the Riverside Water Company. Encouraged by that amicable agreement and by boom prosperity, the directors voted two bond issues which resulted in more than 157,000 dollars' worth of improvements between 1884 and 1888. The land north of Riverside was watered chiefly by the Gage Canal, begun in 1885 and completed in the spring of 1887, while three other boom companies—the Vivienda Water Company, the North Riverside Land and Water Company, and the Jurupa Land and Water Company—supplied adjacent agricultural lands.

Four companies were organized in the Redlands area during boom years: the East Redlands Water Company, formed in 1886, and the West Redlands Water Company, the Domestic Water Company, and the Lugonia Water Company, all established in 1887. The first two of these concerns depended upon Bear Valley sources. Corona was supplied by several small organizations, of which two of the most important were the South Riverside Land and Water Company, begun in 1886, and the Temescal Water Company, incorporated two years later for the purpose of taking over the former's property. The Perris region drew upon Bear Valley waters, and when these failed in the early nineties, Perris suffered intensely; so many of its inhabitants moved to Riverside that the place was sometimes called the "valley on wheels."[4] East of this region, near the San Jacinto River, two rival water companies, the Fairview and the Hemet Valley, conducted a stormy dispute which resulted in near-violence. The former believed in direct action to the extent of filling in Fairview's ditch, but ensuing litigation in 1886 favored the latter. In January, 1887, the Hemet Valley Company, failing to find additional capital, was split into two separate organizations, one for land and one for water development.

[4]Holmes (et al.), *History of Riverside County*, p. 173.

Desert colonies were by their very nature dependent upon water development for success. An outstanding desert-irrigation project was that of the Palmdale Valley Land and Water Company, which tried to colonize the site of the now-flourishing winter resort of Palm Springs. Promoters planned to utilize the Whitewater River and built a small stone ditch in 1886-88. State Engineer Hall thought its capacity, claimed sufficient to supply 6,000 acres, was inadequate, but the developers contemplated adding other sources. The project was unsuccessful, and not until later enthusiasts came were the beauties of Palm Canyon and the winter desert climate exploited.

The San Diego area was especially prolific in boom irrigation enterprises—perhaps because of the secure foundation laid by earlier promoters. Coronado promoters organized the Otay Water Company and planned a one-hundred-foot dam, but failed to act. San Diego investors tried to carry on, and spent $10,000 on roads and dam foundation, but they, in turn, failed to complete their work. On the Mexican border the Mount Tecarte Land and Water Company, formed in 1888, designed a diversion of both Mexican and United States tributaries of the Tia Juana River to irrigate Otay Mesa. The San Diego River mothered two important boom projects. One was the San Diego Flume Company of 1886, whose founders included the chatty publicist, Theodore Van Dyke. The group sponsored improvements worth $900,000, and profited greatly from the increase in value of lands on the mesa at the flume's terminus. The other was the Mission Valley Water Company, incorporated in 1887, which planned a dam in the lower canyon of the San Diego River. The dam, started in the fall of 1887, was backed by San Diego citizens, who were commended by the state engineer for "following the judgment of the . . . priests, who selected this same field for the establishment of their first footing in California and made this the point where the first of many notable irrigation works was constructed, and where irrigation is believed to have been first successfully practiced in the State."[5]

Other southern projects included the Pamo Water Company of 1888, which intended to divert water from the San Dieguito (Bernardo) River to the Poway Valley and Linda Vista Mesa, but never accomplished anything. Up the coast, land operators from San Diego scheduled San Luis Rey River improvements to irrigate the Oceanside area. The contemplated structures, including a submerged dam below Pala, were not completed before the end of the boom, although in 1888 the company proceeded with a 500,000-dollar New York loan despite the contraction of credit facilities. Inland, the Fallbrook Water and Power Company, organized in 1887, projected a storage dam at the head of Temécula Canyon and a flume and pipe line to irrigate 3,000 acres.

The coastal region in general has not been considered in detail, except for the larger projects. It is necessary to add, however, that almost every land company interested in coastal property promulgated plans for augmenting or improving the water supply. As the coast needed less water than drier inland regions, these plans usually involved minor creek diversions or artesian-well drilling. A good example was the work of the Centinela-Inglewood Land Company, which dug eleven miles of ditches, built a short tunnel, and laid out a small reservoir to handle the waters of Centinela Springs. But here, as in other areas near the sea, irrigation was not, as in the arid interior, the *sine qua non* of settlement. If one stream failed, a *ciénaga* with a conveniently high water table could usually be found, and irrigation was seldom given the prominence in coastal advertising that it achieved in uplands like Ontario and Etiwanda.

The general influence of rainfall on boom economy pre-

[5]Hall, p. 85.

BEAR VALLEY, WATER SOURCE FOR THE SAN BERNARDINO REGION—DAM CONSTRUCTION
IN FOREGROUND BEGUN IN 1884

sents an interesting problem that cannot be summarily dismissed. Clearly, the amount of water available for crops in southern California's semiarid climate depended indirectly on rainfall; that is, there were few streams and no large natural lakes from which diversions could be made. Reliance had to be placed upon a scanty supply of ground water, which varied noticeably in proportion to precipitation, and thus there is logic in assuming that rainfall might have had a profound influence upon the developing horticultural economy. Yet, the boom reached its maximum intensity during years of declining rainfall averages, and it collapsed miserably during an increase in precipitation, which in 1890 set a six-year record. Although a prolonged drought preceding 1887 probably would have discouraged many settlements at the outset, no correlation apparently existed between property transfers and the abundance of water available for irrigation. In the face of these statistics, one must conclude that water development—that prime factor of southland habitation—was much more a result than a cause of the great boom. Irrigation received a necessary impetus, but southern California's growing thirst went unslaked until the arrival of William B. Mulholland, and, later, the Six Companies.

A corollary of the great boom was the passage of the Wright Act of 1887. Though not primarily a local measure, it was stimulated largely by southern irrigators like L. M. Holt, J. De Barth Shorb, and Judge North of Riverside. Passage of the act was brought about by the 1886 decision of the state supreme court that common-law principles regarding riparian rights were valid in California; this meant that riparian property owners had sole rights to the flow of streams which bordered their lands—an anomaly in arid regions where rainfall was insufficient to supply nonriparian acreage. Governor George Stoneman showed great interest in the problem and called a special session of the legislature to consider it.

Irrigation conventions were held: one in Riverside in 1884, at which southern irrigators really began the "war against riparianism"; and one in San Francisco in 1886, at which southern influence dictated the selection of Shorb as chairman of the executive committee. Pamphlets were published, and the press became actively interested. As a result, C. C. Wright, assemblyman from Stanislaus County, proposed the act of 1887, which finally defeated the claims of the riparian owners. This was "an act to provide for the organization and government of irrigation districts,"[6] and also for the holding of elections for bond issues to finance irrigation facilities. The law was attacked in the United States circuit court, but the federal supreme court reversed the lower court's decision and upheld the act.

The Wright Act was eminently successful and proved a temporary godsend to southern-California promoters. By 1890 fifty irrigation districts had been formed in the state, and thirty-one of them were in the southern counties. Los Angeles County had eleven, Orange one, San Bernardino seven, and San Diego twelve. Santa Barbara and Ventura counties did not form districts until later. The following table shows the number of acres of irrigated land in 1889, two years after the act's passage:[7]

County	Acres Irrigated	Per Cent of Irrigated Farm Land in County
Los Angeles	70,164	9.23
Orange	31,816	12.00
San Bernardino	37,907	12.00
San Diego	10,193	1.15
Santa Barbara	396	.08
Ventura	3,347	1.03
Total	153,823	Average 5.92

[6]California *Assembly Journal* (July, 1887), pp. 401, 494, 498, 693; *Laws and Resolutions Passed by the Legislature of 1885-86 at Its Extra Session* (1887), p. 29.

[7]From the United States Census Report for 1890, V, 41.

The average percentage of southern-county farm land under irrigation, as shown by the table, compares favorably with the state average of 4.69 per cent.

From the foregoing data it can be concluded that boom finance provided a fertile field for the growth of water-development projects. Like all enterprises started by the flurry, some were successful and made permanent contributions to southern California, while others died with the boom. A few of the weaker organizations that managed to last through the discouraging months of the collapse were given a knock-out blow by the dry seasons which afflicted southern acres in the early nineties. Those that succeeded in maintaining their precarious existence were almost unanimously forced to augment their water supply by pumping plants in near-by artesian basins. Not a few of the companies wasted precious funds in long-drawn-out litigation, and others, not mentioned in this chapter, existed only in promoters' conversation and tract leaflets. Most of them were affiliated with realty groups, which were as much interested in rapid land sales as in the efficient development of an adequate water supply. In general, boom enthusiasm, though sometimes harmful (as in the case of the overdevelopment of the poorly-watered Perris Valley), had more often a beneficial effect upon southern agriculture. By loosening purse strings, the flurry provided for a spurt of irrigation improvement that laid foundations for many subsequent decades of prosperous settlement.

CHAPTER XVII

Encouragement for
Education

B ECAUSE southern California was advertised as a good
place to live, educational facilities were naturally
stressed. Although common schools necessarily profited
from the boom, colleges and universities were considered to
be more picturesque and to have greater magnetism for the
lot buyer. If all the projected institutions of higher learning
had been completed, California would have had more of them
per capita than any other state of the Union. The staid, solid,
venerable character of a "college town" attracted promoters
in droves, and consequently the plans of nearly every community with ambitions included designs for a university.
Often these ambitions resulted, at least, in the creation of a
new school district; sometimes they merely vanished into
ghost-town oblivion. But along with the broken dreams and
shattered hopes many new institutions flourished. Enrollment
and building-construction figures swerved sharply upward

during boom years, but statistics tell only half the story. The real picture of the boom in education is presented by the reports of county superintendents—in descriptions of crowded buildings, laments over inadequacy of equipment and funds, and records of the inception of double-session work to care for both the normal increase in population and, in addition, children of transients and tourists brought in throngs by the great prosperity.

Los Angeles County in 1860 had seven schools and an enrollment of 460 students; twenty-five years later the enrollment reached 11,368, distributed among 200 school buildings. With the increase in property values, the county was hard put, during 1884 and 1886, to find room for its school population, and boom optimism did not contemplate any lessening of the strain. The flurry's height brought an unprecedented increase in enrollment, which reached 12,000 in 1886, nearly 15,000 in 1887, 19,000 in 1888, and 22,000 in 1889. New schools—nearly fourteen per year, on the average, from 1885 to 1888—were hurriedly constructed to house the increase. School-property values rose accordingly, from $467,728 in 1885 to $1,067,344 in 1888. During 1887 the number of teachers in Los Angeles County increased thirty-two per cent, and nineteen new school districts were created.

Pasadena's superintendent was especially concerned: "A number of those enrolled [in Pasadena] were the children of tourists who spent only a part of the year here, hence the average daily attendance [1,036] was not what it would have been otherwise."[1] Pomona was in dire need of new buildings. "To provide accommodation for this remarkable growth," the county superintendent said, "the city of Los Angeles and several other districts have been compelled to resort to double

[1] *Report of the Superintendent of Public Instruction of the State of California . . . 1890*, p. 115.

session work."[2] In the school year 1887-88, twenty-one districts voted school bonds of varying amounts.

The lag between the real-estate boom and the flurry in education was probably natural, in view of their causal relationship. Los Angeles County enrollment, for instance, failed to decline until 1890, two years after realty sales dropped off. Following the same trend, the number of new schools erected dwindled from twenty-five in 1889 to only seven in 1890. Part of the decrease was attributable to the fact that in August of 1889 Orange County began its separate existence, depriving Los Angeles County of 4,000 children, 31 school districts, and 72 teachers. Nevertheless, the boom's effect is evident; in Los Angeles County it resulted in a rapid acceleration of enrollment and building construction, and it raised school-property values to a high figure.

While the public schools profited from the boom, the county was also infected with "college fever." One of the institutions which grew through boom nourishment was the University of Southern California, established under the auspices of the Methodist Episcopal Church. In 1879 Robert M. Widney, attorney and banker, organized a syndicate which decided that real estate in western Los Angeles would form the best endowment for the embryo institution, and through the generosity of three donors—Ozro W. Childs, John G. Downey, and Isaias W. Hellman—the University Tract came into being. Among the provisions of the deed of conveyance were stipulations that no lot should ever be encumbered, that none should be sold for less than one hundred dollars, and that the first $5,000 realized was to be used for building construction. The tract, as finally platted, consisted of some thirty blocks, bounded on the south by Agricultural (now Exposition) Park and on the east by Figueroa Street; the campus was in the center. The initial lot sale was so successful that the college

[2]Ibid., 1888, pp. 72-73.

was opened in October, 1880, with an enrollment of more than fifty. The main structure, now the "Old College," was built between 1884 and 1887, and the rapidly expanding university attracted settlers in such numbers that a new Methodist church was built near by. The post office (University Place) had arrived in 1883, and street railways offered easy transportation to Main Street. In 1887 lot prices rose from $500 to $1,500, and tract additions were numerous.

The boom encouraged the university's founders to inaugurate an ambitious program of expansion. President Marion M. Bovard wanted the institution to be a "cultural center" surrounded by far-flung "units" to form a great "University System," and realty profits nearly fulfilled that dream. The Chaffey College of Agriculture at Ontario was included in the scheme and remained with the university for more than twenty years, breaking away in 1906 to become a high school, and later, a junior college. The funds of the old agricultural college that were retained by the university were used to establish the Chaffey Trust Fund, annually providing ten full scholarships for worthy graduates of Chaffey High School. The Maclay College of Theology was hopefully begun in the San Fernando Valley with a donation comprising 150,000 dollars' worth of stock in the San Fernando Land and Water Company, a three-story building, and seventy acres of valley land, ten of which were to be used for the campus. Charles Maclay made the gift in 1885, and the school opened its doors two years later. The Senator himself assumed the deanship when prospects dimmed, but his efforts were unavailing, and the college closed in 1893, to reopen on the university campus. Another branch to the university was proposed at Escondido, when the local Town and Land Company donated one thousand lots for a seminary. A 40,000-dollar building was erected, but on the boom's collapse became a grammar and high school. In 1888, a San Diego College of Fine Arts was projected as one of the units, but the plan failed when the boom broke. The Freeman College of Applied Sciences, at Inglewood, was to feature hydraulic and mining engineering, wood carving, and metal turning, but, despite its detailed program, did not materialize. Thirty-eight years later Daniel Freeman donated $50,000 to the university for the establishment of a chair of applied science. The Monrovia Young Ladies' College was conducted for a year in W. N. Monroe's home, and the site of the Tulare Seminary campus "remained unbroken desert."[3] Abbot Kinney urged the university to found a school of forestry, but his plans never matured. In addition to these far-flung ramifications, a college of medicine was started in 1888. Just before the boom ended, the University of Southern California "extended from the heart of the San Joaquin Valley to the southern boundary of the State!"[4]

Deflation had deleterious effects upon all colleges in the southern counties, and the University of Southern California was no exception. When land sales ceased, the endowment turned into "frozen assets," and, in "common with Pomona and Occidental, the University . . . passed through a heartbreaking period of financial depression which reached its darkest days in 1893."[5] University property in 1888 had been worth several millions, but most of it was either mortgaged or only partly paid for. President Bovard died of overwork and worry, and enrollment dropped to a pitiful twenty-five. The assumption of Bovard's duties by Dr. Joseph P. Widney led, however, to a revival of hopes, and the change from an expansionist policy to one of extreme centralization made for less expense and more efficient operation. With the subse-

[3]Laurence L. Hill, *Six Collegiate Decades: The Growth of Higher Education in Southern California* (1929), pp. 23-25.

[4]Rockwell D. Hunt, *The First Half-Century* (1930), p. 4.

[5]Hill, pp. 23-24.

quent rise in property values, the university recovered, and in 1930 its holdings were assessed at more than $6,500,000.

A corollary project was the planning of an astronomical observatory on Mount Wilson—first designed by Edward F. Spence in 1887 as an adjunct to the "University System." Spence donated a business lot in Los Angeles, appraised at $50,000; immediately a forty-inch object glass was ordered. When the "System" disbanded, Harvard University investigated the site, and President Eliot arrived in 1892 with high hopes. Scarcity of water and abundance of rattlesnakes caused a second abandonment, and Mount Wilson remained a wilderness for ten more years, until George Ellery Hale and the Carnegie Endowment established the present observatory. The lenses ordered by Spence were installed in the Yerkes Observatory at Lake Geneva, Wisconsin.

If the University of Southern California owed its early growth to the decade of the eighties, Occidental College owed its very existence to the boom. Occidental grew out of three institutions in 1887: the Sierra Madre College of South Pasadena, a Presbyterian school; the McPherron Academy of Los Angeles; and the Presbyterian Church. The college was incorporated in February, and its charter was certified by the state in April. It was originally called Occidental University of Los Angeles, California—an example of the ambition stimulated by boom optimism. The Reverend Samuel Weller was made its first president. "The aim of the Institution," said an early brochure, "will be to secure an education that 'is broad and thorough. Its purpose will be to realize a culture that is practical and Christian. While the University will be under the care of the Presbyterians, its instruction will be evangelical rather than sectarian."[6] The college year was divided into fall, winter, and spring terms; Monday, instead of Saturday, was made a holiday, so students would not be obliged to travel

[6]Robert Glass Cleland, *The History of Occidental College* (1937), p. 11.

on the Sabbath, and the tuition was fixed at fifty dollars per year.

Once the college was organized, its founders approached various landholders in an effort to obtain a good site. The choice was fairly wide; colleges seldom had trouble in obtaining land donations during the boom, because of their advertising value to the tracts they occupied. Finally, a plat of about fifty acres east of the city was chosen, and became Edward S. Field's Occidental Heights subdivision; the chief donors were Mrs. J. E. Hollenbeck, wife of the well-known capitalist and philanthropist; the firm of Wicks & Mills; and Field and his associate, Hubbard. The *Los Angeles Times* reported the event as follows:

About $50,000 worth of land was donated by different persons for the benefit of the school. From this an abundant reservation was made for the college campus, and the remaining lots were put upon the market for the benefit of the institution. By this means it will be able to commence operations not only free from debt, but also well endowed. . . . The location is an extremely beautiful one; a broad plateau sloping gently to the south and east, with a magnificent mountain view and the ocean lying softly in the distance.[7]

The Occidental brochures combined realty advertising with descriptions of liberal-arts courses:

UNIVERSITY HOMES
IN
OCCIDENTAL HEIGHTS TRACT

A beautiful site. Best water in the country piped to every lot. Rich soil. Pure air. An educational center. No better place in the State for a home. Prices $250, $300, $500. Terms to suit. Call on or write to the

PRESIDENT OF THE OCCIDENTAL UNIVERSITY[8]

[7]*Ibid.*, p. 8.
[8]*Ibid.*, p. 13.

Construction of the college building was begun in the summer of 1887 and finished in the following year. It was a three-story, brick, "Elizabethan" structure, which combined under one roof the various functions of a hall of letters, an administration building, a women's dormitory, a president's office, a library, a refectory, a chapel, and a laundry. Men students were to be quartered in cottages on the campus.

The boom's collapse ended the rosy hopes of the founders. Dean Cleland's account reads as follows:

The effects of the crash upon Occidental were scarcely less severe [than on the University of Southern California]. The lots which were to furnish funds for endowment and current revenue could not be sold. Parents, hard hit by the slump, found themselves unable to meet even the modest tuitional and boarding charges then in effect. Equally unfortunate, the friends and sponsors of the college were too hard pressed in their own affairs to come to the relief of the nearly bankrupt institution. It is difficult to understand how the college lived through the overwhelming discouragements of those troubled years.[9]

Enrollment declined in 1891 to twenty-nine preparatory students and six of collegiate rank. The college debt amounted to $23,000, and because of Occidental's relatively late start, only $6,000 was realized from realty sales. President Weller, unable to subsist on his meager income, was forced to resign in 1891, but left behind him worthy advice for the founders of similar institutions: " 'Firstly, study the personnel of the syndicate on whose promises you rely for funds; secondly, do not trust anybody; and thirdly, have a bank account which shall duplicate dollar for dollar the contractor's claims before a brick has been laid or a spadeful of earth turned.' "[10] Only gradually did Occidental emerge from the financial slough in which it wallowed; but, throughout the decline, its Presby-

[9]*Ibid.*, p. 14.
[10]*Ibid.*, p. 14.

terian founders stood staunchly behind the college, and today it is one of the most prosperous privately-endowed liberal-arts institutions on the Pacific coast.

Other collegiate institutions in Los Angeles were affected variously by the boom. The State Normal School, now the University of California at Los Angeles, was founded in 1881 on land formerly owned by Victor Beaudry[11] and at present the site of the public library. The school prospered with the rest of the southland, suffered temporarily in the slump, but maintained its existence, affected less because of its independence of local realty endowments. The West Los Angeles land, formerly part of the Rancho San José de Buenos Ayres, which the university occupies today, had been owned by Benjamin D. Wilson. In 1884 he disposed of it to Joseph Wolfskill at ten dollars an acre, and in 1887 Wolfskill sold it for slightly less than one hundred dollars an acre. The purchaser, the Santa Monica Land and Water Company, founders of the ill-fated town of Sunset, quitclaimed the land back to Wolfskill in 1891.[12]

The Immaculate Heart Academy was started in 1890, at the corner of Pico and Ardmore Streets, as one of the first private high schools in Los Angeles. Its establishment raised land values in Pico Heights to such an extent that streetcar service was resumed, and the realty business began to recover from the boom's crash. Another Catholic institution, St. Vincent's (now Loyola), had been chartered in 1869 and occupied a two-story building on Sixth Street. Boom prospects caused the addition in 1883 of a wing facing Hill Street, and in

[11]The Beaudry brothers, Victor and Prudent, identified themselves with many southern-California activities. Victor invested in Cerro Gordo mines, the Temple Street Cable Railway, and much local real estate.

[12]Joseph W. Wolfskill was the son of William, a Kentucky Argonaut of 1831. The former became a large landowner, platting the famous Wolfskill Tract near the Arcade Station, and managing 3,000 acres of Riverside ranch land.

1887 the school moved, as related in a previous chapter, because
land values careered upward so rapidly that the campus became too valuable for school purposes. The new site at Washington Street and Grand Avenue was occupied for twenty-
five years.

Wilson College, named after the ubiquitous Don Benito,
had been established in 1874 as an educational organ of the
Methodist Church South. Wilson, its chief benefactor, purchased the hospital and officers' quarters of Drum Barracks in
Wilmington and presented them to the college. In these im-
provised lodgings the institution endured for a decade and a
half, but perished in the post-boom slump.

Another suburban academy resulting from boom expansion
was Throop University. Although founded in 1891 at the
depth of the post-boom depression, the institution profited
from Pasadena's relatively quick revival. Endowed by Amos
G. Throop, a benevolent newcomer whose own meager train-
ing made him acutely aware of the benefits of higher education, the university was dedicated to a "higher appreciation
of the value and dignity of intelligent manual labor."[13] It
opened its doors on November 2, 1891, with thirty-five students, in a business block near the center of town, and later,
in 1893, moved to its own campus, and was called Throop
Polytechnic Institute. With further financial and geographical shifts, the academy eventually became the modern and
widely renowned California Institute of Technology.

Whittier College narrowly missed being as typical a boom
institution as Occidental, but the first attempts of its Quaker
founders failed in 1887, despite subscriptions to the amount
of $130,000 and a donated building site. Four years later,
however, it opened its doors as Whittier Academy, with two
teachers and thirteen students. The realty firm responsible for
the development of the town of Whittier was the indirect

[13]Hill, pp. 73-75; see also contemporary newspapers.

cause of the college's growth: the principal stockholder of the Pickering Land and Water Company, Washington Hadley, became the institution's chief benefactor. Hadley, local banker and Rivera walnut grower, presented temporary quarters and a fourteen-acre site, whose improvements were to be financed by subscription. The school grew steadily, and in 1901 was chartered by the state. Hadley in the following year gave $10,000 more to his protégé, with the provision that $50,000 additional be raised.

La Verne College laid its foundations directly upon the wreckage left by the boom in the valley town of Lordsburg. Promoters of that community had built a 75,000-dollar, three-story hotel, which was left empty and forlorn after the crash, and became the first home of the college. Its establishment was partly due to the efforts of the Santa Fe Railway to build up the towns straggling along its San Gabriel Valley line. A propaganda campaign was inaugurated among the German Baptists known as Dunkers; southern-California products were exhibited at their conferences, and excursions were planned. The result was the formation in stagnating Lordsburg of a Dunker colony, which in 1895 numbered 2,500. As early as March, 1891, bankrupt promoters had persuaded the Dunkers to buy their empty hotel, and the groundwork was thus firmly laid for establishing a school. The Lordsburg College Association was incorporated to provide for a non-sectarian institution where young people might be educated "free from evil surroundings."[14] The only denominational restriction was that a majority of the trustees must be Dunkers. The college was opened in September, 1891, with a faculty of eight and a student body of 135; tuition, including room and board, was $137.50. The depression of the nineties was responsible for much financial distress and constant changes in administration, resulting in the school's temporary

[14] Hill, pp. 65 ff.

closing and a subsequent reopening under the sponsorship of a Philadelphia Dunker, W. C. Hanawalt. The ensuing reversion to "first principles" insured the success of the little college.

The Congregationalists were not to be outdone in the matter of facilities for higher learning. In 1887 the Educational Committee of the First District Congregational Association drew up plans for a college in the Pomona Valley. Realtors offered many sites, by-laws were drafted, and prospects gleamed brightly. This auspicious beginning was not, however, followed by immediate accomplishment. "It was not," one writer said, "for lack of faith but of time. Night and day, everywhere, everyone was selling real estate."[15] Failure to ride the crest of the wave led to difficulties. The slump made money hard to find, and only with the utmost effort was the association's secretary, Charles B. Sumner, able to plan a campus and lay out the town of Piedmont on the land constituting the college's endowment. A building was started, but never finished; classes were transferred in 1888, first to a cottage, and then to the abandoned Hotel Claremont, renamed Sumner Hall. Like its collegiate associates, Pomona found lean going during its formative years, but it now rivals Occidental in prosperity, equipment, and beauty of environment.

Although Los Angeles County was the center of the boom in education, as it was the nucleus of the real-estate flurry, other counties also profited. San Bernardino County, during all of the pre-boom years, ran Los Angeles a close second in school population, and its building enthusiasm was nearly as great. An 1885 enrollment of 2,739 rose to 3,436 in 1887, 4,188 in 1888, and 4,671 in 1889. Here, again, the boom's effect is seen in an accelerated rate of growth during the years of the flurry, rather than in a marked falling-off im-

[15]*Ibid.*, p. 42.

mediately afterward. Twenty schools were built in the four years preceding 1886, and school-property valuation advanced from $58,130 in 1883 to $146,888 in 1886. The report of the county superintendent in the latter year announced that new construction to the amount of $25,000 had been provided for. The number of new buildings constructed in each year from 1885 to 1890, inclusive, was, respectively, five, seven, nine, twenty, and four. The boom saw enrollments increase twenty-two per cent, and property valuation fifty-five per cent.

Notwithstanding the enthusiasm of the Baptists in the Los Angeles region, the Baptist college of southern California was finally located in San Bernardino County. Redlands University did not start building until 1909, but its realty endowment can be traced to boom years. Dr. J. D. B. Stillman, a leading Redlands physician and scientist, had bequeathed his vineyards to Stanford University, as a natural consequence of his personal acquaintance with Leland Stanford, and of his son's position as head of the chemistry department of the northern institution. Stanford, however, sold the lands to Karl C. Wells, a Redlands banker, who in turn donated to southern-California Baptists, in 1906, forty acres, plus a 25,000-dollar endowment. The lands of the Redlands campus have thus been devoted to educational purposes since the boom first enhanced their value.

The enrollment of San Diego County's public schools increased from 1,985 in 1885 to more than 4,000 in 1888, and to nearly 7,000 in the following year. San Diego equaled Los Angeles in school-building enthusiasm, and, in proportion to population, far surpassed it. Sixteen new schools were established in San Diego County in 1887, eleven in 1888, eighteen in 1889, and—a record for any southern county during this period—thirty-eight in 1890. The pinch of inadequate accommodations for pupils was felt acutely. Much of the trouble was caused by the lag between population increase

LORDSBURG COLLEGE, LA VERNE (ABOUT 1890)

and administrative adjustment. "With a county," said the superintendent in 1888, "the populated area of which is equal to the State of Massachusetts, and the population of which would call for the tenth class of counties, the superintendent's office is hampered by the laws of counties of the thirty-first class."[16] School-property valuation increased from $65,742 in 1885 to $371,679 in 1888, declined to $310,543 in the following year, and in 1890, because of the construction record set at that time, attained an unprecedented high point of $432,483.

San Diego's boom-time college was the San Diego College of Letters, located at Pacific Beach. The school's first bulletin was issued in October, 1888, and presented three courses of study: classical, scientific, and literary. A preparatory department was included. The institution boasted a seventeen-acre campus, one completed building, and a faculty of fourteen, headed by Harr Wagner, later the county superintendent of schools. There were, the prospectus said, no saloons in the locality, but an enterprising reporter from the local *Independent* discovered plans for opening a "sportsman's resort" there—a project that was, he said, to be deplored in view of the nearness of the college. The school went out of business after the boom, the building later becoming the Hotel Balboa. The property was offered at an appraisal value of $100,000 to the state as an inducement to locate a normal school at Pacific Beach, but the gift was never accepted, the normal school finally going to near-by Vermont Heights.

Ventura County's public-school enrollment advanced from 1,376 in 1885 to 1,881 during the boom, but declined in the years following the collapse. School property rose in value more than $50,000 between 1885 and 1889, and a total of seven new schools were constructed from 1886 to 1888. Santa Barbara County was similarly affected, seeing its largest

[16]*Report of the Superintendent of Public Instruction . . . 1888*, pp. 78-79; *1890*, p. 115.

enrollment growth, amounting to 300 per year, during 1888 and 1889. Five new schools were built between 1886-88, and six more in 1889. Property-valuation increase also showed a lag, achieving its greatest acceleration in 1888. A word should be added with regard to Orange County, which, established in 1890, began its educational history with an enrollment of 3,451 and school property valued at $143,536, including three additional schools begun by the new county government.

The boom's effect on education is therefore definite and well-marked, not only in the field of higher education, which became a natural adjunct to boom promotion, but also in the public-school systems of southern California. Among the chief problems were those of financing institutions founded on shaky boomtime values and of nursing such schools through the difficult years of the nineties, of centralizing and retrenching in order to overcome the disadvantages and extravagances of too-enthusiastic expansion schemes, and of providing adequate housing facilities for a transient school population which, luckily for educational finances, did not entirely disappear after the boom. These problems were hard to solve, and in many cases resulted in the abandonment of cherished plans and the sacrifice of much effort exerted by educators. If, as might have been expected, a universal collapse had ensued, the region's educational future could not have been predicted. Actually, however, the public schools were subjected to no more than temporary strain, and the colleges that merited staunch devotion and financial backing were enabled to weather the storm, with an improvement of morale which perhaps did them more good than harm in later years.

CHAPTER XVIII

The End of the Boom

D ESPITE hopeful prognostications and repeated assur-
ances by both buyers and sellers that the boom had
come to stay, the spring of 1888 witnessed a rapid
decline in land values and in buying enthusiasm. Common
sense told the investor that the end was in sight. The expected winter-tourist influx had not materialized—at least not
to the extent that had been hoped for—and the banks were
becoming more and more cautious in their lending policy.
The boom, says Guinn, did not burst; it "gradually shrivelled
up."[1] The first three months of 1888 saw approximately
20,000,000 dollars' worth of real estate transferred, but, beginning in April, there was a sharp decrease in sales. Conditions became difficult for those who had plunged too deeply.
Interest rates rose, and people who had boasted of the huge
amounts of money involved in boom transactions now became
aware that paper profits, and not liquid capital, had been the

[1]Guinn, in Hist. Soc. of Sou. Calif. *Annual Publications, 1890*, I, 21.

lifeblood of the flurry. There was a universal desire to sell—
quickly, at any price—and consequently, expanded values
deflated like pricked balloons. Persons who had been talking
"land and climate" for two years now regretted intensely the
lack of a stable industrial basis for southern California's economy. Worried citizens looked back upon their frenzied existence during 1887 and began to realize that "never, perhaps,
did a community more completely lose its sense of values
and proportion."[2]

No precise date can be given for the end of the boom. If
banks had permitted themselves to be swept along with the
current, the spring runs of 1888 would have marked financial
collapse in the southland; but the banks withstood the runs,
and did everything in their power to enable the honest investor to pay his debts. Loans were extended, week by week
and month by month, and deficiency judgments were remark-
ably few in number. As a result, the collapse was milder in
its effects than might have been expected. There was no
widespread suffering or want. High interest charges, low
prices, financial stringency, and a glutted market were the
primary results of the finale of the great boom. In 1889
Alonzo E. Davis, supervisor from the Fourth District of Los
Angeles County, applied to the State Board of Equalization
to have the assessment figures for that year reduced. Using
statistics compiled by Valentine J. Rowan, local engineer and
surveyor, Davis described sixty ghost towns, founded after
January 1, 1887, which comprised 79,350 lots—and had only
2,351 citizens. He told of worthless alkali lands, which boom
literature had hailed for their fertility, now deservedly barren
of population but assessed at forty to sixty dollars per acre.
"The figures of the county assessor," he concluded, "are
$14,000,000 less than in 1888, yet property is assessed far
above its value. Everything has been wrecked by the boom

[2]Cleland, *History of Occidental College*, p. 4.

and financial men have gone down by the hundreds."[3] Davis'
spirited plea resulted in a reduction of twenty-five per cent
in the county's assessed realty valuation, and his report made
clear that in a "less hopeful and self-reliant people, the collapse of such a boom would have resulted in complete financial ruin and untold suffering."[4]

Effects of the boom's collapse on individual communities
varied. Pasadena suffered severely. Guinn comments: "As
Pasadena had soared highest in the balloon of inflation, when
the drop came she struck bottom the hardest. Her orange
groves, once her pride and boast, had been mostly sacrificed
on the altar of town lots; and what the boomer had left the
cottony scale had devastated."[5] But, Guinn adds, the Australian ladybug destroyed the cottony scale, and the post-boom
depression ruined the boomers, so that in two years Pasadena
was approaching normal once more. The deflation's effects on
Glendale were both bad and good. On the one hand, the town
stagnated in economic doldrums for many months, the new
hotel lay empty, and the Improvement Society died a quick
death and was not resurrected for more than a decade. Con-
versely, the San Rafael lands were permanently benefited by
the railroad line which had been started, by publicity available in the local boom newspaper, and by the interested activity of many prosperous businessmen who had invested in
Glendale property. Monrovia first felt the decline in the spring
of 1888, when a projected office building failed to materialize.
In May, economic conditions were so bad that citizens signed
a petition requesting the town council to abate license fees
temporarily. "Hundreds of the lots sold in Monrovia went
back to the original owners, as the payments could not be

[3]Netz, in Hist. Soc. of Sou. Calif. *Annual Publications, 1915-16,* X, 67-68;
see also Los Angeles County Board of Supervisors "Minute Book," XII, 249.

[4]Guinn, in Hist. Soc. of Sou. Calif. *Annual Publications, 1890,* I, 21.

[5]*Idem, Historical and Biographical Record of Southern California,* p. 143.

met, and the owners who were carrying mortgages on the property found themselves unable to meet these demands, as there were no more payments coming in and the whole house of cards fell with the mortgagees property poor."[6] The nadir of the depression was perhaps reached when the "garbage wagon was discontinued and the city marshal instructed to employ a wagon once a week."[7] Here also, however, the slump was short-lived. In 1889 signs of reviving activity were evident in the construction of a new bridge over the San Gabriel River and in the establishment of a telegraph office. Times were still dull in 1890, but a "gradual growth" could be perceived.

The effects of the crash on individuals were often disastrous. "Lucky" Baldwin, patriarch of Santa Anita, left landpoor by the boom's failure, was forced to withdraw temporarily from his beloved horse racing, and for a time found difficulty in paying his employees. In Glendale, Harry J. Crow, one of the builders of the Glendale Hotel, was forced into bankruptcy when 200 acres of his land, together with the hotel building, were taken from him by foreclosure. Consequent financial worries caused his death a few years later. Not only the great and near-great were affected. For instance an article in the *Los Angeles Times* on June 9, 1887, told of a Pasadena citizen who took strychnine because he had "sold some property too cheap," and subsequent inflation of values had made him regret his disposal of it.

Criticism of the boom was widespread. The *Chicago Tribune* printed the following article in mid-1887:

The California Swindle
How Settlers are induced to Invest their All
and Are then Abandoned
Maj. Ben C. Truman, chief of the literary bureau of the Southern

[6]Wiley, *History of Monrovia*, p. 70.
[7]*Ibid.*, p. 69.

Pacific Railway Company, was in the city last week. . . . Truman flops around between the Atlantic and Pacific like a railway postal clerk. He said to a friend—an old Californian—the other day: "The Los Angeles crowd has become crazy. That's all there is to it. See this item." He showed a real estate note in a Los Angeles paper, which related that three acres of ground adjacent to the Raymond Hotel in Pasadena had sold for $30,000, or $10,000 an acre! Maj. Truman could only look unutterably at that. "It is all wrong," he said, "to talk or write in such a way. The Southern California boom has taken a great shape, but it is, in my opinion, time to hold it down a little."[8]

Major Truman's sentiments were quite naturally resented by local publications, but their inherent truth was hard to deny. That the boom did have bad effects was recognized even by local publicists. In June, 1887, the *Times* listed three main evils of the boom: (1) neglect of agriculture, resulting from farmers' deserting their trade to engage in the real-estate business, (2) speculation rather than legitimate business, and (3) the fact that Los Angeles was growing so rapidly that municipal improvements were not keeping pace with expanding population needs. To these might have been added the undue emphasis on town lots rather than productive acreage, and the failure of boom leaders to develop a secure industrial foundation for further expansion. There was plenty of talk about industrial development, but little actually was accomplished.

Yet the boom was not entirely detrimental. The economic flurry was California's characteristic mode of development, and, like the comber carried by a rising tide, it always receded—but never quite so far as its starting point. Netz argued:

. . . the great real estate boom of 1887 was not built wholly on air. It was run to mania to be sure. It must be remembered that the frontier town of 1885, with its business at the Temple Block, was transformed into a flourishing city in 1889. . . . Our real

[8]From the *Los Angeles Times*, June 9, 1887.

estate boomers went a little bit faster than the country, that was all. . . . Our intrinsic resources have sustained us through the reaction which followed the wildest real estate excitement which ever attended the building of any American city.[9]

Another cogent evaluation of the boom was made by L. M. Holt, the Riverside promoter and irrigation expert:

It is true that during the boom years of '86-'87, there was a considerable amount of wild speculation that had little or no foundation. . . . and yet during this wild speculative craze there was established many solid improvements that have since been turned to good use in building up the country and making it attractive to eastern people who are seeking homes in our midst.

There is no section . . . where good cement sidewalks in cities and towns begin to compare with those of Southern California. There is no other section where cities and towns have so good a supply and system of domestic water service, it frequently being found that the domestic piped water system under pressure is established before there are people to use the water. There is no other section where there are so many rapid transit motor railroads. . . .

The boom was not an evil in all respects . . . as a whole there was more money made than lost and the country as a whole forged to the front in a manner that could not be equalled under any other circumstances in less than several decades.[10]

The boom greatly affected the caliber of southern California's population. Newcomers arrived from everywhere, especially from the Middle West. In September, 1887, the Springfield, Ohio, *Republican*, stated: " 'It will only be a short time until the whole of Southern California will be settled as closely as Ohio or New York. If all the cities of the Union send as large a proportion of their population to California and Florida as Springfield does, it is small wonder that

[9]Netz, in Hist. Soc. of Sou. Calif. *Annual Publications, 1915-16*, X, 68.
[10]*Ingersoll's Century Annals of San Bernardino County*, pp. 173-74.

that locality is settling up so fast.' "[11] In addition to attracting immigrants, the boom kept many of the southland's older citizens from deserting her for other localities. A mining flurry in Tucson, shortly before the boom, started a significant migration away from Los Angeles. "Plenty of people . . . were willing to bet," says one boom-time resident, "that within ten years Tucson would be the larger city."[12] The boom halted this trend by providing an equally prosperous and more comfortable El Dorado.

Town populations were built up tremendously by the boom. Los Angeles had less than 6,000 citizens in 1870, but the census of 1890 credited it with more than 50,000 permanent residents. Pasadena increased in size more than tenfold during the boom decade, and San Diego and Santa Barbara showed similar growth. The boom's floating population naturally added to census figures during the height of the flurry, although for 1887 and 1888 only estimates are possible.[13]

County population statistics give a fair indication of the number of settlers in rural and unincorporated areas.[14] Los Angeles County's population increased about thirty per cent between 1860 and 1870, doubled in the following decade, and more than tripled during the decade of the boom—notwithstanding the subtraction of 30,000 of its citizens when Orange County was created in 1889. Other southern counties paralleled Los Angeles' increment, although the advance in Santa Barbara and Ventura counties was less spectacular than that farther south. The boom's effect is emphasized when statistics for the succeeding decade (1890-1900) are considered; here, in every case, are only slight population gains, instead of the astronomical acceleration in the rate of growth.

[11]From *San Diego Union*, Oct. 1, 1887.
[12]Brook, in *Land of Sunshine* (Jan., 1895), p. 25.
[13]See Appendix B.
[14]*Ibid.*

❦ The Boom of the Eighties ❧

An important index of boom activity and the general state of business and credit in the area was the amounts involved in realty transactions. As previously stated, such figures are extremely difficult to ascertain, not only because of the huge task of adding long lists of fees in recorders' daybooks, but also because many purchasers were reluctant to state the exact sums transferred, and preferred to temporize by using the undescriptive statement: "For the consideration of one dollar." Estimated totals are, however, available, and the boom's effect on realty transactions is very clear. Conveyances in Los Angeles County rose from $6,000,000 in 1882 to $96,000,000 in 1887. Monthly totals show that the peak of the boom there occurred between June and September of 1887—even though these months were usually dull. Whether or not a large share of these sums consisted of "paper profits," the amount of business entailed in nearly 100,000,000 dollars' worth of realty transactions had a tremendous effect upon the southland's economy.

Another index was the assessed valuation of real and personal property. In Los Angeles city, valuation advanced from $6,000,000 to $49,000,000 during the boom decade, and other towns often equaled or surpassed this record. Comparing proportionate gains in southern valuation with those of the northern part of the state, one perceives that the boom was largely a southern phenomenon. Los Angeles' increase was well over eightfold during the boom decade, San Diego's about twentyfold, and Santa Barbara's (one of the smallest) more than threefold. Alameda, during the same period, exactly tripled its valuation; San Francisco added in the neighborhood of twenty-five per cent; Berkeley and Sacramento approximately fifty per cent. Extravagant rises in land values, therefore, were limited largely to the area south of the Tehachapi, as is borne out by county assessment statistics.

Mortgages were another means of determining the progress

266

of realty activity, and with regard to them the boom curve is graphically very clear. From $700,000 in 1880, Los Angeles County mortgages attained $17,500,000 in 1887, and then declined to $10,500,000 in 1889. Far more of these mortgages were on town lots than on country acreage, showing definitely that the speculative aspects of the boom were concerned largely with town platting. Of the county's ten-year-total, $34,000,000 applied to city and town lots, while $27,000,000 encumbered rural acreage.

A basic reason why the boom's collapse did not utterly ruin southern California's economy was the conservative policy of the banks. In 1888 Los Angeles County had twenty-seven banks, with $3,400,000 on reserve. This was a larger pool than the banks of any county except San Francisco possessed. Southern-California institutions apparently perceived in 1885 the beginning of inflation, and the Farmers and Merchants Bank of Los Angeles led in the inauguration of a policy of caution. Deposits reached $5,500,000 in 1886, $8,000,000 in January of 1887, and $12,000,000 before the end of that year. The banks duly increased their loans, as was natural under the circumstances, but with a steadily rising margin of safety. In 1885 loans amounted to 80 per cent of deposits; in January, 1887, to 62½ per cent. Loans on outside-property improvements were prohibited first; later, no loans at all were made. By July of 1887 less than half of the banks' funds were on loan, and six months thereafter only one quarter. As was stated, the banks successfully withstood runs, and, except for one or two unfortunate and relatively minor incidents, the flurry did not injure the banking structure of the region. The banks' sturdiness in restricting credit raised interest rates which, of course, limited speculation; had that sensible policy not been pursued, the boom would have involved even larger sums of money at its height, and the crash would have been correspondingly more disastrous.

✑ The Boom of the Eighties ✐

Municipal organization was one of the first things to be affected by the boom, as was evidenced in two ways: by the incorporation of communities which were stimulated by the boom and whose civic pretensions thereby expanded; and by the formation of booster groups, primarily boards of trade and chambers of commerce. Cities developed in other ways at this time. Districts which had previously been suburban farmland now became residence tracts, and former residential districts were devoted to business. In Los Angeles, for example, the river land south of Third Street was all platted; brick buildings were erected north of the Plaza in the hope that business would trend in that direction; and the Westlake Park area was given the first of the stimuli that transformed it from farm land to a residential section and then to an aristocratic business zone. Cultural influences were evident, for churches, theaters, and meeting halls became nearly as popular as hotels. In 1892 there were fifty-five Protestant churches in the city of Los Angeles; three years earlier, a park commission had been organized to beautify municipal recreation centers. That the boom of the eighties was largely responsible for making southern California tourist-conscious, and for providing superior institutions of higher learning, has already been demonstrated.

The influence of the boom on publication was tremendous. Not only did it bring forth enormous quantities of advertising literature, some of which was of high enough quality to rank with the best travel volumes America had produced, but it also stimulated the investment of large sums in local newspapers, so that the boom was accompanied by an avalanche of new journals. San Diego, for instance, with a boom population of about 20,000, published five city papers—the *Union, Sun, Bee, San Diegan,* and *Golden Era*—and "each of the small towns," the last-named publication stated in its 1888 supplement, had "one or more good local journals." Altogether, some 160 newspapers owed their beginnings to boom years.

Because southern California is a land of magnificent distances, the transportation problem ranked high in the consideration of promoters. Not only did the boom increase the business of existing lines, but it also emphasized the need for additional road construction; and the eighties may be said to have constituted the initial era of local and municipal railway building in the south. The amount of train travel was, indeed, a succulent bait for businessmen interested in transportation investment. The *San Diego Union* reported on October 4, 1887: "From conversations with a large number of through passengers leaving this city, Mr. Keyes [ticket agent of the California Southern and Santa Fe lines] is of the opinion that fully ninety-nine per cent of them go to their homes in the East for the purpose of making arrangements for a return to this city for permanent settlement." In 1886 arrivals by rail in San Diego numbered 2,000 to 3,000 per month; during the first half of 1887 the average rose to between 3,000 and 5,000; and at the peak of the boom (from July to September), train tourists came at the rate of more than 5,000 a month. In addition, there were well over one thousand boat arrivals in San Diego during 1887, materially adding to the city's population. Parallel figures for Los Angeles were, of course, much higher.

The outstanding event of railroad expansion during the boom was the entrance of the Santa Fe line into California. This involved the previously described negotiations with the Southern Pacific, which resulted in the construction of the Needles-San Bernardino line via Cajón Pass. The Los Angeles and San Gabriel Valley Railroad, comprising a twenty-one-mile route, was combined with the Los Angeles and San Bernardino Railway, being built west by the Santa Fe to connect with the San Gabriel line, and several other smaller lines and franchises, to form the California Central Railway in April,

1887. A later reorganization, the Southern California Railway, was merely a renaming of the Santa Fe's southern-California properties. The consolidation of the Santa Fe and California Southern was a direct outgrowth of the boom, as was the laying of eighty-seven and one-half miles of new southern-county trackage during boom years. The Southern Pacific also expanded, with the result that 147 miles of new track were constructed during the fiscal year 1887-88. Many short lines came into being during the flurry, and more were projected. The San Diego, Cuyamaca, and Eastern Railroad was organized in March, 1888, to connect San Diego with Needles, and within a year twenty-five miles were completed. The National City and Otay Railroad began building in 1887, as did the Los Angeles and Pacific line (Los Angeles to Santa Monica). Other railways started by the boom included the Chino Valley, the Coronado, and the Los Angeles, Pasadena, and Glendale routes. Street-railway construction was also stimulated, some twenty-seven new lines being incorporated during boom years. Los Angeles street railways grew from eleven miles of track in 1880 to more than eighty miles in 1889, the bulk of the construction occurring during 1887 and 1888.

The effect of the boom on industrial development was surprisingly small. Indirectly, of course, the increase in population and the arrival of new capital stimulated later industrial growth, but few new industries were initiated during boom years. The abortive coal-mining project of Elsinore has already been described, as have the terra-cotta and clay works of that region. A watch factory at Otay was unable to survive the boom, and most industries unrelated to agriculture suffered in like manner. Practically all of the real industrial accomplishment came about through new utilization of agricultural products. There were several fruit-drying plants in the Glendale region, and after the boom a short-lived co-operative association consolidated these various companies. Linda Rosa's fruit-packing establishment began with ambitious hopes, and in 1890 the Oxnard brothers founded a beet-sugar refinery at Chino. Mining resembled industry in its unimportance during this era. Although several small gold veins and placer deposits were discovered, especially in the San Gabriel Mountains, profits were small. More significant was the increase of interest in petroleum, whose production in the state rose from half a million gallons in 1879 to 15,-000,000 in 1888. The year 1887-88 was called a "gold-letter" year by one writer on the subject, because 350,000 barrels had been produced by southern-California wells alone.[15]

The influence of the flurry on the larger political units, the counties, was notable. Orange County, formed in 1889 (as described earlier), was the first new county to be organized in fifteen years. After 1890, enthusiasm for county division became pronounced in southern California. Stimulated by new boom populations, there were proposals for four counties—San Antonio (Pomona), San Jacinto, Escondido, and Riverside, but only the last, as already related, was carried to completion.

Another corollary of increased population in the south was a renewal of the agitation for state division. Discrimination against the southland in taxation and representation was strongly resented, and the pre-Civil War movement for the formation of a separate southern political organization was by no means forgotten. Although the eventual shift of the northern districts to activities other than gold mining put an end to the chief difference in economy, there was still a general feeling that basic disparities existed. Southern California's climate made it essentially different both in agriculture and in general outlook, and continual hints in the correspondence and periodicals of the time show that separatism still glowed.

[15] *Annual Report of the Los Angeles Board of Trade, 1888*, pp. 146-49.

◄§ The Boom of the Eighties §►

David Berry, writing in 1873, confidently predicted that "when the state is divided . . . [Los Angeles] will doubtless be the capital and land will advance in price."[16] In 1881 a mass meeting was held in Los Angeles to discuss division, but, as sentiment favoring this move existed only in Los Angeles County, the plan died for lack of support. Seven years later a Ventura congressman followed up the idea by proposing a bill for division, but his suggestion was immediately tabled. Despite nonaction, the Los Angeles Chamber of Commerce announced in 1888 that the "proposed State of Southern California will, if created, probably consist of" San Diego, Los Angeles, San Bernardino, Ventura, Santa Barbara, San Luis Obispo, and Kern counties—a total of 56,576 square miles.[17]

A new trend in the sectional jealousy was seen in boom-time expressions of local patriotism. Whereas before 1880 the southern "cow counties" had been the malcontents and the north the wealthy region, smugly self-satisfied with its speedier progress, now the south overtook the bay area in its rate of growth; and southern pre-boom recriminations changed to patronizing expressions of encouragement when Sacramento, for instance, sent down a representative to learn Los Angeles publicity methods. The *Tribune* dispatched an emissary to inspect the citrus fair at Sacramento in December, 1886, and the reporter mailed back the following depreciatory account of his arrival:

Sac., Cal., Dec. 13.—I arrived . . . this morning and found it exceedingly cold. The presence of mud on the streets indicates that Sacramento has had considerable more rain than Los Angeles. After lunch, and the fog having cleared away, I was shown through the Pavilion. . . . The lemons . . . look well, and would look better were it not for the presence of the red scale on them,

[16]David M. Berry to J. M. Mathews, Sept. 27, 1873.

[17]*Southern California and Los Angeles City and County* (Los Angeles Chamber of Commerce, 1888), p. 3.

272

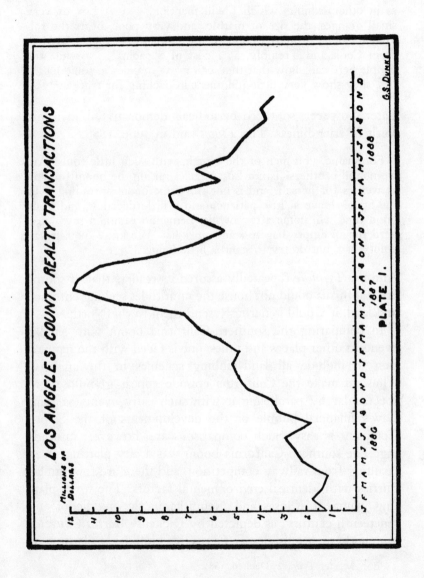

LOS ANGELES COUNTY REALTY TRANSACTIONS

PLATE I.

G.S. DUNNE

273

as in other exhibits which I will mention. . . . A box of very small oranges, the size of marbles and very poor, bears the following label: "From trees bought for budded Los Angeles oranges from Cook and Trembly, at a cost of $ each." . . . while the people here can show that they can grow oranges in some localities, they show very little judgment in packing for market.[18]

Later, however, southern periodicals demonstrated an ironic spirit of friendliness. The *Times* said in June, 1887:

For shame, you men of the North, with such little souls! Are we not all brothers? Is not Los Angeles raising the boom for you as well as for herself, and is not this same boom spreading over the State? Have a little patience and a little decency, and your good time will come after awhile. Benjamin Franklin says "it is hard for an empty bag to stand upright." We know you are an empty bag, but do try to stand a little longer.[19]

And the *Tribune* repeatedly assured its readers that, if southern California could not house the multitudes seeking entrance and land, it would generously send them to the North.

In comparing the southern-California boom with similar events in other places and times, one is faced with the temptation to include all land-jobbing schemes in the analogy. Thus, to make the California episode appear grandiose and spectacular by paralleling it with such early events as John Law's financial bubble or the developments of the Scioto Company is easy. Such comparisons are, however, misleading. The southern-California boom was a city-platting craze resulting from railway competition, and there are few similar flurries with identical environmental factors. The town-platting mania of Kansas and Nebraska in the middle of the nineteenth century, as depicted by Dickens' *Martin Chuzzlewit*, with such episodes as Cyrus K. Holliday's platting of

[18]*Los Angeles Tribune*, Dec. 16, 1886.

[19]*Los Angeles Times*, June 15, 1887. This was printed in rebuttal to an article appearing in the *San Jose Times*.

Topeka, is a closer analogy. An even better comparison may be made with the Florida land boom of 1923-26. Here, although the causes differed, the results were the same: the feverish platting of suburban towns, magnificent land sales, and a building-construction flurry which made Miami a city of skyscrapers. Financially, the southern-California boom is unimposing beside its Florida counterpart. In the West, $200,000,000 was the estimated total for all transactions in the southern counties during boom years; in Florida, three-fourths of that sum was spent on the promotion improvements of a single project, Coral Gables. Where California land prices ran into thousands, Florida prices were counted by tens of thousands. But of course the time element and its effect upon the normal expansion of American economy must be considered. Historically, the boom of the eighties occupies an important place in American economic development, and no similar future events, however important, can detract from its significance as a developmental factor in the expansion of Pacific-coast economy.

"On the whole," says Guinn, "with all its faults and failures, with all its reckless waste and wild extravagance, our boom was more productive of good than of evil to Southern California."[20] True, the flurry overemphasized realty speculation at the expense of more productive development, caused bankruptcies and failures when it collapsed, and was responsible for an artificial level of economic activity which might have been very dangerous to the region's future welfare. But, in general, benefits exceeded harmful effects. The boom brought people to California in ever increasing numbers, and they themselves were the foundation for a greater economic structure. It enlarged transportation facilities and municipal development, settled hitherto barren areas, completed the breakup of the ranchos, and was largely responsible for south-

[20]Guinn, in Hist. Soc. of Sou. Calif. *Annual Publications, 1890,* I, 21.

ern California's modern publicity-consciousness, which has done much to develop the southland. Even in their most extravagant predictions, boom promoters proved to be true prophets, for Los Angeles realty valuation and activity have long since overtopped the highest boom levels. The depression following the boom was not a bad one, for, as a contemporary put it:

> . . . the best and most rapid growth of the city has been since the excitement died away, and during a long process of liquidation so general and severe that it would have made hard times in any other country and in the midst of any prosperity . . . when millions of hands have been hanging idle in the east, every hammer and saw in the city has been busy, and business houses, fine residences and neat cottages are still rising as fast as ever.[21]

The boom was significant, not only for its color, picturesqueness, and uproarious enthusiasm, but also because it wiped out forever the last traces of the Spanish-Mexican pastoral economy which had characterized California history since 1769. The gold rush made northern California a real part of the United States; the boom of the eighties did precisely that for the south. Where once the "cattle of the plain" had grazed in silence over rich acres, now the American citizen built his trolley lines, founded his banks, and irrigated his orange groves. The boom was the final step in the process of making California truly American.

---

[21]Theodore S. Van Dyke, "Los Angeles since the Boom," *Land of Sunshine* (June, 1894), p. 15.

Appendixes

APPENDIX A

Assessed Valuation of Southern Counties and Cities, 1880-90[1]

	1880	1890
Los Angeles County	$13,731,872	$60,012,280
Orange County		7,780,523
San Bernardino County	2,156,253	17,188,555
San Diego County	2,382,795	24,451,740
Santa Barbara County	4,395,076	13,074,112
Ventura County	2,711,630	5,752,840
Los Angeles city	4,775,373	45,066,436
San Bernardino city	470,000	3,720,702
San Diego city	614,500	14,678,101
Santa Barbara city	469,826	2,894,833
Ventura city	504,404	1,189,775

[1]From United States Census Reports for 1880 and 1890.

⋇⋚ Appendixes ⋚⋇

APPENDIX B

City Population Statistics[1]

Year	Los Angeles	Pasa- dena	San Ber- nardino	San Diego	Santa Ana	Santa Barbara	Ven- tura
1870	5,728	....	....	2,300	....	....	....
1880	11,183	391	1,673	2,637	711	3,460	1,370
1888*	80,000	6,500	8,000	15,000	4,000	8,000	....
1890	50,395	4,882	4,012	16,159	3,628	5,864	2,320

*Estimate

County Population Statistics[2]

Year	Los Angeles	San Bernardino	San Diego	Santa Barbara	Ventura
1870	15,309	3,988	4,951	7,784	....
1880	33,381	7,786	8,618	9,513	5,073
1885	72,500	17,000	19,500	15,000	8,000
1886	80,000	20,000	35,000	17,000	10,000
1887	100,000	30,000	50,000	20,000	13,000
1890	101,454	25,497	34,987	15,754	10,071
Increase, 1880-87	200%	285%	480%	110%	156%

Population Increment in Fourteen Southern Counties[3]

Years	Population
1850-1860	25,332
1860-1870	15,477
1870-1880	54,184
1880-1890	156,530
1890-1900	114,766
1900-1910	496,976

[1]From United States Census Reports for the specific years.

[2]*Ibid*. Mid-decade statistics are from Douglas Gunn, in *San Diego Union*, Oct. 2, 1887. The Los Angeles 1890 population does not include Orange County (13,589).

[3]John Walton Caughey, *History of the Pacific Coast* (1933), p. 397.

278

Bibliography

GENERAL SOURCES

A S STATED in the Preface, the only full-length book written about the boom of the eighties is Theodore S. Van
Dyke, *Millionaires of a Day* (1890), and the sole
scholarly account is William Bell Langsdorf, "The Real Estate
Boom of 1887 in Southern California" (MS, Occidental College, 1932). Taken together, these items present a good picture of the boom—Langsdorf giving the facts, and Van Dyke
painting local color in a stimulating manner. Several articles
have been written, the best of which is James M. Guinn, "The
Great Real Estate Boom of 1887," in Historical Society of
Southern California *Annual Publications, 1890,* I, 13-21. Joseph
Netz, who grew up among scenes of the boom, presented
"The Great Los Angeles Real Estate Boom of 1887" in the
same *Publications, 1915-16,* X, 64-68. General works having
sections on the boom include John Walton Caughey, *California* (1940); Robert Glass Cleland, *A History of California:
The American Period* (1922) and *From Wilderness to Em-
pire* (1944); Aaron M. Sakolski, *The Great American Land
Bubble* (1932); and Frank J. Taylor, *Land of Homes* (1929).

Most boom material must be culled from the various collections of California documents in libraries and government
archives. The Huntington Library possesses the finest collection of southern-California material, including: the Thomas
Balch Elliott letters, dealing with the foundation and early
history of Pasadena; the James De Barth Shorb letter books,
which illustrate the development of real estate and the wine
industry in the San Gabriel Valley; the James F. Crank col-

lection, describing railway and business affairs during the
boom era; and the H. A. Barclay papers, dealing with irrigation and ranch-land development near San Bernardino and
Los Angeles. Other useful Huntington collections are the
Solano-Reeves papers, including boom-time maps and plats,
the Horatio N. Rust collection of Pasadena material, and the
Charles Maclay documents, part of which relate to the early
history of San Fernando. The papers of Abel Stearns, Benjamin D. Wilson, and Robert S. Baker cast light on an earlier
period, but contain valuable background material, and the
Pierce, Prinz, and Crank photograph collections make an
older decade seem more real. The Huntington's array of boom
maps, plats, and surveys is also very extensive.

Other aggregations of Californiana are widely scattered.
The Bancroft Library at Berkeley contains the Bancroft
Pamphlets and the Bancroft Scrapbooks, both of which touch
here and there upon southern-California affairs; here also can
be found an excellent general collection of southern newspapers for the period. The Los Angeles County Museum
houses the Coronel Collection, which includes a useful series
of tract pamphlets, and the Museum has, as well, another excellent collection of southern newspapers. The Robert E. Cowan
Collection at the University of California at Los Angeles and
the Max Hayward Collection at Occidental College are valuable groups of Californiana. Libraries in smaller communities
possess many unduplicated items, and city and county archives, especially miscellaneous records, map books, and tax
rolls, are productive of much information on the boom.

Bibliographical material appears in both Caughey and
Langsdorf, and *A Union List of Newspapers in Offices of
Publishers and in Libraries of Southern California* (Publication
No. 2, 6th District, California Library Association; 1936
[mimeographed]) locates elusive files.

CHAPTER I

Southern California's Economic Flurries

The best accounts of the boom of the sixties are found in Robert Glass Cleland, *The Cattle on a Thousand Hills* (1941), and in James M. Guinn, "Los Angeles in the Later Sixties and Early Seventies," in Hist. Soc. of Sou. Calif. *Annual Publications, 1893,* III, 63-68. Land advertisements for this flurry can be found in the California Immigrant Union's *All about California and the Inducements to Settle There* (2d ed.; 1870). The upswings in San Diego and Santa Barbara are best discovered in local histories of those counties and cities (see bibliography items for Chapters XII and XIII).

CHAPTER II

Agriculture in the Southern Counties

See Caughey, *California,* for a general discussion, and Cleland, *The Cattle on a Thousand Hills,* for a specific and more detailed application to the southern counties. James M. Guinn, "Some Early California Industries that Failed," in Hist. Soc. of Sou. Calif. *Annual Publications, 1906,* VII, 5-13, discusses the abortive experiments, while the Shorb letter books and the Elliott and Crank papers describe early developments in wine manufacturing and citrus growing. Hubert Howe Bancroft, *History of California* (7 vols.; 1884-90), lists statistics on other crops; and Ludwig Louis Salvator, *Los Angeles in the Sunny Seventies: A Flower from the Golden Land* (tr. Marguerite Eyer Wilbur; 1929), describes earlier developments in agriculture and transportation.

CHAPTER III

Railroad Competition

The history of the Southern Pacific is set forth in Bancroft, *History of California*, in Rockwell D. Hunt and William S. Ament, *Oxcart to Airplane* (1929), and in Stuart Daggett, *Chapters on the History of the Southern Pacific* (1922). The Santa Fe's arrival is treated in Glenn Chesney Quiett, *They Built the West: An Epic of Rails and Cities* (1934), and in Lewis B. Lesley, "The Entrance of the Santa Fe Railroad into California," *Pacific Historical Review*, VIII, 89-96 (1939). Its junction with the Los Angeles and San Gabriel Valley line is treated in Glenn S. Dumke, "The Career of James F. Crank: A Chapter in the History of Western Transportation," *Huntington Library Quarterly*, VI, 313-32 (1943). The rate war is best described in the *Los Angeles Times* for March, 1886. Minor lines and earlier agitation are discussed in Lewis B. Lesley, "A Southern Transcontinental Railroad into California: Texas and Pacific versus Southern Pacific, 1865-1885," *Pac. Hist. Rev.*, V, 52-60 (1935), and in William E. Smythe, *History of San Diego* (2 vols.; 1908). Statistics and dates are available in the *Commercial and Financial Chronicle*, and railroad propaganda is adequately treated by Edna Monch Parker, "The Southern Pacific Railroad and Settlement in Southern California," *Pac. Hist. Rev.*, VI, 103-19 (1937), and in contemporary newspapers. See also Paul F. Allen, "Tourists in Southern California" (MS, Claremont Colleges, 1940).

CHAPTER IV

Advertising

The advertising literature for southern California's formative years is enormous. Nearly four dozen books and a much larger number of articles printed during this period were consulted with a view to analyzing publicity methods. All of the items are strikingly similar, and only a few of the best are here listed: Charles Nordhoff, *California: For Health, Pleasure, and Residence* (1873); Theodore S. Van Dyke, *Southern California* (1886); William Henry Bishop, *Old Mexico and Her Lost Provinces* (1883); Benjamin F. Taylor, *Between the Gates* (11th ed.; 1883); Ludwig L. Salvator, *Los Angeles in the Sunny Seventies;* Walter Lindley and Joseph P. Widney, *California of the South* (1888); Charles Dudley Warner, "The Golden Hesperides," *Atlantic Monthly*, LXI, 48-56 (1888); and, by the same author, "Our Italy," *Harper's Magazine*, LXXXI, 813-29 (1890).

Newspaper publicity may be examined in the files of the Los Angeles County Museum Library, the Bancroft Library, and in scattered issues at the Huntington Library. Newspapers utilized in this chapter were, chiefly, the Los Angeles *Times, Tribune,* and *Express,* and the *Pasadena Daily Union*— the last-named on file in the Pasadena Public Library. Good secondary accounts of publicity methods are in Van Dyke, *Millionaires of a Day,* and in Harris Newmark, *Sixty Years in Southern California* (1926). Advertising through correspondence is illustrated by the Benjamin D. Wilson papers and the letter books of J. De Barth Shorb at the Huntington Library, and in John Walton Caughey, "Don Benito Wilson: An Average Southern Californian," *Huntington Library Quarterly*, II, 285-300 (1939).

CHAPTER V

The Boom in Los Angeles

The progress of the flurry in urban Los Angeles is best traced in county documents, especially the Los Angeles County "Miscellaneous Records," VI-XXXVII, and in contemporary newspapers, notably the Los Angeles *Times*, *Tribune*, and *Express*, and scattered numbers of the *Los Angeles Advertiser*. The *Commercial Bulletin of Southern California* and the annual reports of the Los Angeles Board of Trade (title varies) present useful statistics. Secondary accounts are available in William A. Spalding, *History and Reminiscences of Los Angeles City and County* (3 vols.; 1931); Charles Dwight Willard, *The Herald's History of Los Angeles City* (1901); Newmark, *Sixty Years in Southern California;* and James M. Guinn, *A History of California and an Extended History of Los Angeles and Environs* (3 vols.; 1915). Additional facts may be gleaned from Harry Ellington Brook, "Reminiscences of the Boom," *Land of Sunshine*, pp. 25-26 (Jan., 1895), pp. 46-47 (Feb., 1895), p. 102 (May, 1895); J. W. Browning, *Los Angeles City and County Guidebook for Tourists and Strangers* (1885); and *Los Angeles City and County: Resources, Growth, and Prospects*, an 1890 publication of the Los Angeles Chamber of Commerce. The Solano-Reeves and Coronel collections are useful in locating various subdivisions, and William E. Howell, *Real Estate Tract Directory and Land Purchasers' Guide of Los Angeles County* (1888) lists every recorded subdivision for that year. James M. Guinn, "Romance of Rancho Realty," in Hist. Soc. of Sou. Calif. *Annual Publications, 1911*, VIII, 234-42, has information on price fluctuations, and Edwin O. Palmer, *History of Hollywood* (1937), recounts the inception of that suburb.

The best maps are in the Huntington files: Stoll and Thayer (1886), Valentine J. Rowan (1887), and Henry J. Stevenson (1884). *Los Angeles, Illustrated* (1889) is a book of views.

CHAPTER VI

Speculation on the Shore

For Chapters VI-X, the Los Angeles County "Miscellaneous Records," VI-XXXVII, give fundamental information on

tracts, subdivisions, and new towns platted. A good secondary
work which covers the entire area is William W. Robinson,
Ranchos Become Cities (1939). For the coastal district speci-
fically, see Luther A. Ingersoll, *Ingersoll's Century History
of Santa Monica Bay Cities* (1908); Josephine Kingsbury,
"The Establishment of Inglewood, 1887-1890" (MS, University of California at Los Angeles, 1941); *Ranchos of the
Sunset* (1925); H. L. Sherman, *History of Newport Beach*
(1931); Mrs. M. Burton Williamson, "History of Santa Catalina Island," in Hist. Soc. of Sou. Calif. *Annual Publications,
1903*, VI, 14-19; and contemporary newspapers. An excellent
boom-time plat is *Plan of Redondo Beach, Los Angeles County, California* (1888), designed by State Engineer William
Hammond Hall.

CHAPTER VII

*Suburban Centers of the Boom: The San Gabriel Valley
and Pasadena*

Special references for the San Gabriel Valley include Carl
Burgess Glasscock, *Lucky Baldwin* (1933); John L. Wiley,
History of Monrovia (1927); Harold D. Carew, *History of
Pasadena and the San Gabriel Valley* (3 vols.; 1930); and Los
Angeles and Pasadena newspapers. Pasadena is treated in
Carew, in John Windell Wood, *Pasadena, California: Histor-
ical and Personal* (1917), in the Elliott, Shorb, and Crank
collections, and in Jeanne C. Carr, "Pasadena, the Crown of
the Valley," in Hist. Soc. of Sou. Calif. *Annual Publications,
1893*, III, 80-87. Altadena's boom period is discussed in Sarah
Noble Ives, *Altadena* (1938).

CHAPTER VIII

Glendale, Burbank, and the San Fernando Valley

Newspapers and county records maintain their rank as the
best sources for this chapter. On Glendale's growth, see John

285

✑§ Bibliography §✑

Calvin Sherer, *History of Glendale and Vicinity* (1922). Near-by areas are discussed in Grace J. Oberbeck, *History of La Crescenta-La Cañada Valleys* (1938); Frank M. Keffer, *History of San Fernando Valley* (1934); *A Daughter of the Snows: The Story of the Great San Fernando Valley* (1923); and Robinson, *Ranchos Become Cities*. See, also, scattered items in the Elliott papers and the Coronel pamphlets.

CHAPTER IX

Pomona and the Irrigation Settlements

For the Pomona area, see Guinn's various works; Frank P. Brackett; *History of Pomona Valley, California* (1920); and *This Is Claremont* (ed. Harold H. Davis; 1941). J. A. Alexander, *The Life of George Chaffey* (1928), traces in detail the careers of both George Chaffey and his brother, William Benjamin, but emphasizes the Australian phase at the expense of the California enterprises. Newspapers and Los Angeles County records are important. Benjamin F. Arnold and Artilissa Dorland Clark, *History of Whittier* (1933), gives the story of Whittier's boom origin.

CHAPTER X

Creation of a County: The Boom in the Santa Ana Valley

Boom records of present-day Orange County are found in Los Angeles County files and newspapers. Other information may be obtained from Samuel Armor, *History of Orange County* (1921); the *Orange County History Series*; and Mrs. Joseph E. Pleasants, *History of Orange County, California* (3 vols.; 1931). County division is discussed by Owen C. Coy, *California County Boundaries* (1923), and H. W. Slavin, "History of the Boundary of the County of Los Angeles" (Department of the County Surveyor, 1938 [typewritten]);

the latter quotes legislation pertaining to the subject. *The Statutes of California and Amendments to the Codes Passed at the Twenty-eighth Session of the Legislature, 1889,* may be consulted for the laws themselves.

CHAPTER XI

The San Bernardino County Flurry

As Riverside County was not formed until 1893, documents for both it and San Bernardino County are found in the latter's files. Miscellaneous records and map books are the best sources. Good secondary accounts include Luther A. Ingersoll, *Ingersoll's Century Annals of San Bernardino County* (1904); Elmer Wallace Holmes (*et al.*), *History of Riverside County, California* (1912); and Rose L. Ellerbe, "History of Temescal Valley," in Hist. Soc. of Sou. Calif. *Annual Publications, 1920,* XI, 12-23. Arthur Kearney, *San Bernardino County: Its Resources and Climate* (1874), is a piece of early promotion literature. The Barclay and Elliott papers contain pertinent items.

CHAPTER XII

"Bay 'n Climate": The Boom in the San Diego Area

Bancroft Library, Huntington Library, and Los Angeles County Museum files, including those of the San Diego *Union, Bee, Progress, Free Press,* and *Golden Era,* plus Los Angeles newspapers, were heavily drawn upon in constructing this chapter. James M. Guinn, *A History of California and an Extended History of Its Southern Coast Counties* (2 vols.; 1907); Smythe, *History of San Diego;* and Harry C. Hopkins, *History of San Diego: Its Pueblo Lands and Water* (1929), are good secondary works, and Walter Gifford Smith, *The Story of San Diego* (1892), draws a picture of the town as it existed immediately after the flurry. Holmes, *History of Riverside County*, contains a chapter on the Temécula Valley settlements. In 1872 the *San Diego Union* published a booklet entitled *San Diego: The California Terminus of the Texas and Pacific Railway*, which describes the enthusiastic reception accorded Col. Tom Scott. Realtors Judson and Hamilton issued, in 1885, *San Diego County: Land Register and Business Directory*, which contains revealing land advertisements. The local chamber of commerce sponsored *San Diego: the City and County* (1888), including a useful sketch map, statistics, and a list of the larger towns; and the annual reports of the San Diego Land and Town Company (1887-93) present the story of a realty firm which appraised its extensive assets at $9,600,000 in 1887. It published in 1888 a *Guide to the San Diego Bay Region, California*. The Sanborn Map and Publishing Company printed a large folio volume of San Diego block plats (1888-97), a copy of which is now in the Huntington Library; and in 1874 the chamber of commerce published *Descriptive, Historical, Commercial, Agricultural, and Other Important Information Relative to the City of San Diego*, with twenty-two photographs. The Coronel pamphlets stress Coronado advertising.

CHAPTER XIII

The Rural Boom in the North: Santa Barbara and Ventura Counties

The Santa Barbara *Weekly Independent* and *Morning Press*, the *Ventura Free Press*, and Los Angeles newspapers describe the flurry here in detail. See also Santa Barbara County "Map Books," "Map Indexes," and "Miscellaneous Records," and Ventura County "Miscellaneous Records" and "Tax Rolls." Secondary accounts include Owen H. O'Neill, *History of Santa Barbara County* (1939); Yda Addis Storke, *A Memorial and Biographical History of the Counties of Santa Barbara, San Luis Obispo, and Ventura, California* (1891); John R. Southworth, *Santa Barbara and Montecito, Past and Present* (1920); and Solomon N. Sheridan, *History of Ventura County, California* (2 vols.; 1926). Boom literature is represented by Rev. Abraham W. Jackson, *Barbariana* (1888); Mary Camilla Foster Hall Wood, *Santa Barbara As It Is* (1884); Edwards Roberts, *Santa Barbara and around There* (1886); *Ventura County, California: Its Resources* (1885); and *To the Senate and House of Representatives of the United States. Petition of Citizens of San Buenaventura, California, for Harbor Improvement* (1888), which contains a good map of the Ventura region.

CHAPTER XIV

Ghost Towns

County records and newspapers, with plats from the Coronel and Solano-Reeves collections, again head the list of major sources, and most of the general accounts of the boom stress this phase of promotion activity. Two articles exist on ghost towns as such: Blanche Collings, "Fairview, Boom Town," in *Orange County History Series*, II, 67-71; and C. C. Baker, "The Rise and Fall of the City of Gladstone," in Hist. Soc. of Sou. Calif. *Annual Publications, 1914*, IX, 188-94. Guinn describes Hamburg's developments in his "Great Real Estate Boom," *ibid., 1890*, I, 13-21.

CHAPTER XV

Men and Methods

General promotional methods are discussed in nearly all of the general references cited, Newmark and Van Dyke (*Millionaires of a Day*) being especially noteworthy. The California

289

Immigrant Union is described in its own published pamphlets, the best of which are *All About California and the Inducements to Settle There* (7th ed.; 1874) and *Opinions of the Press of San Francisco and Sacramento on the Value and Importance of Immigration and the Necessity of State Aid* (1870). State-society affairs and district agents are best discussed in Los Angeles newspapers of the period. For boom personnel, the biographical histories, especially those by Guinn already cited, together with his *Historical and Biographical Record of Southern California* (1902), furnish much information. Alexander's *Life of George Chaffey* and the correspondence of various pioneers, such as Elliott, Shorb, and Wilson, augment these data. Bancroft's footnotes in his *History of California* and *Chronicles of the Builders* (7 vols.; 1891-92) contain much otherwise unavailable information. Newspaper articles often supply biographical hints. Fraud, corruption, and shady business methods are all given more than their share of attention in the general references and in newspapers.

CHAPTER XVI

Irrigation Improvements

The boom's stimulus to irrigation development can be traced in William Hammond Hall's classic *Irrigation in Southern California* (Part II of the *Report of the State Engineer of California on Irrigation and the Irrigation Question* [1888]), and in four "Water Supply and Irrigation" papers published by the United States Department of the Interior and written by Walter C. Mendenhall: *Development of Underground Waters in the Central Coastal Plain Region of Southern California* (Paper No. 138; 1905); *Development of Underground Waters in the Western Coastal Plain Region of Southern California* (Paper No. 139; 1905); *Development of Underground*

Water in the Eastern Coastal Plain Region of Southern California (Paper No. 137; 1905); and *Ground Waters and Irrigation Enterprises in the Foothill Belt, Southern California* (Paper No. 219; 1908). Alexander's life of Chaffey describes San Antonio Canyon and Ontario mutual water-company development; and the Los Angeles area is discussed in Gaylord Reid, "The Zanja System of Los Angeles" (MS, University of California at Los Angeles, 1941); Edward M. Boggs, *A Study of Water Rights on the Los Angeles River* (repr. from U.S. Department of Agriculture, Office of Experiment Stations, Bulletin 100, *Report of Irrigation Investigations in California*, 1901); and items in the Barclay collection. See also Hallock F. Raup, "Land Use and Water Supply Problems in Southern California: The Case of the Perris Valley," *Geographical Review*, XXII, 270-78 (1932); *idem, Piedmont Plain Agriculture in Southern California* (repr. from *Yearbook of the Association of Pacific Coast Geographers*, VI, 1940). The Pomona College Library has an extensive collection on water development.

Information on the agitation for, and passage of the Wright Act of 1887 is obtainable in the California *Assembly Journal* and *Statutes* for that year, in Bancroft's *History of California*, and in three published pamphlets: *Addresses of the State Irrigation Committee to the Fresno and Riverside Irrigation Conventions and to the Anti-Riparian Voters of California, with Opinions of the Press* (1886); *Proceedings of the State Irrigation Convention* (1886); and *Proceedings of the State Irrigation Convention Held at Riverside, California, May 14, 15, and 16, 1884* (1884).

CHAPTER XVII
Encouragement for Education

Effects of the boom on the public schools of southern California are disclosed by the Reports of the Superintendent of

Public Instruction of the State of California. Expansion of facilities for higher education is dealt with in: Laurence L. Hill, *Six Collegiate Decades: The Growth of Higher Education in Southern California* (1929); Rockwell D. Hunt, *The First Half-Century* (1930), a history of the University of Southern California; Leslie F. Gay, "The Founding of the University of Southern California," in Hist. Soc. of Sou. Calif. *Annual Publications, 1909-10,* VIII, 37-50; Mrs. M. Burton Williamson, "A History of University Town," *ibid., 1895,* III, 19-22; Robert Glass Cleland, *The History of Occidental College* (1937); *This Is Claremont;* and contemporary newspapers. Plats of the University Tract may be found in the Los Angeles County "Miscellaneous Records."

CHAPTER XVIII

The End of the Boom

Consult general references on the boom, and contemporary newspapers, for symptoms of the decline. Assessed-valuation changes may be sketchily traced in the Los Angeles County Board of Supervisors' "Minute Books." The boom's effect on population is best set forth in United States Census reports, while statistics on property transfer are available in the realty columns of southern-California newspapers, in the annual reports of the Los Angeles Board of Trade, and in *The Tribune Annual* (1888). Mortgage and assessment fluctuations are also included, in various forms, in the census reports. Effects of the boom on local institutions, municipal government, and industry must be gleaned from local histories and newspapers. Railway development is detailed in the census Reports, and in Glenn S. Dumke: "Early Interurban Transportation in the Los Angeles Area," in Hist. Soc. of Sou. Calif. *Quarterly,* XXII, 131-49 (1940); and "The Career of James F. Crank," in *Huntington Library Quarterly,* VI, 313-32. The problem of state division is set forth in James M. Guinn, "How California Escaped State Division," in Hist. Soc. of Sou. Calif. *Annual Publications, 1905,* VI, 823-32; local sentiment on the subject occupies much space in the newspapers of the time. Bases for comparison with other land booms are found in Sakolski, *Great American Land Bubble;* and the Florida frenzy is described by Kenneth Roberts in a series of *Saturday Evening Post* articles, including "Florida Fireworks," CXCVIII, 12-13, 82-83 (Jan. 23, 1926), and "Good Warm Stuff," CXCVIII, 12-13, 78-82 (Jan. 9, 1926). Theodore S. Van Dyke reminisces on the aftermath of the boom, in "Los Angeles since the Boom," *Land of Sunshine,* p. 15 (June, 1894).

Index

·§ Index ȝ·

296